Character Reading from Handwriting

CHARACTER READING *from* HANDWRITING

A Newcastle Classic

by Louise Rice

Newcastle Publishing Co., Inc.
North Hollywood, California

Originally published in 1927 by Frederick A. Stokes Company of New York.

ISBN: 0-87877-232-4
A Newcastle Classic
First printing 1996
10 9 8 7 6 5 4 3 2 1
Printed in the United States of America.

TO

MY PUPILS

WITH FRATERNAL GREETINGS

"National and personal character is as strongly marked in the handwriting of nations and of individuals as it is in their moral and physical attributes. The modern nations of Europe can never suffer the varieties and changes in their handwritings which fell to the lot of their ancestors. The printing-press has rendered such possibility impossible. Yet the printing-press itself, with all its power to enforce uniformity, at least in literary works, has been powerless to repress the national and individual character, which breaks out, and will continue to break out, in the domestic handwriting of the day. This assertion of character will last to the end, whatever mechanical influences may rise up to check its natural course. Undoubtedly such mechanical changes as the abandonment of the quill pen for the steel nib and the introduction of the stylographic pen have affected our modern current writing very much for the worse, and other inventions may serve to give it a still worse turn in the future; but the natural hand is not to be expelled. Character will persist, though the writing may become villainous. Whether the palæographer of the distant ages will direct his researches to the elucidation of the national hands of his day we need not stop to consider. We do not envy him his task, content as we are that the lines have fallen unto us in pleasanter places."

—Sir Edward Maunde Thompson, in *An Introduction to Greek and Latin Palæography.*

LR

CONTENTS

THE HISTORY OF HANDWRITING

CHARACTER READING FROM HANDWRITING

WHAT GRAPHOLOGY IS

The knowledge that character is revealed in handwriting is so old that we find the Emperor Nero writing to a friend that he fears a certain man at Court—"his writing shows him treacherous." The Chinese and Japanese both have a popular belief that goodness and purity, as in a lovely young girl, for instance, will show in the "handwriting," which it is more accurate to call hand painting.

Literature is full of the expressions of this idea. Graphology was, up to a certain period of the world's history, like many of the other sciences, only the hobby of the curious and the preoccupation of the very few, who lacked data with which to pursue it in exactitude.

We must remember, always, that writing is, in itself, the crown of man's rise from the beast. Hundreds of thousands of years went by while man did no more than painfully teach himself to manipulate a writing-instrument. The period of time in which writing has become the possession of much of the world, as a facile and accustomed operation, is so little that it is but a tick of the clock compared with all the dragging hours of the previous slow struggle for facility in writing.

Therefore, the science of writing, so slow to develop, so swift to rise to an art after all its early days, must be to many of us like electricity was before we learned to understand it. There is no doubt that men had "a feeling" that certain matters would one day be opened to the light of the sun, and that certain inventions would ultimately be made. Men dreamed of flying hundreds of years before there was the slightest comprehension of how it might be done.

With handwriting, then, there has been the feeling all over the world and at all times, that it was a mysterious thing and that it was, to an exceptional degree, the emanation of the maker. There is not a nation in the world which does not have ideas about what a man's writing shows of his character; but of a system of deduction or of anything more than the most nebulous theories we have little trace until 1632. People made their own theories as they went along, either coloring them by what they thought they *knew* of the character of a writer or fancifully inventing characters and then ascribing certain handwritings to them.

Sir Walter Scott, in *Chronicles of the Canongate,* has a paragraph which is remarkable, in its clear conception of the truth:

"I looked at the even, concise, yet tremulous hand in which the manuscript was written . . . could not help thinking, according to an opinion that I have heard seriously maintained, that something of a man's character may be conjectured from his handwriting. That neat, but crowded and constrained, small hand, argued a man of good conscience, well regulated passions, and, to use his own phrase, of an upright walk in life, but it also indicated narrowness of spirit, inveterate prejudice and hinted at some degree of intolerance. The flourished capital letters, do they not forcibly express the pride and sense of importance of the author?"

This was good graphological deduction. The only trouble was that Sir Walter did not know that he was using well-defined formulas in making that deduction nor did he realize that in such formulas there lay the measuring-rule for other deductions.

This has been true of a great many people, from the time of Baldo down to this present day. In each instance they have "felt" and "guessed" and theorized. That was what the Brownings, Elizabeth and Robert, did, along with a good many other intelligentsia of their time. They made a separate estimation for each specimen and did not try to work up any scientific law or set of laws.

An instance of the wrong sort of deduction, based on absolutely nothing, can be found in Rider Haggard's *When the World Shook.*

" . . . was an uncouth . . . ragged person, with a mind almost incredibly simple. He was not fastidious . . . yet he was good, so painfully good that one felt . . . that his guardian angel had tied his ticket to heaven around his neck at birth."

Haggard then goes on to say that he wrote a "large sprawling hand"—which is exactly what he would not do, this simple, yet not fastidious and yet so good creature. He would have written a good deal of a copybook hand, with heavy pressure and with ordinary letter formations, too small capitals and *a, o* and *b* in sloppy construction.

While the world in general was making individual estimations with no effort at laws, a handful of people in France and Germany were trying to reduce all the generally accepted ideas about writing to a system, and then carefully testing the system. They took nothing for granted and weighed each slight advance in positive knowledge.

The man who began this process and who is the father of graphology—although he never heard the word—was Camillo Baldo, who, in 1632, published a little book at Capri, or perhaps at Florence. The long name of this book was *Tratto come una lettera missiva si cognoscano la natura e qualità del scrittore.* (How to know the nature and qualities of a person by looking at a letter which he has written.)

Another man in the same century wrote a rather unimportant little treatise on the way in which character was shown in handwriting; and there the matter rested, so far as books on the subject were concerned, but people all over the civilized world were now casually discussing the matter. Mostly, it was thought that being able to tell anything about character from handwriting was a gift, something accomplished by an extra use of the power of intuition.

About 1830 a learned Frenchman and churchman, the Abbé Flandrin, became the head of a movement which took up the small book of Baldo and proceeded to elaborate on it. The Bishop of Amiens and other men of scholarship and leisure were attracted to this study, and enthusiasm for it spread.

Before that, Goethe, his friend Lavater, Moreau, Hocquart, Delastre, and Schwiedland had written exceedingly generalized booklets on the matter of character as shown in handwriting, but their conclusions had been based on nothing much more than their own reflections on the subject. The Abbé Flandrin took nothing for granted. He compared, sorted, systematized, investigated, slowly building up a more definite picture on the outlines furnished by Baldo. He gave the science its name, *Graphology*.

His pupil and eventually his master was the Abbé Michon, who carried the work much farther, clarified the classifications and passed the mastership on to Crepieux-Jamin, with whom modern graphological work really began, about 1880.

Crepieux-Jamin wrote many works on the subject, the best known of which are: *L'âge et le sexe dans l'écriture, L'écriture et le caractère, La graphologie en examples, Les élements de l'écriture des canailles, Les bases fondamentales de la graphologie et de l'expertise en l'écriture.*

In Germany Hans H. Busse, Doctor Ludwig Klages, with Meyer, Barthe, Engelmann and many others, all set upon the task of working out the details of the new science with characteristic Teutonic thoroughness.

England and the British Isles have given very interested study to graphology, but the most valuable of the written work will be found in English periodicals, and not in books.

In America there is a very small but competent array of writers on the subject. Harrington Keane, whose pen name was "Grapho," was a man of special worth to the science here, in the days when it was struggling hard to escape from the charge of charlatanism. So were Hugo von Hagen, and Leslie French and Mrs. Franklin Hall. Books by these writers (and my own book, written twenty years ago), although out of print now, are occasionally to be found on library shelves and undoubtedly did much to bring the science to the attention of thinking people; and to clear it of the aura of superstition which still clung about it.

In the past five years or so newspapers throughout the English-speaking world have taken up the idea, common to France and Germany for the last fifty years, of running character delineations in their columns. The general public, through this, has become acquainted with the science to a degree which was never true before. Graphologists of standing have little trouble in getting pupils who are intelligent and talented. Physicians and teachers and those who deal with vocations and human aptitudes are awakening to the fact that in every stroke of the pen we have information, priceless and accurate: something not to be denied by the writer, not to be hidden, not to be tampered with.

There will be much more done with graphology, of course, as soon as there are the thousands of investigators engaged on it that there must be for any science which is kept active. Its expansion will be in the direction of specialized branches, as, for instance, in the matter of the detection of disease in handwriting, which phase of graphological deduction is still in its infancy. Records kept by physicians all over the world, by medical and surgical and health institutions, are needed before we can have full data on this phase, our present data being merely fragmentary.

A great deal can be deduced from the handwriting of children when we shall have had the cooperation of teachers for at least twenty years, in investigating the many questions yet unanswered. How soon can we begin even faintly to predict the special line along which education will most easily proceed for the child's benefit? How soon can we tell, from the writing of adolescents, the emotional temperament which maturity will bring to flower? How soon and how can we tell the delinquent, deficient and "different" child from the normal one? What are the distinguishing formations which may tell us of the very abnormal child, who is, almost from its tenth year, a menace to the community? These are the most serious questions that human beings have to face, for they concern the rising generation. If properly answered, such questions would solve fully half of the troubles of the world. They should be answered. Graphologists can, in some instances, answer them now, but to do so with scientific sureness and accuracy, and for all cases, we shall have to have a vast mass of work done, not by graphological practitioners alone, but by amateurs and dilettantes, by teachers and educators and parents, who will contribute the infinitesimally small detailed information out of which all science is built, no matter which science it may be.

It is perhaps unnecessary to add that the narrow-minded and the illiterate and the people totally ignorant of the complexities of life are not fitted to be professional graphologists, nor are their estimations of character as shown in handwriting apt to be entirely correct, no matter whether they draw the right deduction from the specimen of writing or not.

In graphology, as in every other science, the practitioner needs field and laboratory experience with which to supplement theoretical training. To a person who has no knowledge whatever of any save the most conventionalized life, the writing of a full-bodied, lusty adventurer must come as a shock, no matter if the adventurer be gallant, heroic, courageous and unselfish. A wide knowledge of the lights and shades with which the picture of Life is painted and the ability to estimate both truly, should be the equipment of the practising graphologist, *before* actual professional work is attempted.

For the casual user of graphology the mere mechanical end of it will often give light on the perplexing questions of the day.

Turn to the chapters on *Legibility* and *Illegibility* and see how it is possible to begin roughly stacking up human beings according to their appetite for detail, or their aversion to it. Read *Pressure* for light on the temperaments of people; read the *Basic Line* for the explanation of the real reactions to hope and despair; read the *Angle of Inclination* for the explanation of the latest divorce, the newest marriage, the scandal of the moment, the wonder of a marriage which is as beautiful at fifty as at twenty; read *Size, Margins* and *Capitals* to see how vocation is shown in handwriting. These direct and positive indications of character in handwriting need no interpreter. "He who runs may read."

It *does* need the skilled practitioner to paint the complete portrait of the intricate and baffling character, the abnormality, the defective, the genius, the emotional pervert. *They* all need, what the average person has not, the field and laboratory experience of human nature which the skilled graphologist should have.

The letter forms which have descended to us through the many avenues—Babylonia and Egypt, Crete, the Hittite country, Phœnicia, Greece and Rome—belong to all the western world. The national twist is given, in each country, of course.

Germany gives us a more involved letter, which corresponds to the heavy, meticulous and yet far-sighted movements of her mind.

Spain gives us the ornate capitals of stately pride and the long connecting-strokes of letters which express her charm and quickness to respond to the stir of beauty.

Italy, with flowing capitals which are somehow gay, united to her small and precise small letter forms, epitomizes the two aspects of her: the music-loving which has brought joy to the world, and the accurate mind which has given us magnificent mechanics.

France, exquisite in letter forms, which are nearly always small and as clearly read as print, with small and intellectual capitals, expresses her superb mental qualities, cool, keen and logical, only the very forward slant of her angle of inclination telling of her fine sensibilities.

Russia, with letter forms that are only two-thirds those of the western world, sprawls when she writes, overornaments the capitals, and uses the long connecting-stroke which means talkativeness. No better national picture exists in handwriting than that of the typical Russian script.

"The Back of Europe"—all the Balkans, all of Czechoslovakia, leans a little toward the East in national handwriting.

In the British Isles and dependencies we have the upright hand prevailing—the writing which shows a nature not too apt to show its feelings, and usually with the characteristic "incurve" of clannishness!

In the United States there is not, properly speaking, a handwriting which is characteristic of nationality. Graphologically, we are not yet welded together. In almost any specimen of American writing which we take up there peeps out at us the Englishman, the Frenchman, the Spaniard, the Italian—as well as all the other nations of the earth, in decreasing ratio. The nearest that we get to a type which is characteristic is that of the typical salesman—a fine example of the Vital type, with medium pressure, quite far forward leaning, even, rather long *t* bar, even basic line, letter formations accurate, capitals not individual, letters wide, rhythm rapid.

This is the beginning of the "American" hand.

That it does not express the actual individuality of the moment, that it does not, in fact, do justice to it, is due to the way in which handwriting records. Thus, character has to be bitten deep on the profile of the soul before the handwriting registers. That which is shown in the handwriting is not a temporary thing. It is a fundamental. And it is not to be denied that, with all the culture, learning and refinement which have been attained in America, the foundations are still of the hustling "go-getter" sort which first made possible the hewing of this great country out of the vast virgin forests in less time than it usually takes a country to settle a thousand miles of coast.

So far, then, this is all that the United States has given in the way of a nationally characteristic handwriting, if we except the fact that the writing of the schoolgirl here is like no writing of any other schoolgirl in that it is so extremely individual. In it there has begun another characteristic hand, which may ultimately fuse with the salesman type and thus start our real American nationalistic handwriting.

No matter how much handwriting may be changed in the different countries, the basic letter formations remain the same. This is even so of the Arabic and the Turkish, which are remotely allied to our letter forms, having started away from our stem, centuries and centuries ago. Observation will show that pressure, horizontal and perpendicular lines, size, width, and so on, can be applied to them, as well, and to all their tributaries.

When we come to consider Chinese and Japanese and all their tributaries we have no system that can be applied to them. Chinese and Japanese scholars have always professed to be able to tell a good deal of the character of writers from the pictographs which constitute the "writing" of these nations, but this is often largely a matter of feeling which may or may not strike close to the truth.

At the present day, the science of graphology is just coming into active practise. The rules which govern it have been tried and tested for a hundred years.

Many men of science and the most sincere characters have spent a lifetime in verifying such rules and in making comparisons, tedious and prolonged, which have added, little by little, the bases for the establishment of yet another rule or two. There will be no change in the rules now laid down, but only a great extension of them, as the work of investigation goes on.

WHAT GRAPHOLOGY DOES NOT REVEAL

One of the most persistent questions of those who know little about graphology is: "Is this writer a man or a woman?"

This is exactly what the graphologist cannot answer; what no one can answer.

So far as handwriting is concerned, we must remember a rule already laid down, which is that nothing can make a real impression on handwriting until it is a fundamental element of the character of the writer. From Crepieux-Jamin down to the present author, every graphologist has realized that sex simply does not exist in handwriting. (See note on sex indications in the chapter on "Types.")

Students of racial characteristics will remember that, as we go lower and lower in the human family of races, the differences between the women and the men are less and less. The differences may, in fact, become so little as not to be noticeable, except for the biological fact that the men are fighters and the women are mothers.

In the higher branches of the human race we have accentuated what are called the secondary sex indications. This means, in ordinary language, that we have accentuated the boy's instinct to fight and the girl's instinct to cry. As in clothing, which seeks to emphasize the difference between the sexes, so in conduct. We encourage the boy in fighting and in "running wild," and allow him early sophistication, whereas we pen up the girl, pet her when she is a coward, encourage her when she is lazy and a flirt, and stir her personal vanity from the day that she is old enough to demand her "p'etty clothes" in her lisping baby accents. Thus we have built up a lot of tradition about the sexes which is not true.

Handwriting, rejecting all this, proceeds to show us that men are often tender, sensitive and fearful and that women are often hardy, adventurous, bold and independent—yes, and this in spite of the unknown length of time in which the exaggeration of secondary sex indications has been going on. Old Nature is stubborn. She remains pretty much what she is, no matter how we deck her. So it is practically impossible to tell anything about the sex of a writer. Spread out fifty specimens of handwriting and let ten intelligent and observant people try to choose the men and women represented there. They cannot do it.

Let three graphologists of experience analyze the characters of those fifty. It will be impossible to do more than make a rough guess at the sex of the writers.

One of the most striking things in considering the matter of handwriting as a revealer of character is that, so long as women led a life apart, so long as they were shut off from participation in almost everything except matters having to do with their womanly duties, they did actually write a hand which showed some slight difference from that of men. In grandmother's time, it might have been possible to run through fifty specimens and be successful in choosing the women writers, in at least some proportion. But this is not true to-day. Observe the capital *M* that grandmother used to make and look at the one that granddaughter employs! (See the chapter on capital letters.) This modern *M*, which is but three perpendicular strokes topped with a horizontal one, is used by grandson too. In the writing of the parents of the present generation there is a slight shadow of distinction between sex; in the writing of the boy and the girl of to-day—not the faintest distinction.

Crepieux-Jamin, who wrote a good many years ago, declaring that sex positively could not be told from the handwriting, was slightly ahead of his time—but he could foresee, no doubt, that the element of sex fluctuated and that it would do so more as time went on.

It is to be expected that with the ban on employment and occupations lifted from each sex, we will have greater and greater individuality in handwriting and that even the little difference in occupation which still exists between the sexes will pass. When I began to practise graphology over twenty years ago, the graphologist really had to know the sex of a writer before giving vocational advice. No matter how much a specimen of writing might belong to the Constructive type, you could not tell the writer to go to a technical school and become a builder of bridges until you were sure that it was a "he" to whom you were writing.

No matter what feeling for color and fabrics you might see in a handwriting, you could not advise the writer to become a designer of gowns until you were sure that he was not a husky young fellow who would feel insulted by the suggestion.

These phobias are passing. Not only are occupations open to the girl, which used to be closed to her; many are open to the boy which used to be thought unsuitable or degrading for him.

It is therefore of little moment that we cannot tell sex from the handwriting. Other ideas which students of humanity have lately exploded is that parenthood is more innately the possession, as an emotion, of the woman than of the man; and that women are always home makers; and that men are always adventurous; and that women are always good guides for children; and that men are always physically brave.

Another thing that cannot be expressed in handwriting is age.

Physical weakness is, of course, distinctly shown, and failing eyesight, unsteadiness of the hand due to any one of a number of causes—failing memory, failing energies and so on; but these depreciations of the human frame and spirit may occur at any time.

That age is not revealed in handwriting is not surprising. Age is not revealed in the face or figure with any great accuracy. Old age may easily be seen in the person and in the writing; but there is a tremendous difference in the way in which people mature, as well as in the way in which they grow old. The precocious boy or girl does not go through that long and steady progression of increasing powers which marks the child who remains immature even up into the later twenties.

Handwriting faithfully records the difference in these types, causing precocious children to write the steady, assured hand of forty, and immatured people of almost thirty to write the straggling, unformed hand of normal fifteen. Obviously, any effort to judge the ages of these different types, by their handwriting, would be futile. Handwriting *does* reveal the maturity or the immaturity of the writer and does accurately show the amount of vitality possessed.

When handwriting remains "old-fashioned"—*i.e.*, when the writer continues to use letter forms which belong to a past generation—we may take it that that person is one of those who have been early to mature and with whom progression has more or less stopped with the forties.

Handwriting does not show *race*. Look at the writing of a group of Chinese, born in America, who have learned to write with American children: it is utterly impossible to see any indication of their race. Educate a Spanish girl in England: she writes like her English chums. Educate a Japanese in the Dutch schools: he writes like a Dutchman.

This is true in youth. What happens as such persons grow older is one of two things: they totally lose their feeling of oneness with their own race or they slip back wholly into it. If the former, their handwriting remains stamped with the insignia of the adopted country. If the latter, there is a strange reversion to odd letter forms later in life.

Unlike race, nationality *is* reflected in the handwriting. Where the alien does not take kindly to the adopted nationality, the writing does not, either. There are children in the polyglot sections of American cities who react against the new land in which they find themselves and whose writing persists in being that of Europe or whatever part of the world they came from; and there are children who, while yet the burr of some other tongue is on their English, are already part of America and already using letter forms which are typically American.

It is nationality which gives the world its color and variety. Therefore, we will find it most strongly reflected in the handwriting of those nations where the conception of nationality is rather narrow and intense. Obversely, in democracies, and especially in those which have world-wide affiliations, we find less and less of nationality in the handwriting.

LEGIBILITY

It is the custom for people, who do not understand that handwriting expresses character, to estimate legibility as the one chief virtue of the writer.

It is, of course, true that writing is meant to be read, and that any use of it which frustrates this aim renders the action futile; nevertheless, legibility of writing which proceeds from a colorless habit of letter formation, shows the character and the mind which are also colorless.

The least observant person must realize that with the development of individual writing (and with the consequent difficulty of reading the writing) the individuality of the writer rises. Comparison of the writing of young people of good education with the writing of mature people of equally good and sometimes better education, will show that deviation from the copybook formations is greater, in exact proportion as the mind, character and achievements of the writer are greater than mediocre. Even the least observant person realizes this; and yet, it is still to become part of the world's actual and applied knowledge, for, from the hirer of clerical employees right up to the door of the lecture-room in colleges, people persist in regarding legibility, *per se,* as a proof of both mental and character worthiness. There was never a dictum farther from the truth.

The fact is that legibility shows *nothing* of moral worth or turpitude, and nothing, in and by itself, of mental qualities. It may be the expression of any one of a number of states, conditions or tendencies in the writer.

The effort of children is to write legibly, of course, since their whole attention is focused on the formation of the letters. The effort of the person who is naturally a detailist will also be to write legibly, since evading the formation of any of the details of a letter would seem to that person a slovenly piece of work. Detailed workers cannot be expected to be innovators, iconoclasts or individualists and so it is not in their nature to alter the formation of the letters, as they have been taught to make them, and, as detailists, they have patience. Hence, the clear, accurately formed letters, without individuality, the whole forming the appearance of mechanical accuracy, is the indication of the love of detail and the ability to perform work in which detail is the one matter to which attention must be given.

The difference between the legibility of children's writing and that of the legibility of the detailist's writing is that the latter has the greater freedom and force in using the writing instrument and that the slow and careful action of the hand is replaced, in the adult, by assurance. The difference between the writing of the adult detailist and that of the child or young person who is endeavoring to write clearly can usually be seen by the aid of a good reading-glass, the slight shake of the slowing pen betraying the child.

Size of the writing affects the deduction to be made from legible writing, and so does the character of the letter forms.

Small writing which is very legible is the indication of a mind which has been trained along special lines.

The minor scientist, the microscopist, the maker of medical "slides" for pathological investigations, the maker of lenses for eyes and cameras—all workers in minute detail which has to do with science, will exhibit this characteristic of the legible and small writing, their letter forms often tending toward the Constructive type.

Kindly send details
reading of handwriting
Yours truly,

Precise writing which is moderately large and very legible and in which the letter forms are wholly with-

out distinction expresses the capacity for dealing well with set routine.

It is not surprising to find that a certain type of school-teacher, who is honest, attentive to the duties of the work, careful, punctual and conscientious, and yet entirely without teaching inspiration, should be heavily represented in this sort of writing. A great many excellent clerks, bookkeepers, housekeepers and salespeople who sell over the counter use it. (Note that the traveling salesman will be found in the classification which also includes the promoter and the publicity worker and publicity writer; not in this one.)

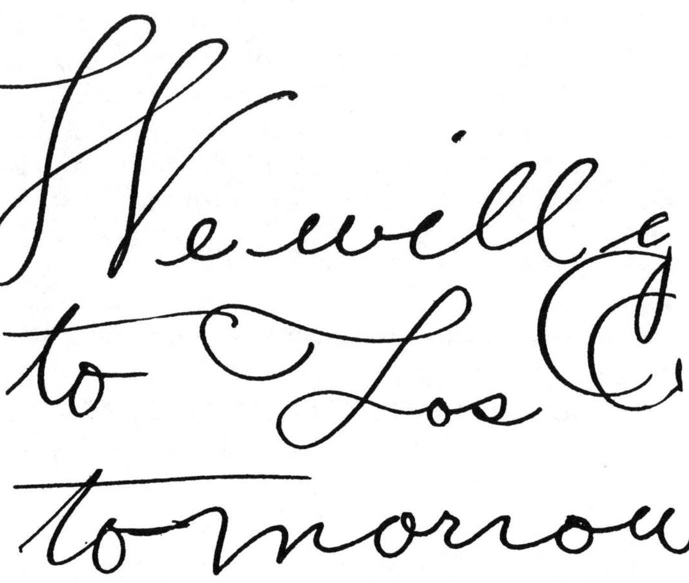

Legible writing, in which the letter formations are rather beautiful, without being extremely artistic,

shows a practical nature in which there is the appreciation of beauty and perhaps the ability to do some "applied art" work.

Turn to the chapter on the small letters and observe that the *i* which has a circle for a dot belongs in this classification, as a rule. (For definition of "applied art" see chapter on vocations.)

Dear Madam—
Please to
send me your
illustrated booklet
as per your advert-

Legible writing which is all but printed and in which the capitals are severely plain but beautiful belongs to the Constructive type.

Teachers of exact science, exceptional inventors, architects, the highest type of constructing engineers, analytical poets and writers of very fine and exact prose may be found in this classification.

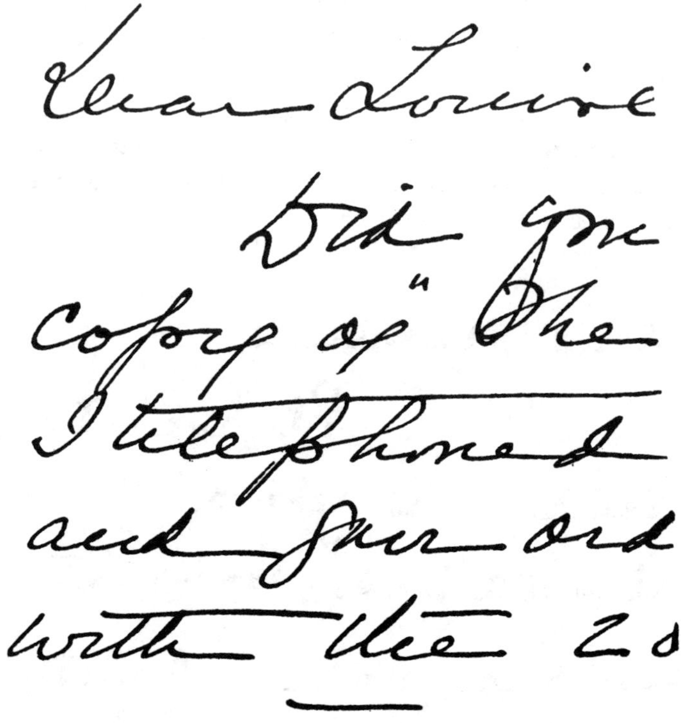

Moderately legible writing, forward leaning, very flowing, written with ease, with gracious capitals which are a good deal larger than the small letters, expresses ease in speech and considerable adaptability.

Singers, orators, "talking" politicians, clever and well-educated "confidence men," the supersalesperson, the promoter and publicity worker, all use variants of this writing, veering off to less and less of smooth, flowing movement and graciousness with the development of eccentricity and illy regulated personalities.

Dear Dissolver of Troubles:—

Your very attractive booklet has strong text appeal for preventing divorce between two great principles of life, namely, the fathering of ideas and the mothering of

Legible writing which is obviously manufactured must be studied in conjunction with the other, or "natural," handwriting.

The "library hand" which people are taught to use in the public libraries and which is also taught by a great many of the carding and filing and secretarial schools, is strictly a mechanical achievement, closely akin to the flourished birds, foliage and Arabesques which used to be taught the teacher and expert practitioner of the Spencerian hand. There is a deduction to be made from any of these mechanical forms of writing, however, which is that a great many persons cannot learn them. Those who *can* are innately of the routine type of mind, to whom detail is not tiring and whose enthusiasms are *for* routine and detail. We do not find, for instance, that the girl who writes a fine library hand also writes a very individualistic hand, when "off duty," so to speak. The more that the natural hand approaches this mechanical hand, therefore, the more will the nature show lack of spontaneity, initiative and individuality, but the more valuable will it be for the intelligent routine of work which is above the level of mechanical routine. A good many expert users of the human hand exhibit this formality and mechanism of writing.

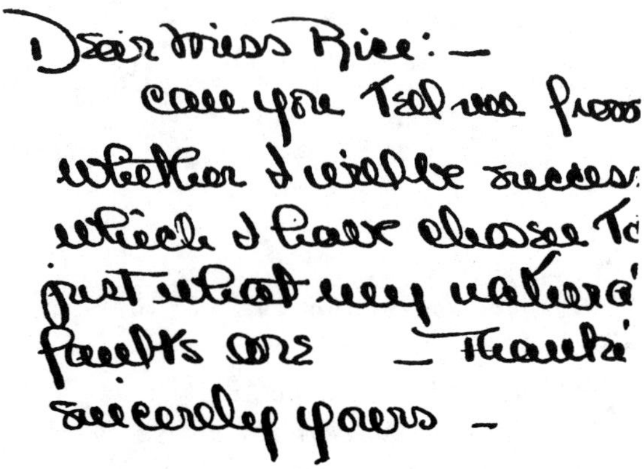
Dear Miss Rice:—
Can you tell me from
whether I will be succes
which I have chosen to
just what my natural
faults are — Thanks
sincerely yours —

Legible writing which is awkward and ungainly shows unfamiliarity with the writing implement, and, nearly always, untrained mental forces.

This is more or less the uneducated hand, but is far more promising of future mental development than the corresponding level of the illegible, *when* there is the occasional exceptional letter form, as in a capital, for instance, in which case the whole level is greatly lifted —away above the ordinary indication; for, the occasional exceptional letter formation in the very commonplace and somewhat ill-educated hand shows the mind of great promise, which is struggling to break into life and growth.

Legibility which is apparent only after we have become accustomed to the writing, is "Legible-Cryptic" and is very rare.

This means that the writer has invented forms of the alphabet which do not correspond to the known forms, and that those forms are strictly adhered to in the writing. The effort, on the part of the reader, therefore, is to memorize these forms and once that is done, the writing may be as easily read as any which is legibly written in the usual forms. People who do this, it is needless to say, have the most exceptional minds and are, almost without exception, authors, statesmen and world-known diplomats. The indication is not only of tremendous independence of thought and action, but of a personality which is lifted far above the common level—and is very outstanding.

ILLEGIBILITY

Illegibility belongs, first of all, to the utterly uneducated writer. This form of illegibility needs no explanation. It is purely a matter of training. However, it is to be observed that a certain degree of education does not, necessarily, result in the same amount of improvement on illegibility. Many people who cannot spell or express themselves, save with the utmost awkwardness, form their letters fairly well; and many who express themselves with an ease and fluency above the level of their education, find it almost impossible to write a legible hand.

The innately *legible* writer, on this level, is the person who corresponds to the neat, accurate and colorless writer on the next level upward. That is to say, individuality and originality and spontaneity are absent, but the mind and hand are capable of direct and accurate motions.

The innately *illegible* writer, on this level, is the one who would be illegible, also, on higher levels, the individuality of the mind or nature being such that it is difficult to keep to set forms.

Generally speaking, it can be said that the illegible writer gives the graphologist the worst problems and makes the solution of those problems the most difficult. The illegible writer is the joker in the human pack of cards—he may be anything! It all depends—on about fifty other things. It is therefore very much harder to give definite statements about the various types of illegible writers; but some of the generalized estimations can be given, always with the proviso that the student be exceedingly careful to add up the fifty other things before making a final decision.

Illegibility which is accompanied by an appearance of great disorder, so that the effect of the page of writing is displeasing and disturbing to the eye, is the indication of mental confusion. There is no exception to this rule.

However, it must be insisted on that a careful estimation of the level on which the mind of the writer operates is necessary before any true deduction can be arrived at; for illegible and disorderly writing in which the letter forms are manifestly those of the uneducated hand is the indication of a very different nature from that writing in which the illegibility and disorderliness are manifestly those of the highly educated hand. It it to be borne in mind, too, that it is at these extreme poles of mental development that we find this illegibility and disorderliness, but the effect produced is, of course, very different, as the causes are different.

The poorly educated, incoherent and disorderly writing is the least promising of all forms of writing, and the highly educated, incoherent and disorderly writing is the expression of the highest qualities of the mind and character, which are in a state of inextricable confusion. For the latter writer there is hope—great hope—if only the will-power can be brought into action and the self-understanding can be developed. For the former, the best thing that can happen is that the writer be put under severe discipline which is also intelligent and kindly. A great many writers like the former can be found in the ranks of the army and the navy, where they receive invaluable training—training which is worse than useless for almost every other type.

It is not surprising to find that domestics, manual laborers and those occupying the lowest level of intellectual activity should have the unformed, unlettered and illegible hand—therefore, when on such a level we find a writing which varies from this, we may at once predict for the writer the possibility of moving up a level or two, at least.

This low-level illegible writer is a routine worker but not a detailed worker. He must be supervised in work and must have imposed upon him only the necessity for the slow and monotonous repetition of the same motion; he cannot perform a duty in which skill and great speed are required in the handling of a detailed motion. Taking the writing of a certain number of factory workers as an example, it will always be interesting to see that the more legible writers are the speedier workers. This may be due, at times, to the fact that the more legible writers are better educated, but investigation will show that this is not always the case; that the man or woman with speed and efficiency in the *character* will tend to make the writing clear and readable, even though awkward and ungainly.

Illegibility which is marked by extremely ordinary letter formations and by straggling, sprawling capitals (which form of illegibility is by no means confined to the uneducated hand) *is usually accompanied by uneven pressure and a weak* t *bar, and is the indication of a nature which is without strength, direction or determination, in either character or mind.*

The capitals are the clue to the real meaning of illegible writing. If the capitals are commonplace then we may feel discouragement as to the ultimate development of the mind and character, but with fine, expressive capitals, we have the nature which is perfectly able to cure itself of its ills.

"Cryptic writing" comes under the heading of legibility, despite the fact that it is so hard to read, for the reason that it really *has* set letter formations. The difficulty is simply that of getting used to these formations.

A good many specimens of writing which are hard to read and yet have great distinction and charm of formation are erroneously called cryptic, when a little close observation will show that the letter formations are about the usual ones, with the exception that they are either slightly ornamented or slightly cut, in formation; or that the legibility of the writing is affected by the fact that the small letters continually vary in size; or that the words are written with their letters too close together; or that extraordinarily long connecting-strokes between the letters of words confuse the eye; or that the letters are indicated, as to form, rather than drawn.

The true cryptic writing, if analyzed, will show that the letter forms are *always the same* and that they vary greatly from the forms usually in use—thus, *a* will be  and *f* will be  and it is impossible to mistake them, once they are recognized.

A good deal can be said, on the matter of legibility and illegibility, from the standpoint of what the interpreter *thinks* is legibility and illegibility.

To people to whom a good bookkeeper is about the height of efficiency, the slightest lapse in legibility will show up as a bad fault; in other words, the matter-of-fact Materialist, who thinks in terms of concrete actions and deeds, will underestimate legibility which he will consider only normal and overestimate illegibility, since the latter is anathema to him. On the other hand, the person of the Mental type, who is used to regarding more than material facts, will underestimate illegibility and admire legibility, being led thereto by the reverse action of the Materialist; the Materialist finding it hard to admire anything which is not like himself, and the Mentalist often finding it hard to admire sufficiently that which is a good deal like himself!

Much of the careless illegibility of the writing of well-bred and well-educated men and women corresponds to the attitude that too great a degree of punctiliousness belongs only to the *bourgeois,* taking that word, in this country and largely in the British Isles (despite their alleged distinction of classes) to mean a mental and temperamental distinction and not a family one. For it is distinctly the lesser mental lights who are proud of writing good "hands." The greater subordinate legibility and allow the letter formations to fall as they will, so long as they are characteristic and without affectation.

This attitude can be carried too far, of course. We need to take some thought as to the formation of writing and not leave our readers groping about as for the deciphering of some long-buried inscription, all but obliterated by the flight of time. But it is also true that too meticulous attention to the conventionality of the letter form has the stigmata of vulgarity—even as has too great attention to form of any kind.

Another consideration in this matter of illegibility is the fact that rapid thinkers have great difficulty in training their minds to the careful observation of the action of the hand which gives legibility. The rapid thinker finds it hard to keep the eyes fixed on detail and for this reason many a writer is astonished to find the extreme illegibility of his writing, when he looks back over what he has written.

In estimating illegibility, then, we will have to consider carefully the rate at which the hand has traveled and the *tempo* with which it has traveled. Thus, it is clear that a smooth and uniform tempo of the action of the hand will give us a more legible writing than when the same rapid rate of writing is used with a ragged and jerky tempo. The student of graphology should never fail to seize opportunities to *see* people write and should often try to imitate the tempo of writing with which he is familiar.

This matter of tempo and illegibility gives us another clue by which we may estimate the character of writers, for the even, smooth tempo of the rapid and somewhat legible writer will tell us of a mind working rapidly but accurately and pinning its efforts to something tangible, whereas the ragged, jerky tempo of the rapid writer shows us the reverse, to which is usually added emotional disturbances, uncertain temper and great and excessive sensitiveness.

The diplomat's handwriting is often very illegible because of his tendency to make each letter of a word less and less distinct. For explanation of this, see the chapter on "Words."

PRESSURE

Those who have not given careful thought to the matter of pressure, as exerted by the human hand and forearm, in using a writing implement, are apt, when considering the matter, to ask: "What kind of pen do you use?" To this material fact they ascribe whatever of heavy pressure or lack of it may be found in the handwriting, when what they should ask is: "What pen do you *choose?*"

It is the *choice* of pen which does actively affect the matter of pressure in handwriting, and that, in turn, depends upon whether the action of the hand in writing is heavy or light.

So far is even the intelligent average person from thinking intensively on this subject, that it is hard to convince him that his choice of the pen does depend on the anterior fact. Remembering that it does, and that, therefore, the matter of the choice of a pen is only part of the whole question, let us consider what evidences of the character and temperament we may find in the fact of heavy, medium or light pressure in handwriting.

The first thing to take into consideration *is* that it is only the character and the temperament which are expressed by pressure in its varying degrees. There is nothing as to mental condition to be deduced from the matter of pressure, save in one particular which is dealt with in the chapter on "Diseases as Indicated in Handwriting."

In the matter of the pen, then, it is to be said that heavy-pressure writers instinctively choose the heavier stub, as allowing them to use most easily the pressure which is natural to them; and light-pressure writers choose the sharp-pointed pen, as admitting of that very thin line which is natural to them.

Heavy pressure denotes, not only the actual physical strength which allows the pen to be borne down on heavily, but the temperamental ardor which gives nervous vitality to any action of the body.

This gives us the actual heaviness of the physical type and the added or extra heaviness which expresses the heat of the spirit. We may rate the writer of heavy pressure, then, as belonging to those who are either sensual or sensuous—and this is a rule which has no variant and no exception.

The matter is one
in which we can
have no interest

The degree of attachment to matters of fleshly gratification, then, can be registered by the heaviness of the pen-pressure. Heavy pressure, with commonplace letter forms, will show the very sensual person, since there is so little evidence of mental action in the nature (the letters revealing this) and therefore there is little to distract the attention from its appetites of the flesh.

The degree and kind of sensuality in this case have

Sir,
Will you kindly
send mentioned
advertisement?
Respectfully.

to be estimated from the extremity of the pressure and from the commonplaceness of the letter forms, and from the perhaps added indication of actually vulgar tastes (see the chapters on the small letters and the capitals). If the objection be brought forward that a great many fine men and women use a heavy pressure in writing, the reply is, first, that letter forms will often mitigate the indication of sensuality, as showing it struggled against, modified by altruism and so on; and, second, that sensuality, while not pleasing to the idealistic temperament and not on a very high level of human feeling, nevertheless is not evil, in and of itself, except that it is rather more of a bestial instinct than we like to believe exists in humanity.

That it does exist and that, from the standpoint of the purely animal in man, it is not abnormal, is well understood by all students of psychology. It need not surprise us, therefore, that a good many perfectly good citizens—yes, and good parents and loving mates—reveal themselves to us as distinctly material and as sensual and earth-bound. Heavy pressure can be found in many types of handwriting.

Heavy pressure, with interesting and unusual letter forms, brings us at once into a different stratum. These are the people whose appetites may or may not be hearty, who may or may not be actively sensual, in the matter of sex relationships, and who may or may not be good citizens.

The unusual letter forms, added to heavy pressure, give us temperamental fervor to replace bodily fervor, and add subtle and contrary elements of thoughts and feeling to the ground-plan of the character, which remains that of the Materialist. A good many artists, musicians, writers, orators and statesmen will fall into this classification. Such people can never be as fine in caliber as if they used by preference a lighter pressure, but they have undoubted power. It is not surprising to find that these heavy-pressure-important people are more aggressive rulers and more aggressive success-getters than the light-pressure-important people, but that their ultimate place in the memory of man is less, unless they have been in such key positions in the world as to have their names carried aloft by that accident. Napoleon and Alexander, Darius and Herod, Queen Elizabeth—some of these we know to have had the heaviest of pressure and those of whose writing we have no sample could not but have had it.

Unusual letter forms at once lift the temperament of the heavy-pressure writer out of the trough in which animal reactions are the most powerful of all stimuli, and transfer sensuality to keenness of appreciation of many things which are on a higher plane. Love of perfume, music, color, the dance, and acting, all are the transcendent children of instincts which are sunk deep into the primal recesses of man's ancient ancestry of sensual reactions.

Muddy-looking writing in which the letter forms are uncouth or have the suggestion of deliberate crudeness about them shows conscious sensuality: the sort of thing which deliberately seeks indulgence and which recks little of the consequence to self or others.

Murderers through sex jealousy, debauched and abandoned people, the lowest class of criminals and vagrants, have writing which conforms to this classification. A few examples, once seen and studied, will fix the type indelibly upon the mind. It is, of course, quite possible to find such writing coming from the hands of alleged reputable citizens, but the graphologist will not be deceived by this, although it is really quite rare to find such a wolf among the sheep.

Pressure which is uneven, varying in different specimens of writing, expresses a character which is still in the process of settling to its level, as to character and temperament; and probably is just in the throes of emerging from the materialistic stage, in which heavy pressure has been uniform.

This can be seen very often in the writing of the young man and woman of from eighteen and twenty onward. They have started out with a nature materialistic and innately sensual; but good education, wise restraint of self-indulgences, on the part of parents and teachers, and the awakening of idealism through inspiration from both kinds of mentors, have all done their good work. The appetites of the body are giving place to the delights of the mind and to the tenderness of true loving kindness, which may not be free from sensuality but which does not willingly give it room. The more that the type of letters is changing, also, and other and better letter forms are supplanting commoner ones, the better is the indication.

This changeable state, as shown in handwriting, is very interesting and promising, but may produce writing which looks disorderly and which must be carefully estimated, in order that the truth of it may be understood.

Pressure on horizontal strokes and not on perpendicular strokes gives a strong will-power and an eager interest in all gratification of the senses, but does not lay the emphasis of life wholly on such gratification, as is the fact with "muddy" writing.

These people usually have strong magnetism and usually use the forward-leaning angle in their writing. They are lovers of Life, which they embrace with fervor and yet with a certain wholesomeness, having the will-power with which to control their appetites and passions and therefore accepting them with something whole-hearted and lusty and yet not lustful, in their attitude.

Heavier pressure on horizontal lines than on perpendicular lines, in a heavy-pressure hand, expresses a nature which is dominating and which will never be brought to see that the degree of materialism possessed needs to be lessened.

These are the people who actively hate idealism and who are apt to scorn any of the arts which are not rooted in delight of the flesh. Love of money, desire for power, possessiveness and aggressiveness, mark this division of the Materialistic type.

Sudden pressure on an occasional stroke is the indication of temper and of illy regulated passions and appetites, with self-control far from developed.

It is quite obvious that this covers a good deal of the writing of children, and traces of it are to be seen in the writing of those whose professions allow and even demand expansiveness of emotion, such as the lower grade of actors, many artists, and a great many of the emotional type of religious followers.

Heavier pressure on perpendicular strokes than on horizontal expresses passions and appetites which are probably without expression, save as they ravage the inner nature, and which are not either controlled or expressed through the will-power (which would be shown by the horizontal strokes being heavier than the perpendicular).

These are the "inhibited" people, the persons who secretly long for a great deal which they never dare to take or do, and who are apt to be "soured" by this, cynical, and alternately defiant and cringing.

Light, wavering pressure, with indefinite letter forms, irregular basic line and weak t *bars, shows vacillation, lack of real purpose in life, and the tendency to whine, complain and evade responsibility.*

This is the type of person who is the most exasperating of all types to those who have any real will-power and character-strength. It is usually found in the whining and complaining and shiftless wife or husband, or employee. With a good deal of really fine feeling—which does little except make the possessors wretchedly conscious that Life is not all that it might be!—they are never to be relied on, have little endurance, and are apt to have various physical ills and mental complexes. Jealousy, of a most disagreeable sort, is apt to characterize these persons.

Pressure which is both light and semi-light shows the nature which is probably developing into true self-control; the fluctuating letter forms will usually confirm this.

The letter forms, in such a case, will be different in style, so that the effect is that the "hand" is just in the process of formation. A tendency to use differing angles of inclination will usually be found, too.

Very even pressure, which is light and delicate and yet conveys the feeling of virility, is the finest indication of character development.

This, united to unusual but not exotic letter formations of the small letters and to definite and fine-looking capitals, will reveal the very highest type of character, united to a rare and fine-calibered mind. Note that the letter forms have a good deal to tell us, as to whether this fine self-control, evinced by the light and even pressure, is an indication of moral development only, or of mental development as well.

Softly rounded and flowing writing, of exceedingly even pressure, without distinctive letter formations, will give us the idealistic, tenderly unselfish and perfectly controlled moral nature, in which the mentality plays an unimportant rôle.

Light pressure, in which there is an occasional thickening of the horizontal and down-strokes, shows a nature which is idealistic, but in which impatience and temper are strong, and in which self-control is apt to have seasons of inactivity.

Irritability is shown by this sign, too, and an odd sort of abashed jealousy. Such people are more or less of the Nervous type and are the prey to their own emotional and nervous reactions. They make good workers, as they have good memories and are extremely conscientious, but they are not fitted for positions of authority and bear responsibility very ill. Usually they are affectionate but without virility in their emotions.

Pressure which is heavier in the signature than in the body of the writing is an indication of the desire to rule.

This is something which is often amusingly clear when we know the person. A good many business men, of very ordinary mental caliber, have the most assertive and forceful-looking signatures, but a glance at the body of the writing is enough to tell the graphologist that this signature is literally what the slang expression "front" means. It is a grandiloquent gesture by which a little man seeks to hide the fact that he is less than normal in stature. (Other phases of this will be considered in the chapter on "Signatures.")

When the signature is light in pressure and the body of the writing is heavier, we may have any one of several indications. The personality may not do justice to the real force and power of the mind or character; the personality may be beautifully and marvelously modest through refinement of feeling; the personality may be affected by an "inferiority complex" behind which there lurks the aggressiveness which is shown in the body of the writing.

To make this deduction and to make it correctly will require great care. If the personality does not do justice to the mind and nature, the letter forms of the signature will be quite different and far more commonplace than the body of the writing. If the personality is really modest, through spiritual aspirations and extreme refinement, the letter forms, even though unassertive, will be even more exquisite than in the body of the writing. If there is an inferiority complex, the letters forms in the signature will be cramped and the angle at which they are written will often be changed from that of the body of the writing.

As a general rule, we are to observe that heavy pressure expresses the more materialistic characters of humanity and that light pressure expresses the more idealistic characters.

There is no exception to the fact that heavy pressure shows materialism, but there are quite a number of exceptions to the fact that light pressure usually shows idealism.

Light pressure, *unless* marked by exotic letter formations, does show idealism, but we must look with a sharp eye to see whether the letter formations are consistent, whether the capitals are normal, suave and flowing, whether the *t* bar is rather long. Light-pressure writing which has involved, tortuous letter forms and in which there is either the appearance of an extraordinary disorderliness or constant change of angle of inclination, gives us the abnormal person, in whom the normal sensual passions are replaced by pale and unhealthy subterranean growths which lead to strange vices and perversions.

For instance, the habitual drunkard—even though his letter forms are attacked by unsteadiness and even though his basic line of writing wavers, and even though his nerves and bodily health are, in the most expressive metaphor, "shot to pieces"—will *still* manipulate his writing implement with something of the lusty force which was the element in his character which started him on the abuse of an appetite. That very element is the thing on which it is possible to build the reformation of almost any drunkard. The forces of his being are still normal, though their equilibrium is shaken.

The drug-addict, however, starts out with a light pressure. I am not willing to state that there are no exceptions to this rule, for researches on this point, although I have carried them on for over twenty years, still leave a great deal to be desired in the way of adequate data (it being frequently impossible to get hold of the writing of a drug-addict *before* the formation of the habit); but it would seem almost within proof, even from this brief time of investigation, that the person whose temperament leads him to the taking of drugs is innately the light-pressure writer, with odd and exotic letter formations. In other words, the drug-addict is already abnormal, by constitution, intent and leanings, before the formation of the habit.

The heavy-pressure drunkard, on the other hand, is usually a very materialistic person, with lusty and healthy appetites. The only trouble is that one appetite has been allowed to swallow up all the rest. This would explain the extreme difficulty of breaking a drug habit. Men who have been actually debased "sots" for years can cure themselves, almost without outside assistance, whereas the drug-taker, even at the start of the habit, needs medical attention for the breaking of the enslavement.

Among light-pressure people, too, we are *usually* apt to find the sex perverts and the whole batch of unhealthy degenerates of all kinds.

The objection which will be offered is that certain famous people who are or have been more than under the cloud of suspicion in this respect use heavy pressure; indeed, I can, myself, show the handwriting of a famous man, noted for his degeneracy, which belongs to the classification of the extra-heavy pressure. In this case I knew the man and his family and therefore had inside knowledge of the development of that which made him infamous—and of the development of his talents, which coincidently made him famous.

This man was a son of New England and was what science likes to call an extravert. That is to say, he was ceaselessly occupied with the thought of how he might, could, or should appear to the world, and early, even at the age of sixteen, was such a pushing, assertive and aggressive youth that he was conspicuous, although of a poor family, in which there was little culture.

Of an unpleasant personality and possessed of a bad temper, he had no chance at all, until there went to that town, for the summer, a European, also famous and infamous. The boy deliberately set himself in the way of that man, having heard the gossip—and the two became inseparable for years.

This man, now dead at an advanced age, developed a really remarkable mind and was able to dissect himself. He declared that early habit had fastened on him what was not natural to him and that he hoped that "death will slough off this body and give me the fighting, eating, lusty but healthy nature that I started with."

This story is given to explain the fact that graphologists have too often stated that the degenerate uses heavy pressure. As a rule, *and when he is innately degenerate,* he *never* uses it. The instances in which famous characters have seemed to prove the matter of the heavy pressure, were no doubt similar to the history just related.

On the other hand, the hundreds of drug-users, drug-addicts, and criminals who were drug-takers, whose handwritings have passed through my hands, have used light pressure, with the exception of about a dozen. In seven of these cases out of the dozen, I was able to verify the fact that the drug-taking and the consequent degeneracy more or less, and in different degrees, paralleled the instance mentioned above.

(Light pressure, as indication of disease and degeneracy, will be considered in the chapter on "Diseases as Indicated in Handwriting.")

That children should almost universally use heavy pressure is to be expected, since the child, far from "trailing clouds of glory," is more or less the little animal and his handwriting slides back down the trail of man's slow climb upward. When, therefore, we have the child whose pressure, even as he learns to write, is delicate, light and true, we can be sure that we are dealing with a high caliber in both character and mind.

Old age *ought* to bring light and even pressure, in which the unsteadiness of the hand might be reflected in the wavering of the stroke but not in the degree of pressure; but life—as no one can know better than the graphologist—is not always what would meet the expectation. It is no rare thing to see, in the shaking hand of age, the lusts of the body and the surge of the blood despite the fact that the actual condition has passed. Life has not put out the fires, although they are banked. If self-discipline and spiritual development have not come at mid-channel, it is my experience that they do not come at all, and that it is only the body's power to carry the voltage, which is impaired. The handwriting often shows that behind the fading flesh the big elemental forces are still pulsing.

(The matter of racial characteristics, as shown in pressure, is discussed in the chapter on "Graphological Indications of Race.")

THE BASIC LINE

By this is meant the line, real or imaginary, on which every letter is based, those with lower loops cutting through it and all others supposedly touching it with the points which depart from and return to the line.

The way in which writing is arranged, either on or off this basic line, has a great deal to do with the appearance of the writing and tells us much of the character of the writer.

A good many people use guide-lines. These, of course, invalidate our deductions based on the line; but a little acquaintance with various specimens of writing will soon tell us when such lines have been used. There is an invisible but almost tangible *beat* in handwriting, which is violated when we use guide-lines, and this is something which the graphologist will not be long in discovering.

Writing which has a very straight basic line (which is obviously not attained through the use of guide-lines) shows an even disposition.

This will be affected, of course, by the roundness or angularity of the writing, by the evenness of pressure, and by every possible consideration that the graphologist can bring to the study of the specimen. Despite everything else that can be found, however, the very straight basic line is always the indication of at least the *capacity* for holding the disposition to an even keel. If the writing is filled with hurried formations, and unequal pressure, and the basic line is *very* straight, we may presume a natural bent toward an even disposition, which is much shaken by events.

When the basic line slants upward somewhat, the indication of a happy disposition and of a tendency to be optimistic, is strong.

Just how much to depend on this will depend, in turn, on whether the writing is rounded, angular, flowing, and so on. It is always the indication of a tendency to be cheery in manner.

If the basic line slants upward sharply, the writer is rather too optimistic.

This is all the truer if there is extravagance in the outspread letter forms and large and aggressive capitals, in which case we have a fine instance of the man who, without foundation, always hopes for millions to be made "next year"—in oil stocks or in mines and so on, when he knows nothing whatever of even simpler businesses. These are people whose business judgment is very poor, although they are the last ones to think so. In business, they need partners who will hold them down to actual conditions. Their personalities are usually pleasant and their manner convincing.

The downward slant of the writing, in great or little degree, shows the like degree of depression.

This downward slant may be customary or transient.

If customary, it is practically impossible for the writer to make a line of writing which does not sag. If temporary, concentration on the matter may bring the line of writing up to the level for part of the letter. Whether temporary or not, this indication is one which is serious. It means the let-down of courage, the slackening of resistiveness and the tendency to accept what fate brings, with either resignation or despair.

If the *t* bar is long and strong there is every likelihood that this state is only temporary; but disordered writing, with letters in variable sizes and the angle of inclination vacillating to right or left, shows the state as more or less permanent. Many people who use this discouraged basic line, which accurately reflects the state of mind in which they allow themselves to be, so often complain that they never have any success—that they are always running up against misfortune—not realizing that it is their own lack of forceful enthusiasm against which they run.

Quite another sort of thing is the basic line which is fairly straight for part of each line and then drops abruptly at the end. This is the record of profound temperamental difficulties, of "inhibitions," of innately sad and sensitive souls who are almost predestined to be unhappy.

Fully two-thirds of the "suicide notes" have this sudden dropping of the basic line. When found in what seem to be normal hands, it is to be regarded very attentively. People who use it, no matter how serene they seem, are in great need of help, cheering, and bringing up to the normal level of consciousness.

It is not surprising, of course, that a great many

highly talented people display this trait. The graphologist need not hesitate to attack such writers with the assertion that they need cheering, no matter how much this is denied!

The basic line which is produced by practically every letter seeking a different level is a faithful representation of irregular waves. These people have all sorts of moods, in rapid succession and sometimes at the same time!

This is often a temporary condition, but there are many people in the world to whom every breath of emotion is a disturbing factor, and who are always in the clutch of some only half-important emotion or other. It is needless to say that people of whom this is true have little reliability and are changeable, but they often have personal charm, and, if not required to do routine work, often are quite successful, since the very receptiveness which causes their moodiness also gives them a quick understanding.

Eccentric basic lines always point the finger of "danger"—of either a nervous or mental breakdown. When the basic line sags in the middle, when it represents the waves of the sea, when it is never twice alike—the graphologist looks carefully for the *t* bar, for the pressure and for letter formations, in order to estimate the probable degree of the threatened condition. This does not properly belong to the indications of disease in handwritings, at all times, since it is often a temporary indication and not a fixed one.

(For other rules for the basic line see the chapter on Words.)

ROUNDED WRITING

Rounded writing consists of formations which are softly rounded in many places where angularity is to be found in other specimens of writing.

This definition leaves something to be desired in the way of exactness, but exactness is rendered difficult by the fact that the "roundness" of writing is such an indefinite matter, although something which the least thoughtful can understand.

The copybook will give us examples of many rounded formations, which the average person turns into angular formations; that is to say, the average writer will tend to angularize the copybook model rather than to follow it. This is natural, since few of us are without at least *some* individuality.

Therefore, when we have a piece of writing which is so softly rounded as to disclose itself to the eye at once as such, we have rounded writing which is extreme.

Very softly rounded writing, in which the capitals are of a like character, is the indication of a nature which is without aggressiveness of any kind. (See the second illustration on page 43.)

The first instinct of the careful, gentle and not-too-individualistic child is to round all the formations of writing. That a child should do this (even when the specimen is produced by quite young children) is the indication that the character is *apt* to grow into the mild and unassertive one which will continue to use the very rounded formations.

Very rounded formations will not give us assertive capitals of any kind, nor capitals which are very definite, nor horizontal strokes which are strong. *If* any of these are present, then the mildness, gentleness and unassertiveness of the rounded formations are greatly mitigated and modified. The perfect example of the rounded writing has none of these modifiers and is expressive of a nature which has remained childlike in many ways. Some of the most lovable of people may be found in this classification, however.

Partly rounded writing, with weak horizontal strokes and without positive capitals is less indicative of childlike sweetness of temper and more indicative of weakness of character, gullibility, and so on.

(See *credulous b* as special exponent of this indication in roundness; and note in the chapter on angularity the distinction in this special point between the angular writing, with weak horizontal strokes and without positive capitals, and the rounded.)

Rounded capitals and partially angular small letters show the instinct to appear more credulous and confiding than is the actual fact.

These are the people whose personalities are suave and tactful, bright, cheery—confiding in manner, but who really have a good deal of shrewdness in their natures. It is to be noted that the rounded capital—which also includes the "flowing" capital—is always the indication of personal suavity and assurance and tactfulness of manner.

Rounded small letters associated with angular capi-

tals are not often found, but this is not an unknown type. These are the people whose manner is crusty and aggressive, but who are really "easy-going" and who have little of the aggressiveness which they try to use as a shield between themselves and the world.

It is never to be forgotten that handwriting is more or less of a gesture. To be sure, the antecedents of it lie rooted so deep in the primeval history of the race that they are lost, but the shadows of those antecedents are still occasionally to be seen. In the present case, the instinct to make the capitals more aggressive-looking than would be natural and consistent is essentially the same thing as the gesture of scowling to show that we are strong and fearless. It is the instinct to "put on" a personality.

Rounded handwriting which is large and almost machine-like in its regularity, gives us the seemingly mild person, who is really "set" in opinions.

These are the people whose tyranny is none the less positive because covered by a shield of extreme mildness. There is no other type of writing in which narrow-mindedness is so pronounced an element *if* the mind is narrow at all: that is to say, some of the individuals using it may remain merely confident about ordinary matters and not too assertive of opinions, but the general thing is to find the mind firm on what may be antique, outworn and aggressively unprogressive ideas. People of this type cannot argue. They can only restate their own opinions.

Very rounded writing which is excessively small is most uncommon. It is the indication of an acute mind, united to the mildest and least assertive of characters. (See the first illustration on page 21.)

This is sometimes used by the typical "absent-minded professor," the figure who has been the subject of so many amusing tales, the man or woman whose thoughts are so fixed on some one subject that all other matters are excluded. The small size of the writing and the usually precise formation of the letters show the concentration and the scientific bent, and the roundness of the writing shows the lack of worldly sophistication.

ANGULAR WRITING

Angularity of writing gives sharp angles at places in the writing where the majority of people use rounded or curved formations.

The instinct of the angular writer is to use heavy pressure, and this, of itself, will tell us that angularity is the accentuation of more or less material tendencies. Thus we have the first rule:

The union of angular handwriting with heavy pressure and with heavy horizontal strokes tells us that the writers are interested, emphatically, in things of this world and in matters which pertain to personal satisfaction. (See the illustration on page 50.)

On the other hand, the angular writer is never as stupid as the rounded writer about matters of practical life. The judgment is usually rather good. Values are easily approximated. The opportunities for success are not only seen but seized.

It is not surprising to find, therefore, that the angular writing with heavy pressure is most often found in strictly commercial circles. Many business men who have really idealistic characters, yield to the pressure of the commercial world and model their personalities on its notions of what a man should be, which is easily shown in the angular signature they use —against the far more interesting and less angular formations of their writing in general.

Angular writing which is very small and in which

the capitals are also angular is the indication of an acute mind, to which is united the ability and the tendency to concentrate—otherwise, to specialize.

This is the "professor" type, but there is not a great deal of absent-minded good nature in *this* type. These writers are quick to see what is to their own advantage and frequently have the type of mind which, for instance, can invent a thing and market it too. In their personal relationships such writers are apt to be clannish—showing partiality for those who are allied with their own interests and not showing much interest in those outside of such interests.

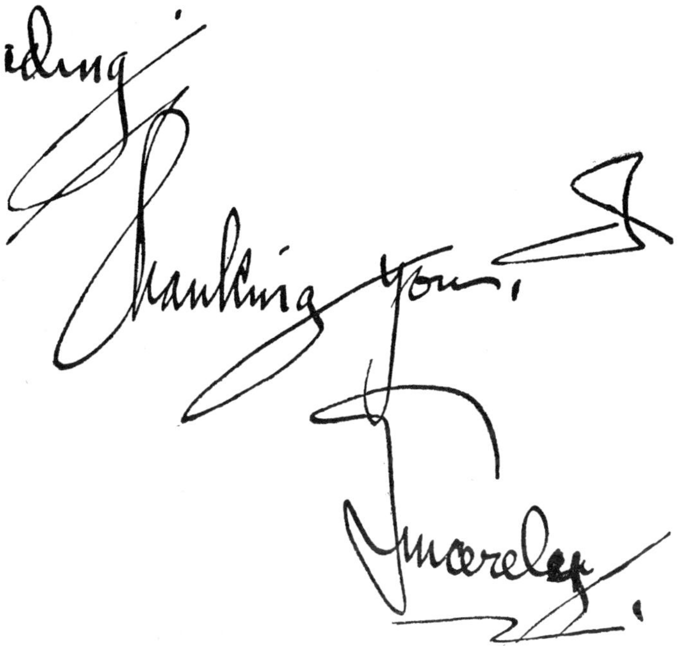

Large, irregular writing which is angular, in which

there are eccentric capitals and unusual letter forms, may belong to the selfish and clannish person with purely mental perception which replaces emotional and artistic perception.

Some of the emotional actors and actresses use this type of writing. They will never be found to be quite as smooth and easy in their work as the forward-leaning type and are *always* the victims of contradictory and disturbing personal states of feeling; something which is not true of the forward-leaning emotional type. From this type we also get the painter, at times, the stage director, and so on.

Angular writing, in which the letter forms are all but printed, and which is distinguished by especially beautiful, and severe, letter forms, is the indication of a high development of Constructiveness.

The architect is usually a striking example of this,

the constructive engineer is, too; and often the builder, cabinet-maker, toy-maker, and designer of such small art objects as jewel settings. These people often have the reputation of being unfeeling because they are not demonstrative and because they cannot help but think coldly even about things which affect their emotions, but the truth is that they are as ardent as some of the types which graphologically express it more frankly—the trouble being that they cannot help giving the lead to their minds rather than to their emotions.

Appealing to these writers from the standpoint of the emotions alone, is futile. Appeal to their conceptions of right—wrong—justice—good judgment—reason—and their emotions will assert themselves; but, appeal directly to the emotions and the mind will, involuntarily, take an antagonistic attitude. They take orders very well, *from their superiors,* but are aggressive and often insolent to inferiors, since they must respect thoroughly before they can accept any coercion at all.

Men of this type are supposedly more just and stern in dealing with women than they are loyal or patient, but—given a woman whom they respect—they are the most patient of men.

Small, angular writing, squeezed-looking, with constrained capitals, with o, a *and* g *tightly fastened, is the indication of real stinginess and moral pettiness.* (See "Small Letters" for these formations.)

The true miser, the man and woman who love money for its own sake, the persons in whom human feelings have atrophied—write like this. As a tribute to human nature, I can state that seldom, in even all the extensive correspondence which has been mine, have I seen this type of writing, in all its wretched completeness. Modifications of it—yes. An occasional line of it—yes; but seldom a whole page. The one perfect example of this writing which I have was written by a man who lived in a shack on the outskirts of Brooklyn some years ago. He was found dead in the shack, which also contained bankbooks showing balances of some forty thousand dollars. The man died from malnutrition due to his persistent effort to live solely on potatoes and rice. He was a man with quite a fine mind originally; but avarice became his besetting sin, and with the gaining of that sin in his soul his writing shrank and contracted until it become almost the epitome of the type.

In considering the matter of the rounded and the angular writing we may estimate that these distinct formations have something definite to tell us about temperament, in its special application to mating.

Rounded-letter users like the demonstrated affection of a type which is not too strongly colored with sex. They are the people who pet children, kiss babies, coo over puppies and kittens, love to be appreciated with words and bloom under praise. It is obvious that it is the affection of home ties, and the pleasant relationship of the shared shelter and food and pleasure which will appeal to the rounded writer.

Angular-letter users are more passionate in temperament and their affection is more exclusively for the mate and their interest more centered in him or her. They are jealous and possessive but devoted, ardent and demonstrative at times.

The rounded-letter user can forget the loss of a mate if children are left, if the home is left, if friendship is left, but the angular-letter users are the people who sometimes die when the mate is lost and they are almost universally the people who get into print through shootings and stabbings of jealousy and through the tragedies which attend passional relationships. It is obvious that marriage between the very angular-letter user and the very rounded-letter user is a most precarious affair. (For further discussion of this matter see the chapter on "The Angle of Inclination.")

THE ANGLE OF INCLINATION

The angle at which writing inclines either to the right or the left—or the fact that it does not incline at all—is of the utmost importance, from a graphological standpoint.

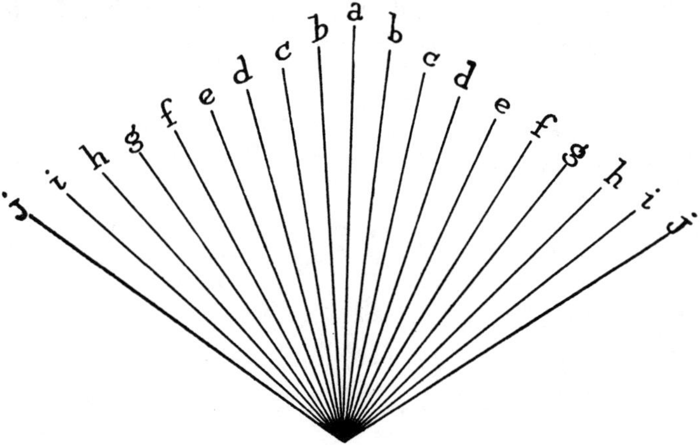

In a jesting spirit, I have sometimes called this angle "the love register"; and to a large extent, that is a very good name for it, for the emotions which have to do with the affections find their outlet, as to handwriting, in this inclination at which the hand lays the writing on the paper.

Let us start with the angle which is no angle at all, but is upright writing. This is the norm—the key of C, as it were, to the gamut of human emotion. It is the "no-ardor" indication. Rightward from it, sloping more and more, until the most extreme forward-leaning angle possible is reached, lie the openly ardent people and those to whom the *expression* of that ardor is a desperate need. Leftward from it, forming the various angles of the so-called "backhand," lie the reserved, unexpressive, inarticulate people, who are, some of them, quite as intense as the forward-leaning, but who have not the ability nor, often, the wish, to express their emotion, and who are sufferers from all sorts of phobias and inhibitions which have to do with attachments for their fellows.

Upright writing, when rounded, of medium size, and with pleasant but unobtrusive capitals and moderate t *bars, is the expression of the good child: obedient and sweet-tempered, willing to learn, interested in everything and attached to others only by the gentlest and purest of ties; the passions of the adult being embryonic only.* (See the second illustration on page 43.)

The good child. That is what these writers are. Lovely people, pure in heart, adaptable to ordinary life; patience and kindliness their innate traits. Put them in positions where this is wanted and they are the mortar which will hold together the fabric of society. As mothers and teachers for little children and as nurses for the sick the type is perfection. Not good for surgical nurses—cannot stand the strain. Not good as teachers of higher grades, for they lack the understanding of the complexities of adolescence. Unfortunately, this type causes a great deal of unhappiness in the world, for the reason that, the personality usually being sweet and loving and the character fine, all sorts of people are drawn to it—marry it—and almost immediately regret the step. This angle of inclination can marry successfully only with its own angle and sometimes with the angles which lean at one or two degrees away from it to the right or left—but that is all.

Upright writing, very angular, the letters narrow, the pressure heavy, show the writer to be extraordinarily efficient, cold in temperament, interested in power. (See the illustration on page 50.)

This type should not marry at all, unless a person of exactly the same type. The ability to work hard is really unusual; the sincerity and truthfulness is usually good (unless contradicted by other indications); and the loyalty that of a "good pal"—never anything more. This type cannot marry even the preceding. The ideal of attachments is the union of interests, the loyalty which keeps the secrets of the other, the physical loyalty, the bravery which endures for the sake of the other. To this type caresses are childish when they are not disgusting. He or she will prove a good friend; invariably a poor parent; never much beloved but always greatly trusted.

Upright writing, small fine letters, light pressure, accurate letter forms, very small capitals, without distinction, is the indication of indifference to the usual passions and of very faint physical appetites. (See the first illustration on page 21.)

Quiet and scholarly men and women who live alone and prefer to do so, never having married, or having continued the married state only a short time, are very often of this type. They love a well-ordered home, serenity of life, well-served but not highly spiced meals, good service—all the sensuousness of which the nature is capable being poured into such reactions. They should not marry the preceding type, whose ambition, aggressiveness, and efficiency, would make them very unhappy. They may, however, marry the first type, who will pet and mother them and not recognize that there is a good deal of indifference on the part of this type to that fact.

Forward-leaning writing, one degree from the upright, medium size, mixed angular and rounded formations, well-placed t *bar, capitals not unusual but very often the* i *dot which shows humor.* (See "Small Letters.")

This is the handwriting which is found in a great many people, in all ranks, and which reflects the normal good sense and lack of aggressive individuality of the traditional "man in the street." The affections are expressed with ease, but are not intense or complex enough to demand unusual expression. It is in this type that we find a great many of the good-natured and rather inefficient people, the plain truth being that they are too easy-going to get the best out of themselves.

Forward-leaning, two degrees from the upright, increases fervor. From this degree, away over to the angle which is inclined so sharply to the right that it seems to be falling, so to speak, we have the constantly increasing degree of fervor.

It is not possible, in these angles of inclination, to make the more or less standardized rules which are possible in the previous instances. From the second degree of the rightward inclination we have the most intensely individual and assertive of temperaments, with all possible complications of mentality and character. Therefore, in considering the matter of the angle of inclination, we have to make some general rules, such as the two following:

Extreme angles of inclination show temperaments which are never as indifferent to sex attraction as the lesser angles, and which include extreme individuality of concept as to sex attraction.

It is obvious that the heavier pressures on the very forward-leaning angles of inclination will increase the sensuousness or the sensuality of these attractions, and the light and very light pressures will carry all sex feeling up to planes of idealism which are practically not sensuous at all, although the intensity of feeling is present, and in a high degree.

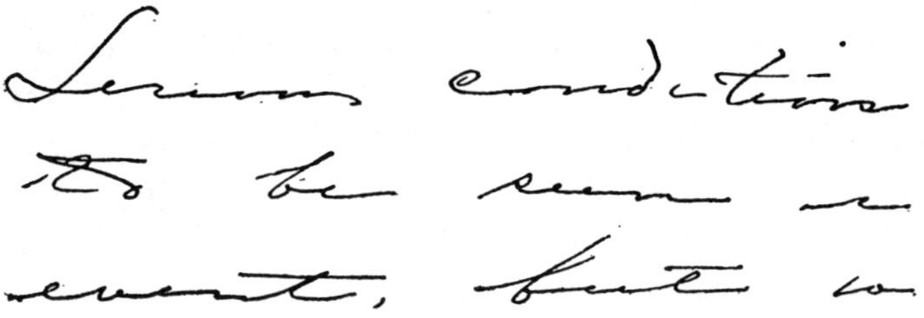

The most extreme angle at which writing can be inclined to the right, and if there is extremely flowing writing, is often used by emotional actors and actresses, sometimes by musicians and nearly always by those who are imaginatively ardent.

It is folly, of course, for us to subject every alleged emotional actor and actress to this test, or to state that this is the only form of handwriting in which emotionalism can be found. The more intellectual of the emotional stage folk transmute their emotional intensity to the mental plane, and this is reflected in their writing. It is also a very delicate question as to whether many who have the reputation for emotionalism are not merely good mirrors of the emotional playwrights and directors to whom they owe their fame! Nevertheless, taking all this into consideration, it is possible to state that this extreme forward-leaning and flowing writing is always the expression of the capacity for expressing emotion, *in some form.* Sometimes we have the painter of high color—the "intense" painter, using this type of writing. It is almost impossible to find such a writer as this with a colorless personality. The personality is always able to *flow*—to send out its waves of magnetism—and this is true, even when, as once in a long while may happen, we find this type of writing is the uncultured and all but uneducated.

All the angles of inclination which lean leftward away from the upright show variations on reticence, reserve, inhibition, self-consciousness, lack of self-expression and other forms of being which are the reverse of expansive.

It is true of the first- and second-degree angles leaning leftward from the upright—as it is true of the same degrees leaning away from it to the right—that they approximate the general types of humanity. Among these types—the upright, and the first and second degrees of inclination to the right and left—there is great community of interests. They will frequently be found to be of the Philoprogenitive type and are never iconoclasts, reformers or innovators, *unless* extreme and unusual letter forms distinguish them; and extreme and unusual letter forms are not to be found, as a rule, in these angles of inclination.

It is in the more extreme leftward angles that we get nearly all of the greatly involved and sometimes morbid temperaments—the people who cannot find proper self-expression and who are afflicted with many personal and internal difficulties.

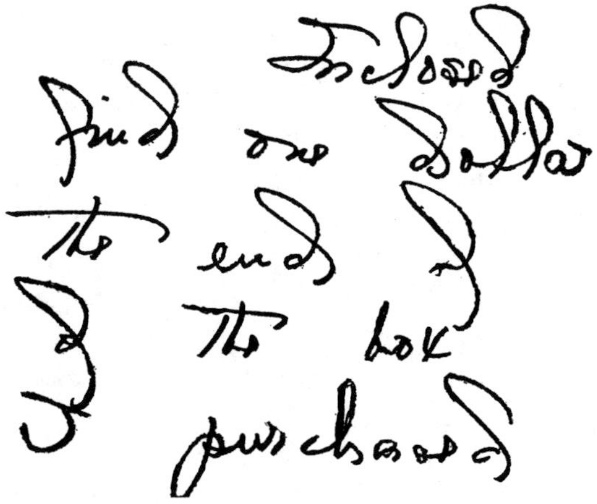

In proportion as the writing is "backhand," angular, eccentric, jerky in rhythm, uncertain and varied in letter forms, in just that proportion is the writer a tortuous and complex nature, with a temperament which makes his (or her) life a burden and which causes him to be an object of perplexity and worry to those who care for him.

It will be found that the leftward or "backhand" writer is apt to have a far more baffling personality than the extreme rightward angle of the corresponding degree. Charm is often theirs, and sometimes a perverse charm which holds affection and yet does not reward it, which demands affection and yet does not seem to return it.

Marriage between the various angles of inclination: The one thing which the graphologist is asked more frequently than anything else is, "What is the writing like of the person whom I should marry?" The angle of inclination tells more about this than any other graphological point; although of course everything else has to be taken into consideration too. The angle, however, will give the clue. (See the statements on mating in the chapters on rounded and angular writing.)

In general, the norm, or upright, may marry with angles one and two either to the right or the left. These people, although very different from each other, approximately dwell in the same world and will have common meeting-grounds, especially as to their emotional reactions; but they will not have many meeting-grounds with the more extreme angles of either the right or the left inclination, those extremes usually having not only emotional, but also mental, reactions which are different from the fundamentally simple five.

The extreme angles of the rightward inclination may or may not marry successfully among themselves. It is always safer to have one angle slightly less than the other and to have the extreme individuality of one less than the other. In this case, we have to look to letter formations, to pressure, to variability of capitals and so on, for light.

The extreme leftward angles of inclination do not marry so successfully among themselves. Two ardent and inarticulate people are apt to get to an *impasse* sometime or other. It is to be noted that as the angle of leftward inclination increases the ardor, passion and sensuousness also increase, just as these elements of character increase with the rightward inclination; so varying degrees of the leftward angle of inclination vary in this respect, and so may marry with some expectation of happiness. Generally speaking, however, the extreme rightward angle of inclination can marry the extreme leftward angle of inclination with—ultimately—better results than with any other combination. It is inevitable that there should at first be friction with such a mating. The rightward angle will be demonstrative and expansive and the leftward angle will be reticent and withdrawn; but the thing which will unite the two will be the fact that in the leftward angle of writing the fires of ardor burn quite as high as in the rightward. There is also the strange charm of the leftward-writing people to estimate, which is precisely the charm of the hidden fires—the veiled ardor—the eyes which give a glimpse of feeling and then shroud themselves. This is the personality which is very apt to appeal strongly to the rightward-leaning writer, especially of heavy pressure.

Human nature being the contrary thing that it is, it is not surprising that the writers of uncongenial angles of inclination should often want to marry each other and should frequently do so. It is then the graphologist who may show those people how to get along with each other, what allowances to make, and so on.

The reserved and undemonstrative leftward writer who marries the extreme rightward writer can frequently have a happy marriage if each understands the nature of the other.

When various angles of inclination are to be seen in the same specimen of writing, or when the writing varies a great deal at different times as to the angle of inclination, the writer is still emotionally growing up.

This is frequently seen in the handwriting of young people and is sometimes a characteristic of older persons who have never learned to control their emotions. When the latter is the case, it is impossible to depend upon the mood of the writer for more than an hour at a time, and stability of *emotion* is entirely lacking. It is a mistake, however, to read this tendency as instability all along the line of character. If the *t* bar is strong and other elements do not point to weakness, it is in the moods alone that the weakness exists.

The ability to write different angles of inclination, with extreme ease and facility, accompanied by the ability to make the writing appear quite different, is the indication of rather a dangerous quality in the character. Such people are apt to be "all things to all men."

If the letter formations are indicative of goodness and sincerity, then we have in this facile writer merely the great diplomacy which sustains itself in integrity, though never seeming to be aggressive in so doing.

If the letter forms are not emphatic on the point

of sincerity, then we have to regard the writing with extreme attention, for the determination of its true character. It is so obvious that here we are discussing the type out of which we get the forger that comment is rather unnecessary. Nevertheless, it is to be borne in mind that even the criminal forger is the least disagreeable of the criminal class and that it is rare to find him a person of small and petty faults.

As against this, there is also the fact that the more educated blackmailers, confidence men and untrustworthy employees, are apt to display this rather too great talent in writing. Many factors in the handwriting must be taken into consideration before we allow ourselves to brand a specimen of writing as belonging to this "uppercrust of the underworld"—but we must make sure that we do not underestimate it either.

The ability to write at either the extreme forward angle or the extreme leftward angle—or to write with the forward angle and the upright angle—or to combine easily any two of these angles of inclination, will give us the more or less dual person.

The duality of some people is a matter which is exceedingly interesting. Moreover, it is not as uncommon as might be expected. There are people who are so truly two that, could they appear in one of their aspects to one set of persons and in the other to another set, it would be impossible for those two sets of persons to recognize the different aspects as parts of the same person. This fact explains a good deal about the tantalizing and baffling people who change, at times, for whole days together, into what is practically a stranger.

It is needless to say that such people are not especially reliable, *as to action,* although a certain unity of feeling may prevail. Thus a man may be a good friend and yet be so exceedingly moody that it is impossible to depend on how he will behave at any given time; and still we may be sure that in an emergency, he remains a friend.

One thing we may positively state:

The ability to write with equal facility two angles of inclination is the indication that the personality will be varied in the effect which it produces and that the moods will be many. (Note that this is a different thing from the ability to write *many* hands.)

SIZE

After considering legibility, illegibility, pressure and the points covered in previous chapters, the next step is to consider the size of any writing under observation.

Generally speaking, it is the very small handwriting which expresses the power to concentrate and, hence, to do a few things well.

Generally speaking, it is the very large handwriting which shows the expansiveness of the temperament and the great difficulty in pinning the powers to definite work. There are, however, a great many exceptions and considerations which affect the deduction.

Medium-sized writing, in which the letter forms are ordinary, is about what we must expect from the average person, who is not an exception in any way.

As soon as we have a real deviation from this average size *in average writing* we are sure that we have something exceptional to deal with. When we have a piece of writing which is just this ordinary sort of thing, hardly to be distinguished from hundreds of other specimens, and find it either very small or very large we have the evidence of something decidedly wrong—which leads us to the following two rules:

Ordinary handwriting, without a distinguishing mark in the letter formations, which is excessively small, is the indication of a mentality which is close to the brink of abnormality.

However, be sure that it is "excessively." If it is

cramped and "squeezed" the indication is stronger. Minute handwriting which is very easily read and which manages to preserve a certain amount of rhythm does not fall under this classification. The type will show little or very broken rhythm, is usually squeezed, and the lines run into each other, or are arranged with great disorder.

Here we have the mentality which begets the monomaniac—the slightly unbalanced miser, the hermit, the recluse who hates and fears the world; the men who fear women and have homicidal tendencies toward them; the women who are followed by the delusion of persecution; the people who fancy themselves the victims of strange dangers. Phobias, inhibitions, physical ailments, and so on, are to be expected. These people are offshoots from the Nervous type.

Ordinary writing, without a distinguishing mark in the letter formations, which is extraordinarily large, is not the indication of such a serious state as the preceding; but entirely normal conditions are not shown.

Such writers have often a sort of harmless personal vanity, women dressing loudly and men being loud in their proclamation of their successes. Moral turpitude is not indicated, but the ability to resist temptation is small. Many a girl with mediocre writing, which is amazing only because ten words of it fill a sheet of writing-paper, takes to the primrose path, not because she has any real inclination for it, but because she cannot resist the appeal to her vanity, which is the usual start of such a trip—and also because she is so inordinately fond of dress and adornment that all else sinks into nothing beside the prospect of having that taste gratified. Boys who use such mediocre and very large writing are also personally vain. This indication should be watched for in the young and when found, the writers should be handled with extreme care. (See the chapter on "The Care and Education of Children.")

Exceedingly small writing, with distinctive letter forms, upright or only slightly inclined to right or left, with small and severe capitals, is the writing which is indicative of either training in science or predisposition to interest in science.

"Science" is, of course, a term which is very loosely used. Let us stop, then, to pick out the indications in this representative handwriting and to see where they point. The very small size is the indication of concentration—of specialization; the almost upright angle of inclination shows the emotions under firm control; the small and severe capitals express a severely academic taste. *Therefore,* this type of handwriting gives us the "professorial" type. It makes no difference whether the professor is studying microbes, hydraulics, the history of ancient Greece or modern economics—the man or woman is part of one kind. This form of the small handwriting gives us the indication of high mentality, but of a specially trained mentality, which pours *all* of its powers into *one* line. This is very different from the expansive mentality shown in certain types of large writing.

Exceedingly large handwriting, with virile and interesting letter forms, and with long horizontal strokes, is the writing which is also indicative of the highest mentality, but this is the mentality which does not pin down to one line, nor does it excel in detail, but must operate on a large field.

To this rule there are all sorts of addenda, however. In the first place, the very small, fine and individual handwriting does not show the ability to do detail work with the hands, that we might think. As one of the curiosities of contradictory human nature, we may call to mind the fact that miniature painters usually have very large hands, and that the makers of the most gigantic monuments ever erected by man were the Egyptians, who had the smallest hands of any historic race. The concentration which is shown by very small and interesting handwriting has to do with mental action and is hardly ever accompanied by extreme physical manual skill, *except* when such skill is exercised in the doing of work which has to do with the mental action. Thus, a microscopist may handle the instrument and his fragile objects of observation with a sure touch, but he would never do any other kind of detail work.

The large handwriting coming under the rule just given does not attend to *mental* detail well, but would attend to big schemes well, and handle the executive detail of such schemes. To clear up this distinction:

The small, interesting writing belongs to the class of "professorial work." The large writing, with interesting letter forms and long horizontal strokes, belongs to the executives who manage detail but do not, themselves, want actually to do it.

The excessively small writing, which is so clearly written that it is not hard to read, despite its size, and which has capitals which are in proportion to the size—that is, has capitals which are the right size, according to the size of the small letters—is usually the indication of the person whose personality is unostentatious but by no means effacing, and whose mentality is accurate in its deductions and keenly critical.

These people are natural connoisseurs. They have the instinct for expertness. They are found in some editorial positions, frequently as wonderful "readers" for publishing houses, so long as they have a working-mate who will add the enthusiasm and far-sightedness which they usually lack. The type should not be censured for short-sightedness, however. It is not possible to observe everything right at hand and keep looking down the road, too!

Large and flowing writing in which the capitals are gracious and assured is the indication of highly developed personal traits and of the power to magnetize others.

Social success, success on the stage and the lecture-platform; a liking for all pleasant forms of pleasure and a dislike for sordid things; the affections expressed with frankness and with normal intensity, without sensuality—are indicated.

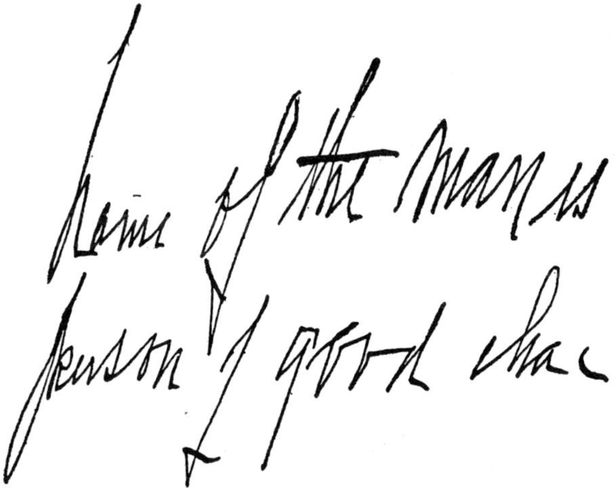

Large, cramped writing, with angular formations and heavy pressure, shows extreme conventionality, resistiveness to influences, and the tendency to be narrow-minded.

It is very difficult to get writers of this type to agree to anything which is not a result of their own experiences. And it is especially hard for them even to approximate an understanding of other types who are very different. The instinct is to abide by the letter of the law and to fail of comprehending that the spirit of the law is a finer thing. The instinct to conserve is intense, so that such writers are almost always reactionaries and are usually out of tune with their age. They are the singers of praises for "the good old days." Nevertheless, their place in the world is exceedingly important. If it were not for the drag that they put on us, collectively and individually, this world would be a wilder one than it is.

Such people work steadily and steadfastly; have high standards of *deeds*—are not so able to understand ideals of *feeling*—and are usually a little hard on young people.

Small and flowing writing, in which the capitals are very gracious and the individual letters individualistic, is the indication of strong individuality, united to an original and well-trained mind. (See the illustrations on pages 24 and 68.)

People who write in this fashion are able to do scholarly work and yet have also the "extrovert" tendency, which enables them to make their personalities outstanding. In this type, especially if the letter forms are unusual and the *t* bars long, we have the exceptional and exceedingly individualistic person who is also exceedingly human. Such persons are not limited as to the kind of work which they can do, but are limited in one thing, which is that they make poor employees, being too aggressive and too sure of themselves for subordinate positions, which they do not fill graciously.

If the writing is heavy, the passions and appetites are keen, but controlled by good taste and by persistent interest in the world in general. If the writing is light in pressure, then the passions and appetites have either never been overly developed or—what is far more likely—have been beaten down to subjection through counter-development of the mind and the spirit.

A good many authors are found in this type of writing; but humanitarians, teachers, a few actors, a very few religious teachers and some artists are also in it. If this type of person is so unfortunate as to be beaten down to subordinate positions, the failure made is greater than that of any other type—for such people, although far from arrogant, find it very hard to take orders, usually being able to give better orders than they can receive—and being better fitted to give orders than a good many other types. It is not surprising, therefore, to find some of the most conspicuous failures of the world in those who use this writing, as well as some of the greatest successes.

There is a natural variation in the size of writing which corresponds to what is the cause of the writing being done. Thus, notes being taken of a lecture will usually be small—because the notebook is, as most people will declare, but some experimenting will soon convince any one that the writing of notes which are to be preserved *and which are to be aids to mental action* will produce the smaller handwriting, no matter whether the notebook be large or small. Thus, the making of a writing smaller when the mind is concentrating is an evidence of the graphological law that small writing expresses concentration, and the sprawling formations in which we pen casual, gay notes to our intimates express the state of mind in which they were penned.

The fact that such a change in size is due to temporary causes, then, does not invalidate the graphological law but, rather, confirms it.

Large capitals and small small letters show that pride is high and courage positive.

People of whose writing this is a characteristic are

apt to be imperious in manner when aroused or opposed. The more that the writing is rightward and flowing in rhythm, the more will there be the ability to beat down opposition, to carry things onward with a flourish, to dominate by sheer weight of the personality.

Capitals which are too small, taking into consideration the size of the smaller letter, show the reverse of this: the personality which does not have weight and the pride which is not strong enough.

People of whose writing this is a characteristic are utterly unassertive. Of course, this does not prevent them from being noble in character. Some of the most spiritual of persons show this characteristic, which is quite in keeping with their other-worldliness and indifference to anything which has to do with personal aggrandizement. When the writing is not highly spiritual, then, we have in this use of very small capitals the entire lack of the fighting soul. Such people, it is needless to say, are often the unfortunate sports of circumstance.

WIDTH

In considering size, width also must be considered, but there are many ways in which the width of letters bears little relation to the size of the writing.

Width is the breadth of the letter from side to side.

It is too often the fact that, because the connecting-stroke between letters is long, we get the impression that the letters are wide. The first thing, then, is to see whether the letter actually is wide.

Width is a matter of relativity. The letter which is spread out to double the width of the average letter shows diffused interests and emotions and passions which are apt to be marked by inconstancy.

These are the people who "fall in love" easily and as easily fall out again. They are often kindly and friendly, but never passionately attached to only a few people. They like contact with the world and are usually successful in social life, though apt to be less tactful than many, especially if the *size* of the letter is not great—i.e., is not high.

Wide letters which are of a good size are more indicative of poise, balance, and endurance than the wide letters which are not high.

The tendency is to be frankly interested in the world everywhere, but not to be inconstant to personal attachments. These people, who usually belong to the Vital type, and who use a pronounced forward-leaning angle, are frankly fond and tender, but can soon forget bereavement. Such people can marry happily several times, no matter how much they have seemed to care for the partners whom they lose by death.

Very wide letters which are very large must be read in the light given by the capitals of the writing. Capitals which are wide and bear normal relation to the small letters in character, tell of a childlike nature which is complicated by egotism.

A good many people who can be found in the show business, in minor capacities, have writing like this. Acrobats often do, and so do the lesser lights of the circus. The width of the letter gives them that instinct to seek association socially with the world which the width always shows.

Angular, wide letters are more apt to give active bad temper and real selfishness than rounded wide letters, in which credulity is always shown.

Angular wide letters give a dominant note to the selfishness which is so pronounced that it is blatant and bland. Rounded wide letters give a dominant note to the gullibility, which is partly selfish and partly mere stupidity. In making both of these deductions, however, we have to remember that the graphological rule, that no one indication must ever be studied by itself, is in full force here, where the many other elements of writing may well affect the deduction.

Medium-wide letters, with wide and rather sprawling capitals, show the innate judgment of the writer, as evidenced by the small letter, struggling with the instincts and emotions, which are shown in the capitals.

Medium-wide letters with capitals which are slightly compressed as to width, show the instincts as cautious and the judgment as not being invalidated by the emotions.

This is the average handwriting, of the average good citizen.

Letters which begin to seem slightly compressed and therefore narrow, are leading off into the type where we find self-expression difficult, and self-consciousness and inhibitions present.

As the width of letters decreases, the instinct of the writer to be credulous decreases. This rule, however, is somewhat hard to put into active practise in the delineation of character, since very often the people who use the very, very wide letters affect a cynicism which is not really theirs, while the rather narrow letter writers—who often use the extreme forward leaning angle—are so warm-hearted and kind that the innate shrewdness of their judgment does not appear until there is some special reason for it.

It is worth noting that the really cynical person often takes care to appear not so much so, and that the really credulous person is usually the one who most loudly proclaims his sophistication.

Extremely narrow letters which are also small in size may belong to the Mental type or the Constructive type, if the capitals are "printed," the d *and* e *and* t *distinctive, and charm and beauty of the writing strong.*

In this case, the narrowness of the letter is to be read as indicating mental powers accentuated and concentration strong.

Narrow letters which are also high, the capitals narrow and the t *bar pronounced, show the tendency to tyrannize over others and to hold narrow-minded views.*

We are apt to find executive ability, too, in this handwriting, but ability which is dealt out with the "iron fist." Such people are sure to draw the bitter enmity of many and the active hate of others. They seldom have many friends, but usually have a few close and trusted associates.

Many of the conditions surrounding such people either accentuate or lessen their natural tendencies. When possessed of cosmopolitan training and mellowed by happy home lives these people are often great organizers.

The letter without width is seldom rounded and is often extremely angular, but when at all rounded, the indication is of greater affection and unselfishness than is shown by the angular formations in the same width.

Generally speaking, the narrow letter expresses some compression. Stricture of the emotions, concentration of the interests, the ability to think with great directness and force, are all found in the narrow letter. So, too, of course, are the elements of miserliness, petty meanness and lack of ardor, sometimes.

As a rule, wide letters show that the emotions are rather near the surface and that both happiness and sorrow can be soon forgotten.

The more or less narrow letter is tenacious. It holds what it gets. It is the letter of bitter, unforgiving animosities, but it is also the letter of passionate attachments, of faith that will not allow itself to be broken, of deep, patient and possessive loves.

RHYTHM

This word usually occasions a good deal of confusion on the part of the student, and many are inclined to think that it means the length of the connecting-strokes of letters.

To see what rhythm really is, get a dozen people to sit down before you and ask each one to write about twenty lines of something—not a quotation, as the hand instinctively changes its natural rhythm when the mind is groping for set words. Have this done so that you can watch them all writing at the same time—their right hands being on a line, so that the comparison of the movements of the hands is easy for you.

You will see that there is something very distinctive about every hand. Some jerk. Some glide. Some creep. Some get along in a series of little leaps.

This is what is meant by the rhythm of the hand in writing.

The rhythm of the hand in writing becomes more and more a set thing as the character matures.

You may find the young person and the totally formless character person using different rhythms at different times; but the older person, and especially the person whose character is a definite one, will use the same rhythm, even when the style of writing has been either deliberately or involuntarily changed.

This explains one of the mysteries of the criminal

world, which is that the cleverest forgers are usually not men of any positive character. They have a genius for manipulating money, perhaps, or for accounting and figures, but mentally they are usually about fourteen. It is no wonder that this is so, and it would be the greater wonder if it were not. The forger, taking on the rhythm of other hands, would have to have only the faintest rhythm of his own.

Women have more decided rhythms than men and more individual ones.

For this reason, it is harder to classify the rhythms of women than it is of men, and this generalized distinction is the only graphological sex distinction. In fifty representative men, chosen from any social stratum, two-thirds may be found, not only to be using rhythms which are similar, but which are more or less characteristic of their special stratum. This is not true of women, who, in this as in almost everything else, are less standardized than men.

This shows why we seldom have successful women forgers. The rhythm of different writings is exceedingly difficult for the woman to control. When she can, when she is innately a forger, by possibility if not by intent, she is never a woman of especially reliable character in word or deed. On the other hand, absolute divergence between the sexes, on this point, cannot be relied on as sure.

Long, swinging rhythms belong to emotional people who are frank in the demonstration of what they feel.

It is, of course, natural that the long, swinging rhythm should usually acompany the forward-leaning angle and writing which is not too angular. The ability both to produce and to enjoy music, color and action is indicated. People of the long, swinging rhythm usually have grace and tact, suavity of manner, and the ability to deal well with strangers. Orators and actors, as a rule, use this rhythm.

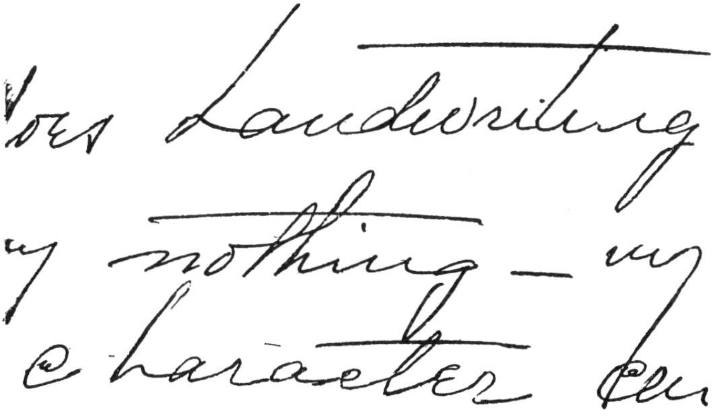

The short, choppy rhythm is always the indication of checked emotion and a personality which has to struggle with reserves.

Many users of the upright and the backward-leaning angle show this rhythm; but occasionally we find writing which lies over as far to the left as it could to the right, and in this there is the long, swinging rhythm. This is really a feat, as any one can see who will try to keep such a rhythm with the extreme leftward inclination of the writing. These people are similar to those who use the extreme forward-leaning angle, but are even more intense and far more jealous and possessive—if that be possible.

An excellent way in which to identify the rhythm in

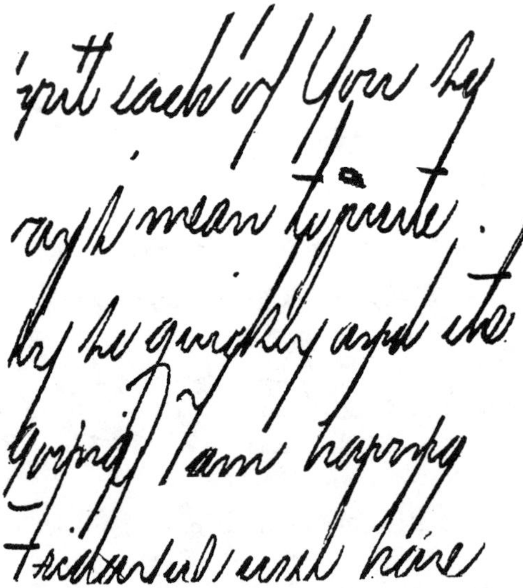

which a specimen is written is to reproduce the writing in the air with the forefinger. It will be found that it is quite possible to do this, and to reproduce the writing fairly well, when it is practically impossible to make a reproduction on paper.

Every person who is a constant or easy writer will acquire a rhythm which is like the beat of music and which, like music, is clear to the accustomed eye, as music is to the ear. Writing in which there is no ascertainable rhythm, which is continually broken as to rhythm, belongs either to very stupid or very immature people or to those unfortunates whose lives have been literally crushed by trouble and privations.

(Other statements as to the matter of rhythm will be found in the chapter on "Diseases as Indicated in Handwriting.")

CONNECTING-STROKES

It is too often thought that a wide letter will give us the corresponding long connecting-stroke of the letters of the word, but this is not always so.

Generally speaking, the *length* of the connecting-strokes of letters in words is the *width* of the letters, and this gives us the first rule in this division.

Connecting-strokes of letters of words which are as long as the letters are wide—no more and no less—show a mind which is accurate and a nature which has a good deal of self-control.

Good judgment marks this writer and very often the ability to be a good valuer. Auctioneers and professional purchasers need to have the connecting-strokes of the letters of their words proportionate to the words if they are to be successful. The woman who is the skilful purchaser for a large family usually has this sign.

Extreme variation in the length of the connecting-strokes between letters of words is the indication of a variable disposition and usually of a highly emotional temperament.

It is impossible to know how things will "strike" these writers; usually they will not strike twice alike! How this will actively affect the personality and the character depends on the *t* bar and the many other indications of strength and moral power. The fact of the variability of disposition and the emotionalism of the temperament is *always* true, even should the personality seem to tell of actual phlegmatism. Sometimes this variation of the stroke is the only telltale sign, in a hand which has been sternly brought down to something which is more or less noncommittal. The judgment of these people is either extraordinarily swift and accurate or without any stability at all. Which it is depends a good deal on the *t* bar and on the character of the capitals.

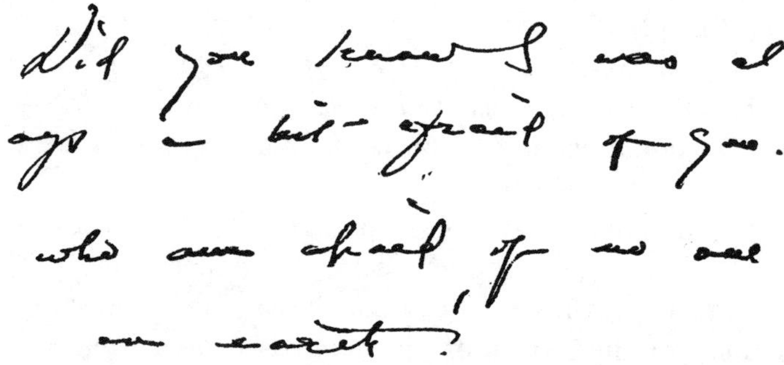

Connecting-strokes of words which are double the length of the width of the letter, and more, express courage and defiance, eagerness for realization of hopes, and a judgment which is often weakened by impatience.

These connecting-strokes are often associated with large and high capitals, with long *t* bars and with rather extravagant spacing of the writing on the page.

The very long connecting-stroke between the letters of words may or may not unite unusual letter forms, but when it does, the mentality of the writer is usually quite exceptional although seldom specialized. Personal pride is nearly always present; the desire to be noticed, heeded, to be paid respect to—to hold the center of the stage. Success, for such writers, must come through gaining a high place and there working, thinking and living brilliantly. There is no success for them in the slow, step-by-step progress.

A break in the connecting-strokes of words expresses the possession of a most unusual faculty—that of intuition.

This quality of the human is one of the great mysteries which science has yet to explore. We have given it a name but we do not understand it. It is more sure than logic, proceeds along paths which we do not know and acts on knowledge which we cannot prove. Intangible as it is, it is as common among the uneducated as elsewhere. People who have it often form opinions which are very hard for them to substantiate with any concrete proofs, and yet they are very often right.

The break in the connecting-strokes of letters of words is the symbol, graphologically, of this quality.

In proportion as the letters of words are all disconnected is the element of logic superseded by intuition.

It is not surprising to find that, where the connecting-strokes are all broken, the writers are supersensitive and often what would appear very illogical. The union of logic and intuition, found in the alternating of connected and disconnected connecting-strokes usually gives us a judgment which is exceptionally keen, logic constantly sitting hard on intuition and intuition constantly demanding of logic that it shall not be too short-sighted.

Variability in the connecting-stroke, so that some letters are tightly connected in a word, and other letters of a word are strung out loosely, shows vacillating judgment.

It is very hard for people of this type to make up their minds and keep them so. The last person whose opinions are heard is the person—of the moment.

When there is frequently a connecting-stroke which does not connect, but leaves off and dashes abruptly downward, there is the indication of real temper, of the rather dangerous kind.

Too often this is a concealed fault which flashes into view at crucial moments and makes trouble.

BEGINNING-STROKES AND ENDING-STROKES

The elimination of the beginning-stroke is the first step that the writer takes in showing developing mental processes.

There are a few really educated people who do not leave off this perfectly unnecessary gesture. This gives us the following rule:

Educated handwriting in which the beginning-strokes are long, shows that the mentality has still a long way to go before it climbs to the second level of mentality, where elimination of the superfluous begins.

It is safe to say, therefore, that the presence of the beginning-stroke in people who are past the first stages of education is a sure indication of the fact that they are not progressing very fast. It is also likely that they are without progressive ambition. The retention of this beginning-stroke into middle age shows the slow and detailed worker, who is not apt to change much from youth to old age.

The total elimination of final-strokes does show the instinct for concentration, but is often, also, the sign of rather a timid and unaggressive nature, if the handwriting is composed of very ordinary letter formations.

These are the workers who do some one thing exceptionally well, and who learn to "speed" in its operation. They usually do not have exceptional minds, but mind and temperament are frequently in better accord than in writers of whom this is not true.

The total elimination of beginning- and ending-strokes, in writing composed of unusual letter formations and of small size, is the indication of the capacity to concentrate and of the natural instinct and the acquired power to think with accuracy. (See the illustration on page 94.)

Many of the purely mental workers—writers, teachers, scientists—will conform to this in their handwritings. It is to be noted that "the unusual letter formations" is the one determining factor. Without them, the elimination of beginning- and ending-strokes will give merely concentrativeness and efficiency on lower levels.

The ending-stroke which curls softly upward and is slightly rounded shows a pleasant disposition and sometimes a sense of humor, if the latter is shown by the i *dot.* (See the second illustration on page 43.)

The ability to enjoy the ordinary routine of life and to find pleasure in small happinesses and to be amused by the little affairs of life are all indicated by these strokes, especially if confirmed by the *i* dot. In proportion as the writing is rounded or angular, too, is the completeness of this finding accentuated, or mitigated; rounded writing accentuating and angular writing making the nature more shrewd in its willingness to be amused and more critical in everything than if the writing is rounded.

When ending-strokes are slashed sharply downward, and especially if they are heavy in pressure, we have the nature which is domineering in some degree.

The addition of the downward-pointed and heavy *t* bar will make this deduction very positive. It is almost impossible for people who use these downward endings and *t* bars not to be dogmatic. They assert much that they cannot prove, fail to allow for the other fellow's viewpoint, often lose temper and sanity when opposed. Yet it is to be observed that there is often the indication of logic in the handwritings where these same signs prevail; in which case, second thoughts bring better judgment. It is needless to say that we seldom have many evidences of tact or suavity of manner in this writing, and that such writers are the last ones who should be placed in positions of authority over others.

Long ending-strokes, in the semi-angular writing, with at least moderately heavy pressure and long *t* bars, express courage which is both physical and moral and a temperament which is aggressive and well able to fight its way through the world. The same indication, it will be remembered, is given by the large capitals with small small letters and we often see the combination of all these signs: long ending-strokes, long *t* bars, medium heavy pressure, large capitals and small small letters. People of this type are always outstanding characters in their times. If accident confines them to a small village, for instance, they will be the chief figure; instinctively painted in high-lights by even the unobservant and partially educated. They are natural leaders and if the letter forms are indicative of culture will be iconoclasts in thought—forerunners of the best thought of the following generation.

Such persons, especially when this combination is

present, are always magnetic and forceful characters.

The use of the long final-stroke, even in much weaker writing, shows the possibility of the writer at least approximating the real leadership of those in whom all the signs are assertive of that possibility.

HOOKS

It is sometimes necessary to use a reading-glass when trying to see whether the often minute formations known as "hooks" are or are not present in a specimen of writing.

These are the small return-strokes made by the fact that the pen is being so firmly driven and held so close that it is, as it were, reluctant to leave the paper.

They occur on the ends of *t* bars, on the ends of ending-strokes, on parts of capitals, and on various parts of letter formations where the pen has to be lifted from the paper.

The psychology of these hooks is not hard to figure out. They are, literally, *hooks,* and they catch and hold, fasten and bind and accentuate whatever are the indications in the handwriting. Whether they register something which is disagreeable, like the tenacity of the prying busybody who is determined to talk about everything which is not his business, or the grim determination of the person who refuses to accept failure as a possibility, will depend on the type of the handwriting, the character of the *t* bar and all the other indications of character which handwriting gives.

Hooks, however, *fasten;* and this is true, no matter what they fasten on. The action is the same. Therefore, when they are seen in handwriting, the instant question which the investigator must ask himself is: To *what* do they fasten? What are the arenas of their action?

It is not surprising to find that the smaller handwritings are more apt to show the presence of hooks than the larger; for tenacity, persistence and perseverance are not often found in the large handwritings and hooks express some degree of those qualities.

It is a mistake to assert that the presence of hooks in handwriting shows irritability. On the other hand, the type of person in whose handwriting hooks are found is apt to be occasionally irritable, and this is quite natural, for the persistent and tenacious person will be constantly annoyed with the world in general, in which tenacity and persistence are all too absent; the fact being that the nature which is tenacious is not irritable in and by itself, but is made so by the lack of its own qualities in the world with which it has to deal.

The hooks, sometimes turned to the leftward, at the beginning of words, show the same quality, in a lesser degree.

It is often true that we find these hooks on the beginning of the first stroke of letters which are the first letters of words when we do not find them on horizontal strokes, where they might logically be expected. This usually transfers the arena of the action of persistence to a less assertive field. Thus, these beginning-stroke-hook people will be persistent and tenacious only about smaller affairs and will lack the deeply imbedded forcefulness and tenacity of those who use the hooks on end-strokes. It is quite logical to find that the rounded-writing writer seldom uses hooks and that the more angular writer, with strong horizontal strokes, does frequently use them.

LOOPS

The loops in letter formations have a great deal to do with giving a specimen of writing its characteristic appearance. As far as the eye can perceive forms, the loops will tell the graphologist much of the temperament of a writer, so that a specimen, too far away for the smaller formations to be followed, will yet give valuable information of the writer of it.

Loops are of three kinds: loops above the basic line, loops below the basic line, and loops which run somewhat horizontally. One letter in the alphabet—*f*—has the distinction of possessing a two-way loop and for this reason a good many of the oddities of human temperament are recorded in it.

Loops which are extended above the basic line to a greater height than is normal show aspirations, of some kind or another.

To aid us in fixing this in the mind we may picture the high-above-the-line loop as reaching up. *What* it reaches for depends altogether on the type of handwriting and on many other elements in the character. Naturally, if we find lack of spirituality, combined with a good deal of pride, in a specimen in which there is the very high loop, we may be sure that the aspiration is for things of this earth: for social place, perhaps, for comfort, for better conditions of education, and so on. The evidences of parsimony and of narrow mental outlook will again limit the matter of aspiration as expressed in the high loops, but aspiration it remains, no matter how low the level on which it expresses itself.

Loops which extend much farther below the line than is normal, sometimes being so extreme as to cut through several lines of writing, are the evidences of interests which are material in their tendencies.

Like the other rule, this also demands careful use. What the degree of materialism, how drastic we ought to be in condemning the character as wholly "of the earth, earthy" will depend on the evidences of grossness, selfishness, small and petty interests, and so on. But, like the evidence of the loops high above the line of writing, the evidence of the loops which are long below the line of writing is that which cannot be disputed. However, a nice distinction should be observed by the graphologist, in that a certain openness, frankness and good-heartedness may exist in the long-lower-loop writer and be absent in the high-upper-loop writer. It is the *trend* of the interests, in other words, which is indicated by this matter of the loops, other matters to be determined by the many other factors of the case.

Loops above the line which are shorter than normal must be carefully estimated. If found in a commonplace hand, they show a deadening of all the aspirations. They take away from the colors of life in which the writing paints the portrait of the writer.

These short and ineffective-looking loops are often found in the commonplace hand, in which the pressure is uneven and the line of writing inclined downward.

They show the instinct for discouragement, the

weakness which succumbs to Life and has little fight in it, the tendency to be "the under dog." It is to be noted, however, that distinction must be made between this point and the following:

Loops above the line which are shorter than normal, in a very fine and unusual hand, *show an accentuation of the capacity for concentration.*

It must be the "fine and unusual," however, to carry this significance. Many of the very rare hands which show extreme ideality have this shortened upper loop, which seems to contradict the general rule, but it will be seen that in such hands the lower loop is greatly shortened too, and is frequently little more than a very light stroke of the pen.

Lower loops which are greatly curtailed by the elimination of the return stroke show mental powers as beginning to be more than ordinary.

No person of extremely ordinary mentality was ever known to make this formation. It shows not only education, but the development of mental individuality—pronounced personal opinions, strong reactions of an emotional nature, positive beliefs and conceptions, which may or may not accord with those commonly held.

Lower loops which have become a mere stroke and which are sharpened at the end by a thinning of the pressure show temper and the capacity for resentfulness.

In cases of this kind it will often be found that the upper loops are greatly curtailed and that *their* return strokes are sometimes eliminated. This is not, necessarily, the person of what we call bad temper, but it is surely the person who is not especially meek!

Very rounded loops in either the upper or the lower forms of loops are apt to show a love of non-extravagant pleasures, and a rather gay and happy disposition. Love of melody, mild sports and company is usually indicated.

These people are, necessarily, not profound thinkers and seldom are possessed of great talent for anything, but are fine companions, often good workers, though never speedy and hardly ever wish to be in business for themselves. Women using these forms like children and the home, but also love dancing and the theater. Men are often amateur musicians. I have frequently found that this type *seems* to like the trade of barbering, probably because of the opportunities for social contact! It is to be noted that love of music, in this formation, does not mean especial talent for it, except in such facility as exists in the person who plays "by ear" rather well, and who has the capacity for "carrying tunes." Generally speaking, something of the happy-hearted child lives in this type of writer.

Lower loops, the return stroke of which are turned to the right instead of to the left, have a very definite name in graphological nomenclature. They are called "altruistic loops" and the people who make them will always be found to have a strong strain of altruistic feeling, no matter whether all of their lives agree to this or not.

As a rule, this sign will be found in rounded handwriting of light pressure, medium size and fair legibility. The student, who has now progressed to exactly that number of points in graphology—so far as this book is concerned—will be able to see how admirably this sign fits in with all the other character indications, in such a case. However, this uniformity of indication is by no means always to be seen.

The graphologist may be confounded by discovering the altruistic sign in a writing which shows shrewdness, stinginess, and other contradictory traits. It is then to be read as affecting some one point of the character. For instance, there are several well-known instances of world-famous "philanthropists" who are far from showing such a trait in any of their private relationships, and who—it cannot be denied—have given with princely generosity in a wholesale way. We all know the opposite type of person, who lives only for others, but only for "others" who have to do with the close personal band of associates.

Look carefully at any specimen of writing, then, in which the altruistic formation is found and do not refuse to believe what it has to tell you because all the rest of the writing contradicts it. Usually, though, there is no contradiction.

Loops which are inflated, in either the upper or the

lower sections, show an accentuation of whatever they indicate, and add the element of pride in some degree: thus, long lower loops, inflated, accentuate materialism.

It is obvious that there may be various kinds of pride and that this deduction will be affected by the *type* of writing in which the formations are found. If the capitals are also inflated or bombastic in formation or vulgarly ornamented, we shall see in this indication the sign of vulgar and ostentatious pride and vanity, but—in a hand which is otherwise conservative and refined, we shall see that this indication shows some self-approbation, but that this is checked by the other pleasant qualities and may even be transmuted to rather strong but not unworthy self-respect. Loops which are only slightly inflated, in a hand which is otherwise of good indications, show the needed self-assertiveness, and sometimes accentuate a sense of humor—a gay, happy personality.

Loops which are squeezed, in either the upper or the lower section, that is to say, which are too narrow across, always show some degree of repression, depression, timidity, unexpansiveness, or other forms of character and feeling which are the reverse of the inflated loop.

This squeezed formation is to be found in the normal loop, the too high loop, the too long loop, and in the horizontal loop. It is a formation which literally squeezes the "air" out of the writing. These squeezed-loop writers lack buoyancy, hope, courage and belief in themselves and others. They can sometimes be found among the money makers, however, for the simple reason that to them one cent is of importance. That is to say, they can be successful in any business where success is built up on the "cent by cent" progress. If compelled to go into any business where foresight and courage are needed they are failures. People who manage chain stores, who deal in products where half-a-cent margin is all that they have, bankers and "safe and sane" investment people, usually have the more or less squeezed loops.

The lower loop which is angular or which has an angular formation in it is the accentuation of what angularity shows.

This is frequently called the evidence of temper and stubbornness, but it is that only when other evidences in the writing confirm it. Most of the people who use this sign have partially rounded writing, which gives gentleness and good temper—the angular formation in the lower loops showing courage, determination and even stubbornness, as present and ready to come to the surface if needed, but not as insistent elements of the personality. *When* this formation is found in very angular handwriting, however, we do have the evidence of aggressive stubbornness—the accentuation of what the writing tells us.

Whether this sign is found in the partially rounded writing or in the extremely angular, we may be sure that it means one thing, at least: that this is a writer who will not readily give up his or her rights.

The loop within the loop is always indicative of some extreme eccentricity, in its mildest indication, and of something which is close to mental disturbance, at its worst.

Graphologists always look with the closest attention at this formation, and well they may. It is a danger signal. It is the indication of some mental "twist" or "kink" which may become serious. If the sign for humor is to be found in the same handwriting, then we will have the mild eccentric, who is often benevolent and philosophic, a specimen of whom can be found in almost every community. In that case, however, we are apt to find, also, the *lasso t.* Disorderly handwriting, associated with this formation, is a pretty bad indication of mental disturbances, or of extreme emotional disturbances, at least. It used to be said that drug-addicts and other weaklings were especially apt to use this formation, and while it is true that traces of it are very often to be found in such specimens of writing, it would not be fair to brand the sign as being that alone. It is sometimes used by very fine characters, as before said, who are merely eccentric. A most careful balancing of all the elements of the character, as shown in the specimen of writing, will be necessary in dealing with this formation.

Horizontal loops—i.e., loops which slant sideways, as often in the loops of L*—do not express so much pride as they do an accentuation of whatever elements are to be perceived as strong in the writing.*

The lower horizontal loops, when well developed, show that vanity is transferred to the plane of proud self-respect; this takes away from direct vanity, but leaves a good deal of desire to have the virtues and talents recognized.

The alternation of various kinds of loops in the writing of one person shows moodiness and that the nature has many aspects.

Such people are apt to be affected by things, people and events which are not noticed by others who are less sensitive.

Suddenly increased pressure on any part of loops shows irritability and excitability.

Many people who are the prey to all sorts of irritations, who "fly off the handle," as the expression is, who have hasty tempers and ill-advised resentments, use this sign.

Lower loops which are very, very long, so that they form the most important part of the picture made by the writing, show either a weak character or a very strong one, according to the length and strength of the t *bar.*

If the *t* bar is long and strong, the character is a materialistic and dominating one. If the *t* bar is weak, short, placed at all sorts of angles, the nature is merely aggressive, grasping and *wishful* of being dominating.

WORDS

The spacing of words on the page is something which has its own special message for the graphologist. Also, the arrangement and formation of the letters out of which words are formed is most significant.

Words formed of letters which are "squeezed"—i.e., narrow—and which have very short connecting-strokes, and are placed close together, without much space between the words, show a mean and cautious spirit which is too greatly engrossed with things, *as against people and ideas and emotions.*

It is quite futile to approach these writers with anything but concrete and tangible and most detailed suggestions. They estimate everything from the practical standpoint alone, and do not even know what generosity means, although, when of good character, they are strictly just. Harshness in judging more emotional types is, of course, to be expected. If heavy pressure is added to this type of writing, the indications are even strengthened.

As against the dour indications here we may count the fact that few criminals are found using it, and that there is sometimes a stern and severe administrativeness about it which is of value. Generally speaking, however, this type of writer is unhappy and makes others unhappy, and is not quite as efficient, in the truest sense, as he or she will nearly always think.

Words which conform to the previous type but

which are rather widely spaced, in relation to each other, and which are rather widely spaced in relation to the various lines of writing, show a great deal more of generosity and openness and understanding than the previous type. (See the illustration on page 91.)

The instincts here are for the close attention to justice, and to the careful estimation of things, but there is a great ability to understand other types and to estimate people. Narrow-mindedness is not so strong, conservatism and moderation taking its place. The affections are apt to have some light chance of asserting themselves. Nevertheless, the dominant element remains—a clear, cold, unfeeling and exacting mentality.

Words which are composed of rounded letter forms, which are closely spaced with reference to each other and to the various lines of writing, thus producing the effect of a closely packed page, although the letters *of the words are widely spaced, show generosity and some indifference to selfish satisfactions, checked and deflected from expression by circumstances, training, environment.*

Such a person, given wealth, would be generous; given power, would not be mean or niggardly, nor abusive of it; given the assurance of love or friendship, is apt to return it. But he or she will often give the contrary impression, being much beaten and subdued by pressure of some kind, which has shoved the words together; it is not a natural tendency. A sidelight on this is often given the graphologist who has the opportunity to see this type of writing expand and the space between the words and between the lines of writing widen, when economic pressure or the pressure of uncongenial circumstances have been removed. We may, therefore, call this the emotionally repressed and subdued writing and may speculate with interest as to what might happen should there come a change in the repressing factors.

Words composed of very small writing, which are widely spaced, in relation to other words and to various lines of writing, show enthusiastic tendencies which have persisted despite rather severe mental training.

In other words, the wide spacing of very small writing shows that the mentality has not absorbed all the emotions, as is so often the way.

When words begin slightly above the basic line of writing and then drop to it with the final letter, and when this trait is continued throughout the specimen, the indication is of people who start with enthusiasm but end with caution.

It is possible to do business with these people or to have relations with them, with comfort, so long as we consider the fact that they will always promptly hedge after the first flush of their impulses has died down. The afterthought and the second statement of these people are what we can positively rely on, and if we make up our minds that that is so, we will never be disturbed by the first fizzing of their ardors! On the other hand, should we not consider this, we will always be expecting of such people the fulfilment of their first promises, their first enthusiasm, and will be constantly disappointed.

When words begin on the basic line and veer upward, and when this trait is continued throughout the specimen, we may be sure that the writer is the type to say "no" and then "yes."

Prudence and reserve are always on top and on tap and it is only after this prudence has had its say that the natural enthusiasm of the writer will be allowed expression. As in the preceding example, these people are not hard to get on with, *if* we have the key: if we know enough to discount the discouragement with which they invariably greet every new thing, and if we confidently wait for the enthusiasm to gather headway. A great many business men show faint traces of this tendency in their writing.

Words which begin with large letters, then dwindle in size to the end, show tact and a gracious manner.

The persistent use of this is usually the indication of a real talent for social life, and it is not surprising to find that it is very characteristic of the writing of the essentially feminine woman, whose instinct it is always to placate, conserve, soothe and render harmonious; but many types of men use this formation, too. These are the people who can usually save a disagreeable situation by the right and often the clever word, who are able instantly to adjust themselves to various social strats —who can be at home in the drawing-room or elsewhere. They are frequently accused of inconstancy because of this, but the charge is unfounded. As a matter of fact, these writers are usually very kind and constant lovers and friends. Perhaps the charge of inconstancy which is so often brought is due to the fact that they are the people of many minor attachments. Such women, for instance, have great joy from their club or church affiliations, and have many friends, not a few.

It is also true that this writing trait shows the capacity to forget sorrow and to form new attachments. Thus a woman will truly grieve if she loses a husband who is loved, but she is especially apt to marry again, since the companionship of the home, gracious and pleasant, is so dear to her.

The ardent, possessive and selfishly jealous man will often feel that all this constitutes inconstancy; but women who write words in this manner are really the most successful wives and mothers, since they are tactful, good-tempered, and loving, and yet never permit themselves to be wholly absorbed by their families.

Words which start with small letters and gradually increase their size are not often found. The trait shows caution as the foundation of the character, but a caution which is constantly being overcome and ridden down by the emotional nature.

This is used only by quite contradictory characters, and the indications in the handwriting, other than this, will confirm that deduction. It is very hard to have to depend on these people, since they are continually fluctuating between reserve and caution and the utmost extravagance. They say "no" and soon change this to "yes"; refuse when asked to spend money and then dash in and spend more than any one else; not satisfactory in any relationship. To add to this we have the fact that the word which begins with the small letter and goes on to the larger and larger one is the indication of that bluntness which takes into little account what the other person's feelings are—the direct opposite to the words which are started with large letters and run down to small ones.

When words start with small but rather well-defined letters, and after the first two or three, end with a meaningless scrawl which is intended for the remaining letters of the word, we have what is called "the diplomat's hand."

This is an accentuation of the use which makes the first letters of words a good deal larger than the remaining. It is moving the peg up much higher—it is taking the tact and cleverness of the words which are larger to start with than to end with, and injecting extreme shrewdness and sophistication into them. Few world diplomats write a hand which is not marked with this characteristic.

Words which start with well-defined letters and then slip and slide into sinuous formations which are all but unreadable, show actual deceitfulness and sometimes criminality.

There is extreme difficulty in distinguishing this writing trait from the tendency just discussed. The truth is, of course, that there is only a thin edge between the selfish diplomatic person and the rather high-class criminal, who uses his cleverness for his own ends, but is not brutal.

We will have to look with the greatest care for evidences of some unselfishness, for high mentality, for strong convictions and for evidences of pride and self-respect.

MARGINS

Margins are called the right and left margins, according to the right and left side of the page of writing, as the page is faced by the reader.

The margin grew out of the first attempt of the monks in the early ages to keep the pages of their precious writing clean by allowing a space at the side of the page, where the thumb or the forefinger of the left hand reposed as the manuscript was held in the hand of the reader. Thus beauty grew, as it does, so wonderfully and so often, from utility.

The idea of the arrangement of writing on a page in such a way as to add beauty to it by that arrangement is one which has occasionally illumined the pages of manuscript, all over the world and at various times. At other times, the idea has been entirely lost. During the period of time rightly called the Dark Ages, writing reverted to some of the earliest conditions, and margins, paragraphing and even the idea of the proper separation of words all disappeared. Gradually, however, the question of the page arrangement became an urgent one.

Out of all this we have the conclusions of to-day in regard to margins and paragraphing, and the first rule concerning them:

The way in which margins and paragraphing are used has a great deal to tell the graphologist about the artistic tastes of the writer.

That is to say, the general interest and feeling and reaction of a writer are expressed in the way in which these matters are handled.

It may be objected that it is not always possible to tell the artist, the man or woman who actually produces art, by this matter of margins. This is true, for the margin and arrangement of writing have to do with the *appreciation* of art.

Those who know the types of producing artists will know that they pour into the actual production of their work that which the connoisseur and appreciator spreads all over life. There are few who, on actually meeting artists, writers, poets, and sculptors, have not been shocked by their seeming indifference to the nuances of the very arts which they produce. A painter's attention was once called to the hideous wallpaper which was on the hall in his house. His reply told a great deal:

"I never see it. Unless I am looking for something to paint, I never notice anything around me at all."

It is this very concentration of attention, *when* the attention is really focused, which distinguishes the producing artist from the artist in appreciation.

Therefore, it is the appreciators and the connoisseurs who are more apt to arrange a page with extreme beauty than the man or woman whose whole soul and being is poured, at times, into the production of the thing which the other appreciates.

We will find the lesser artists, the users and modifiers of great art, much more interesting in their arrangement of a written page, than the masters. Mucha, who a decade ago started a decorative movement in art which was really worth while, but which was many levels below that of real creativeness, had one of the most interesting-looking pages of writing ever seen. Amazing but beautiful capitals, odd spacing, heavily indented paragraphs and great expanses of white paper made it noteworthy. He was a man whose reactions to art ran into the simplest thing that he did, saw or wore. But no great master was ever known to dissipate his powers in that way. Therefore we come to the second general rule about the arrangement of writing on a page:

We do not deduce actual artistic talent or genius from the fact of artistic arrangement of the page or from wide margins, but the feeling for it and the appreciation of it.

On the other hand, it is not correct to estimate the person who does not use margins and whose arrangement of the page is indifferent, as lacking in artistic appreciation. There are some individuals whose sense of thrift is such that they carefully use every available bit of space on a page, their feeling for beauty coming out only in their letter formations. To be sure, this is not the usual thing. The usual thing is for the letter forms *and* the arrangement of the writing to coincide.

Wide margins on the left show innate love of that which is beautiful and the instinct to surround self with beautiful objects.

The instinct for spending money may usually be deduced from this, too; for those who have this instinct do not think of the utility of that which they purchase, nor have they the instinct to save a penny, their attention being fixed upon their own reaction to objects—*i.e.*, to whether they like those objects or not. We will usually find, therefore, that the writing which uses a wide left-hand margin has the evidences of some wastefulness, viewed from the strictly utilitarian standpoint.

Wide margins on both left and right make the matter of art feeling very strong and accentuate the extravagance in the use of money.

With these *two* margins, we are almost sure to find that the letter formations have taken on unusual beauty and that the writing leans toward some actual art feeling—a shade more than appreciation.

No margin on the left and a wide one on the right shows prudence and thrift contending with less utilitarian feeling.

The desire to be thrifty impels the pen to start writing as soon as may be on the page, but the impulse is not genuine and so the pen lags and forgets the penurious instinct as it gets along the line, and leaves the margin which would have been better on the other side; then again the pen starts off thriftily, only to forget again. There is nothing in writing which so definitely expresses the subconscious self coming right to the surface and that wholly without the knowledge of the conscious self.

Very wide margins on the left with the writing crowded to the extreme on the right side—even the letters being made smaller and smaller, so that more can be squeezed in—shows this same warring of thrift and extravagance.

This is an interesting and quite amusing instance of the subconscious self, which, shocked at the prodigality of the artistic self, tries to make up for this by getting onto the line all that would have been possible had the margin at the left not been used. The hand then forgets this instinct and starts out again with the other impulse—only to be pulled down to the mincing gait of economy in the last few words.

These people present great contradictions in character, to correspond with this trait. They will recklessly spend money for, say, a Ming vase, and pinch the household in point of butter and eggs. Sometimes their art feeling runs to clothes, in which case they will wear silk and fine linen, though debts pile about them, mountain high. The discrepancy between this art feeling, in whatever line it may express itself, and their ordinary reactions, will be sharp.

The margin on the left which starts wide and gradually narrows to the bottom of the page is the evidence of economy gradually overcoming art feeling.

This is another evidence of the subconscious self rebelling against that which is, from the utilitarian standpoint, waste.

The margin on the left which reverses this action, starting out to be narrow and gradually widening, is the indication of strong tastes which gradually overcome the check put on the nature by training or environment.

Many who have started life in homes where beauty was never a consideration, or who have struggled hard for a life which should yield them some satisfaction for the love of beauty which is theirs, show this very interesting writing trait.

Margins which are wide but disorderly show some

feeling for what is beautiful, but also show exceedingly poor judgment.

Other indications are apt to be found in such writing to strengthen the indication of poor judgment. If the *t* bar is strong and pointed slightly or positively downward, in such a user of the margin, then we have the person whose judgment is not only poor but is very aggressively used! Employers of this type cause acute anguish to their sensitive employees; in fact, any one of this make-up is a cause of worry and distress to others.

The indentation of paragraphs shows a great step in the artistic feeling of the writing and also an advance in the mental caliber.

Thought is strong—as well as artistic feeling—in those who arrange the paragraphs well on the page, who space the words well—who use capitals in proportions to the size of the small letters—who indent the paragraphs deeply. No crude person ever did all this. It is not a question of education, for many well-educated people contrive merely to fill a page with words, from side to side, and from top to bottom and there is no more to be said about it.

A very unusual arrangement of writing on the page, such as a few lines, paragraphed and oddly placed on a very large sheet of paper, with the additional indication of interesting letter formations, shows extreme preoccupation with art.

Professional art connoisseurs, interior decorators, and those who spend their lives in sensuously, albeit delicately, enjoying harmonious surroundings, beautiful objects, culture and the graces in general, are apt to do this, which is so foreign to the average writer. It would be unthinkable for the *producing* artist to use this arrangement. In him or her it would be a futile gesture, since *all* of the art feeling must be poured into actual production.

THE SMALL LETTERS

It is in the small letters that we find the greatest expression of individuality.

The capitals give us the larger, more fundamental elements of character—the outlines, as it were—which the information afforded by the small letters will allow us to fill with detail.

The first thing to remember, in looking at the small letters of writing, is that size affects a great many of their graphological deductions.

When small letters vary greatly in size, in a specimen of writing, there is the evidence of varying moods and of some degree of sensitiveness, the latter to be estimated by the formations.

It will be found that the smaller writing will give a greater variation of size in the small letter than the larger, for the reason that the small writing is the expression of a more intense development and of a temperament which is more intense.

Large writing in which the small letters vary greatly in size shows the ardent, impulsive and more emotional than mental type, in which the variation in mood and the extreme sensitiveness indicated by the variable size of the small letters is more on the surface than the corresponding traits in the smaller writing.

In reading small letters no proper deduction can be reached without taking into account, and studying closely, each of the following important points:

(a) The angularity of the small letters.

(b) Their roundness.

(c) The basic line, and their adherence to it, or the manner of their departure from it.

(d) The pressure exerted in forming the small letters.

(e) Their legibility and rhythm.

(f) The width of the letters; the connecting-strokes between them; the beginning-strokes and the ending-strokes.

(g) The margins.

(h) The capital letters used by the writer.

(i) The signature habitually used by the writer, if this is obtainable.

With the ground thus prepared, by these observations, and taking care that one indication be "checked up" against another, we may proceed to observe the indications of the individual letters.

(The word "letters" throughout this chapter refers always to the small letters only.)

Letters which are wider at the top than at the bottom show caution. To see whether they actually are wider or not requires careful observation, for the difference between the width at top and bottom is slight —a rare indication.

Letters which are wider at the bottom than at the top show a more confiding nature than the previous formation.

The letter a *which is lightly "closed"* expresses moderation in the giving of trust and confidence and in the impulse of generosity. This is, of course, the most common formation, since most of us belong to the classification of the "average man."

The a *which is "closed" with an extra motion of the writing-instrument* shows extreme caution and reticence, and generosity which responds only to the appeal of logic.

The distinction between these two forms is that the *a* which is tightly closed in this fashion is aggressively cautious and resistive of influence, whereas the lightly-closed *a* is innately cautious but not consciously and deliberately so.

The a *which is "open" where other formations are "closed" more or less tightly* is the expression of the generosity which is responsive to the emotional appeal.

The a *which (in common with other small letters) shows a curious break in the continuity of the stroke at the bottom of the letter* has a formation which will engage the earnest attention of all graphologists.

This is the sign of a love of large sums of money, and its prevalence in a specimen of writing has to be carefully estimated. To find one *a* or other letter which shows this break would have slight significance. The break might be due to a poor pen, weak ink, a sudden faltering of the hand, an interruption. One or two of these breaks, even, might be accidents, but *not when the break is constantly repeated.* The extreme difficulty of even imitating this formation, by the ordinary hand, will be clear the moment it is attempted. For the genuine break is so slight, so minute, that at first glance we merely wonder what has given the writing the peculiar broken appearance.

To carry its full significance it must be persistent, must characterize all the writing. When found in *a* alone, it is less positive in its indication than when found in other letters, but it is seldom that it *is* found alone. Very often, even the connecting-strokes are affected by the formation, showing the characteristic break midway between letters. Sometimes the lower loops of letters are affected by it, also.

This is the sign of the peculiar weakness of human beings which causes them to be tempted, not by any small thing, but by very large ones. The people who write these broken-base letters are the men who do away with trust funds of a hundred thousand dollars, who forge for the sake of getting a fortune, who embezzle large amounts, who seize on huge quantities of cash, who cannot resist the lure of *great quantities* of money.

These men are not the inventors of fake mining schemes, nor are they the "big" confidence men. They do not deliberately seek for the means to steal and are almost never swindlers. Their difficulty is wholly that of the overwhelming temptation, of the one weakness. So long as the makers of this formation are not tempted with *quantities* of money, they are as honest as any one. As a rule, their personal characters are good. They are seldom vicious in their habits, and when they do take the money for which their hands are always itching, they do not fare forth to scatter it on the highway in riotous living, as is the way of the mere ordinary thief. Frequently, they do not seem to know what to do with it, when they have it. Speculation with stolen funds and gambling in stocks are the two ways in which this type is apt to begin stealing.

Now, the importance of all this is that this peculiar formation in the *a* and in other letters is also the indication of real mathematical talent. Such writers, therefore, automatically drift into positions of trust as cashiers and so on—in other words, into the very positions where the weakness which besets them will have plenty of exercise!

Employers should, therefore, learn at least this one graphological sign. It is so unmistakable that it is soon recognized and it is practically impossible for the man who uses it to control his hand so that he shall *not* use it.

This same man, on the other hand, is often a fine salesman and a good executive, and is far safer, as a handler of small sums of money and as a trusted employee, than the majority of people. Just so long as he is kept out of the money-vaults, away from the securities, out of the reach of any hold on large resources, this is a person who is entirely trustworthy.

Knowing this graphological rule and applying it would not be a complicated matter, and its application by employers and personnel managers would prevent at least two-thirds of our big defalcations.

The letter b *has one special formation, which is that of the pendulous "lip."* Graphologists call this the *credulous b,* and it has a physical analogy in the slack human mouth, which has the suggestion of weak credulity. People who use this formation can, it is believed, be successfully sold the Brooklyn Bridge in

New York, or the Ferry Building in San Francisco, for a moderate sum! They are the mainstay of the fake oil wells and of worthless stocks and bonds. The pity of it is that they are so affectionate, as a rule, that they are almost invariably good-natured.

The letter b *which is more "squeezed" than the rest of the letters* shows precisely the opposite trait. These are the people who must be shown, who will believe nothing without concrete evidence.

Too often the question of generosity is mixed into this matter of credulity or its reverse. Credulous people are often stingy, and cautious people are frequently warm-hearted, when they are persuaded that there is a genuine reason for generosity.

When the bulb of the b *has a backward twist this is to be read in the same manner as the extra-closed* a.

The small c, *like the capital* C, *is a test for the angularity of writing.* If the small *c* is angular, then the writing is very angular. If the small *c* is rounded, then the writing, on analysis, will be found to be less truly angular than at first it appears.

When the superfluous first stroke of c, as taught by the copybook, is used by a person of mature years, we may be sure that the convictions, ideals and beliefs of the writer are those which have been learned in youth or adolescence.

The small letter d is one of the most important in the alphabet.

Generally speaking, it is the touchstone of culture.

The letter *d* which is so expressive of culture is the *Greek d* which is closely allied to the ancient formation of *delta.* The writer of this *d* is one to whom precision of speech—education—culture and the higher levels of existence and of mental companionship are of supreme importance. It is not surprising to find stylists among writers and poets using this *d* exclusively, nor to find that college professors and scientists innately take to it. When found in ordinary writing, this formation is the "straw in the wind" which tells of the intellectual possibilities of the writer; and this holds good even though the remainder of the writing be unimportant from a graphological standpoint. The *possibility* is there. On the other hand, a good many writers of fiction and of poetry do not use this cultured *d;* for this is the *d* of precision, remember, and it is a check on spontaneity, and on the expression of emotion. Style, form, constructiveness are all shown by

this formation. On this basis, we will not look in vain for this letter in the writing of good playwrights. It is sometimes an affectation, but the very people who affect it *do not know its graphological significance,* and their affectation of it is therefore the work of their subconscious self.

This *cultured d* also shows good judgment in art, and innately good judgment in literature.

When the last stroke of the Greek d *is not cast back to the left, but to the right*, we have a composite indication which shows culture and refinement as innate, but also shows love of pleasure as strong. These are the people who are fine judges of music and the arts, who have "personality," who have the "gift of gab," and yet are interesting conversationalists; who are usually cosmopolites.

When the beginning-stroke of *d* is used, and when it is very long, all the cultural indications of the other formations of *d* are nullified. The judgment is poor and the outlook narrow. These are the people who will haggle over two cents when there is a fortune in sight: not because they are essentially mean in money matters, but because they cannot visualize; because all they can see is, as it were, the ground at their feet. Such people hang on to "jobs" long after they have outgrown the jobs, and never have the initiative to change their lives until Fate changes it for them.

The letter d *with the beginning-stroke eliminated but without distinction in the formation* shows that the writer is not of the dull temperament of the preceding formation. Elimination has begun and some foresight is to be expected.

The letter d *which begins like the cultured formation but which ends in a lasso formation* is a compound. There is culture in it, and a degree of eccentricity, and some stubbornness. This *d* must always be read with particular attention to other letter formations.

The letter d *which has a very distinct loop* should be read according to the nature of its loop.

The d *which graphologists call a "straddle d" is* a very peculiar formation. Separated from the word in which it appears, it might almost be the protective capital *A*, and in some degree it partakes of the meaning of that formation. It shows kindliness to inferiors, understanding of human nature, and the willingness to learn from experience. It has often been branded as the evidence of a deceitful nature; but this is not true. It *may be* part of the evidence of a deceitful nature *if* found in the "diplomat's hand" or in the writing where other evidences of deceit are strong. When found in the handwriting which is otherwise indicative of sincerity and good feeling, it shows the ability to keep a secret, to act a part, to keep one's own counsel; these writers have "poker faces" and are not to be read easily by the casual acquaintance. In fact, they are enigmas to the ordinary person, though often simple and even guileless to the people whom they trust.

The matter of trust is very important in considering this *straddle d*. The makers of it rank trustworthiness above every other trait; they are usually constant to the few attachments which they permit themselves; they are scornful of the babblers and of gossip; they have the ability to remain silent under pressure.

All this is not necessarily the evidence of a fine moral character. The finer type of criminals sometimes use the *straddle d* and are the ones who never "squeal" on their confederates, and who are not afraid of the officers of the law and are not the ones to "break" under any form of the "third degree." The finer type of spiritually inclined people hear confessions and conceal their knowledge; carry the burdens of their less spiritual neighbors and never tell. The quality is the same—it merely works at different levels.

The letter e *which is made like the capital letter* is also a cultural formation but in lesser degree than that of the *cultured d.* It is not usually found in association with the *cultured d* when the other letter formations, beside *d* and *e,* are indicative of culture. Therefore, we may say that this form of *e* is the indication of the aspiration rather than the realization of culture. It is found, frequently, in the writing of people who desire to be "refined," whose ideals of life are "nice"—by which, of course, the conventional refinement and the conventional niceness are meant. Therefore, in finding this formation in handwriting, we are apt to strike the rather conventional stratum of medium-educated and moderately refined people.

The letter f *is the "two way" looped letter.* When both of the loops are equal in size above and below the line and when their degree of width is the same, we have the indication of the nature which is unusually well-balanced. Close examination of *f's,* however, will show that this is not as common as we might think, and that when it does occur, it is in the handwriting which is rather commonplace, thus taking away from the significance of the formation, since the commonplace person has so little innate one-sidedness, anyway! The formation is very remarkable, then, when it is found, as it is occasionally, in very individualistic writing; the more individualistic, the more remarkable is the indication of poise and mental and emotional balance.

When the lower loops of f *becomes merely a stroke*

there is an accentuation of the meaning of the change from a loop to a stroke in the lower loop. (See the chapter on "Loops.")

The f *which has a "tie" at the jointure of the two loops* shows persistence in small matters. Note that the persistence which is shown by a similar formation in *t* has to do with persistence on a high scale. The tie in *f* is often used by people without really definite aims, those who drift; whereas the persistence which is shown by the *t* tie has to do with real ambitions and purposes.

The letter g conforms, as to its upper formation, to all the rules governing *a*.

When g *is made like an 8* we have the natural accompaniment of the *cultured d*. This is the midway-stop between the rather elementary cultural *e* and the high-level cultural sign of the *cultured d*. People who use this formation never fail to have a certain amount of intuition and instinct; they are the people who innately judge literature and art fairly well, even though not trained for such judgments; they have gentleness "in the blood"; they possess refinement as part of the character, as well as part of the mental equipment. This *g* also shows innate understanding of humanity; and it is almost impossible to find it dissociated from at least some hint of humor in the *i* dot.

For all other formations of g *see the chapter on "Loops."*

The letter h is governed by the rules given for loop-variations, in the chapter on "Loops." The "heart-tick" in the loop of *h* is discussed in the chapter on "Diseases as Indicated in Handwriting."

When the letter i *is always undotted,* we have the graphological evidence of a poor memory.

When the i *is dotted with heavy pressure* there is the indication of assertiveness.

When the i *is lightly but firmly dotted* we have the indication of self-control.

When the i *is dotted very close to the letter* the indication is of caution and a lack of imagination.

When the i *is dotted at a fair distance from the letter,* by a light, firm dot, somewhat in advance of the letter, there is the evidence of good judgment, mingled with some imagination.

When the i *is dotted by a light dot, very high over the letter and far in advance of it,* there is the evidence of imagination, highly developed, which is not controlled by much practical development.

When the i *is dotted with a mark which is club-shaped* the nature of the writer is aggressive and under pressure will become somewhat brutal. Temper, at the least, is the indication.

When the i *is dotted with a mark which is heavy in pressure and which is slanted downward* there is the evidence of opinionatedness and aggressiveness.

When the i *is dotted with a tent-shaped mark* we have a high development of the critical faculty. These people often have the reputation of fault-finders, because it is impossible for them to consider anything, from a human character to a piece of cloth, without appraising, judging, and weighing the value.

When the i *is dotted with marks which are wavy dashes or portions of circles* we have the indication of a happy and fun-loving disposition.

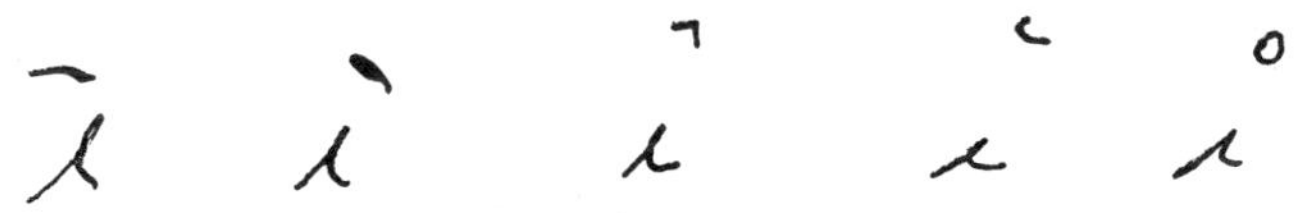

When the i *is dotted with a complete little circle* we have one of the most intriguing and interesting of graphological signs. A good many graphologists have considered this to be the sign of mild eccentricity, of that oddity which borders on the actually unbalanced mind. It is true that there are instances where this seems to apply, but long experience in dealing with the public has shown me that where people using this formation are mentally unbalanced, it is for lack of the kind of life they enjoy and for lack of the kind of work they do best.

These people like the unconventional life; they hate routine in any form. They often are extremely sensitive to their environment. They feel acutely whether or not there is beauty in their surroundings. They are often bad-tempered.

The real meaning of this sign, however, is that it indicates the kind of work these people can do; and once this right kind of work is found, all other problems and difficulties pass away.

These people are the *adapters of art.* They make

wax, and velvet, and paper flowers; lamp-shades; color china and post-cards; design hats, wallpaper and linoleum; sometimes are interior decorators; sometimes sew well; occasionally are fine handicraft workers; become perfumers; make stage costumes; and so on. When given the right kind of work to do, that personal eccentricity which is otherwise so pronounced with them disappears—flows into their work, as it were. They are usually moody, and do not easily make or keep friends. In marriage they are exacting and really do best with those in whose writing is found their own peculiar *i* dot.

The letter j is to be read, as to its dot, by the rules which apply to *i,* and as to its loop, by the rules for loops.

The letter k is to be read for loop-variations.

When the loop of k *is a good deal higher than the loops of the other looped letters* it shows at least a predisposition to spirituality.

The letter l is to be read strictly for loops. Its "heart-tick" is discussed in the chapter on "Diseases as Indicated in Handwriting."

The letter m *when larger than the other small letters* shows executive ability. The tendency to make it with the first "point" higher than the others will give us the accentuation of this trait.

The letter n is to be read in the same manner as *m.*

The letter o is governed by the same rules as the letter *a.*

The letter p has one special conformation, which is that of the very long lower-stroke, when this is a stroke and not a loop. This is the *physical p,* which shows not only physical vitality (an indication of all rather long lower loops) but a special delight in sport and in the development of the body. (Note that this does not mean delight in nature, which is a matter of temperament. Many devotees of sports are almost blind to the beauty of the fields and sands on which they play, and many a passionate lover of the moods of nature is not only indifferent, but often antagonistic, to sports.) This *p* is that of the person to whom the physical side of outdoor life is most appealing and to whom personal participation in it is of prime importance. A curious fact is that many prize-fighters and other professionals of the ring do not exhibit this sign, which would seem to confirm the fact that it has some remote and obscure relationship to the love of nature, although the users are never conscious of this. The professional athlete, it is to be noted, is often not really a lover of physical exercise, and certainly often lacks interest in nature. In estimating the writing of the professional "sport," then, we need not be surprised to find that greed, love of self and a superb self-confidence are the elements of character which we find—and which we find alone, without any of the other traits which one would suppose to be possessed by those who seek the championship in athletics.

The letter q is to be read according to the rules for loops. It is to be noted, as an oddity, that when we have the use of the *altruistic loop*—the loop of *q,* normally turned to the right, is turned to the left, thus becoming a *g*; whereas the loop of *g* will be turned to the right, thus becoming a *q*.

When the letter r *is a good deal larger than the*

other small letters, it is the indication of fondness for dress and general care for appearances. The users of this formation like jewelry, want to live well-regulated lives, in the sense of bodily comfort and ease, and dislike rough clothing and rude surroundings. They adapt themselves well to social usages and usually have suave manners.

All formations of r *which depart from the simple and standard one* (aside from the matter of size) give evidence of a care for detail and a certain tendency to be petty in attending to detail. Thus, the maker of the rather too over-elaborated small *r* will detest people who borrow things and do not return them, even should such borrowing be very petty; these people remember detail and often are offended by actions which are literally unconscious on the part of the other person—they are sticklers for conventions and for the fulfilment of small obligations.

The letter s *which is made with the superfluous first-stroke* is used by those who have never learned anything of the art of elimination of trifles.

The s *which is made with the one movement of the writing-instrument* shows that the mind has had a good deal to do with the development of the character.

The use of both these forms of s *by one writer* is the indication of versatility.

In coming, now, to the *letter t,* the graphologist approaches the most important letter of the alphabet, in so far as the indication of character is concerned.

The real meaning of this letter, with all its many variations, lies in the horizontal stroke with which it is completed. It is so illuminating a letter that it, alone, will often tell us almost the outline of the character of the writer.

The letter t *which is conventionally made*—in which the bar is placed midway of the perpendicular stroke and which is approximately as long as the stroke is high—is the indication of exactly that! That is to say, the individuality is weak, the mentality surely not highly developed, and the personality is without high lights.

The t *which has a horizontal stroke longer and slightly heavier in pressure than the perpendicular stroke* shows a mind which is more active than that of the foregoing writer and a will-power which is less yielding.

The t *which has a very long and strong horizontal stroke* shows strong and assertive will-power and a personality which does not readily take to obscurity or to coercion by others.

The t *which has a horizontal stroke which is club-shaped (heavier at the end than at the beginning) as well as long and strong,* expresses brutality in some degree—just what degree will depend, of course, on the many other indications of the writing; but in some degree, without doubt. This brutality may be physical or temperamental or mental; it may be subconscious, or it may be mere aggressiveness of opinions and indifference to the feelings of others. Whatever line it takes, it is positive and not a mere suggestion of a quality.

The t *which has a horizontal stroke which is spear-shaped (the reverse of club-shaped)* is the indication of a nature to which sarcasm is innate. It is impossible for these people to turn away wrath with the traditional "soft reply"; they are keen at repartee, have always the ready answer, talk too much and do not know the value of silence.

The t *which has a horizontal stroke which flies high over the letter* is the indication of imagination and ardor. People who make this kind of *t* usually have a temper and are impulsive in showing it, but are generous, too, and are always warm-hearted.

When the t, *in a very commonplace hand, has a high-flying horizontal stroke,* the indication is of strong prejudices and narrow-minded opinions, the imagination of the higher type of person being transferred to a lower level in this case.

The t *which has a waved horizontal stroke* is indicative of inconstancy, wavering decisions, too much moodiness, and an unwillingness to assume or carry responsibilities. It is not surprising that in the users of this sign we find the husbands and wives who make a failure of marriage, the fathers and mothers who have not the patience for parentage, and the workers who complain that they find it so hard to settle to any one thing.

When the t *has a horizontal bar which does not quite cross the letter, or which just touches the letter and does not go far beyond it,* we have one of the most positive of graphological signs, for this is indicative of procrastination. Writers of this *t* never do to-day what they can put off until to-morrow, and "delay, linger and wait" is their watchword. It is almost impossible to get decisive action out of the users of this sign.

When the t *bar is continually absent,* the writer is absent-minded. This is usually the indication, also, of a weak will, in so far as practical things are concerned, anyway.

When the t *has a horizontal stroke which is heavy and slanted downward,* there is the indication of obstinacy and of probable argumentativeness. While some people using this sign are not bad-tempered, the majority of them are.

When the t *has the horizontal stroke slanted upward,* the writer is hopeful and enthusiastic. It is to be noted that this is not a sign which gives much stability or firmness of will-power, though, if in a rounded writing.

When the t *has a bar which is in the form of a bow with the ends turned up,* there is the indication of a nature which is rather shallow and too easily affected by stronger wills.

When the t *has a bar which reverses this form and makes a bow with the ends turned down,* there is one of the most interest-compelling formations to be found in writing. This is the indication of the nature which has had strong passions and appetites *which have been conquered.* Sometimes this formation is the first sign that we have that an otherwise selfish and possessive nature is gaining better traits. Sometimes this formation is all that is left to tell us of what has been at some other period of the life.

The t *which has, instead of the horizontal stroke, a "tie" produced near the basic line by the stroke being returned to that position, and then carried in behind and out again, from the perpendicular stroke,* is the indication of persistence and the ability to work right along on one line or to think along one line. This is frequently found in small writing, which shows concentration.

The t *which is formed by an angular return stroke on the perpendicular stroke* is the assertive and aggressive nature which finds it hard to take into consideration the feelings and convictions of other people, of other types of people.

The t *which is formed, at the ends of words, by making, not a horizontal stroke across the upright, but by a partially straddled formation, with a final stroke at right angles,* is indicative of a certain ability to deal well with practical problems.

The t *which is "straddled"* is to be read as is the straddled *d*. It has the same significance and is usually found in association with that *d*.

The lasso t, *which is made by a return stroke, usually very graceful, over the letter,* is indicative of some degree of eccentricity and also of tenacity about personal wishes, desires and convictions. The personality is usually "quaint" and the manner very individualistic.

The eccentricities of t *are more alarming in their import than many of the eccentricities of other letters.* The small *t* being the point at which strength or weakness of will registers, and the point which is the peak of the expression of self-control, strange and unusual formations show the will-power as greatly affected, weakened or perverted.

The t *which is made by going back, putting on the horizontal stroke over a low straddled formation and then adding a perpendicular stroke over that, to complete the formation,* is invariably the indication of serious inhibitions and oddities of mind and temperament which need to be controlled and eventually eliminated.

The letters u, v, w, *and* x *are to be read according to the general laws of legibility, pressure, size, width and so on.*

It will seem at the first glance that there are formations in these letters which call for special interpretation, but care in estimating these formations will show that they fall into step with other formations of other letters.

The letters y *and* z *must be read according to all the various general indications and also for all rules having to do with loops.*

It is to be noted that *y* lends itself especially to distinctive formations, such as the altruistic loop and the eccentric loop, which is a tie within the loop, and so on.

THE CAPITALS

The A *which is made like the small letter* has to be read according to the rules for the small letter. Elimination of the beginning-stroke is a good augury for simplicity of tastes.

The A *which is made like the printed letter* is to be read for its severity of formation, as to whether it is wholly of the Constructive type or only partially so.

The ornamented A shows bad taste and a tendency to be too vain in small personal matters.

The A *which is softly rounded and has a curved line for a bar* is called the *protective A* and is one of the significators of graphology. It shows a tendency to protect the weak and the poor and is always interested in those who are less than normal in any way.

These people seldom have passionate loves or ardent friendships, the intensity of their emotions pouring out to humanity in general, rather than to their own small circle. They are often of the Philoprogenitive type and are frequently poor judges of human nature, knowing little of the complexity of life. Their instincts are to save and rescue without much regard as to what it is that they return to life. It is therefore not surprising to find them antagonistic toward rather sterner ideals, such as capital punishment, birth control and severe tests for human fitness and efficiency. The *protective A* people are always thrilled by misery in the mass and are ardent "joiners," eager to form societies for the assistance of the weak and suffering. They send money to Armenia, work for the benighted Eskimo, and are as close to passions as they can get when they talk about babies and work for the preservation of them.

On the other hand, this type does not understand the unusual individual and will often miserably fail of doing the very "protecting" over which they so yearn, because of this.

The *protective A* is usually found associated with very softly rounded writing.

B, *which has the beginning-stroke ornamented,* so that it consists of a curlicue of some kind or other, shows aggressive pride which is apt to concern itself with externals. These people love to dress well, have a keen regard for appearances, and loathe being laughed at. They do not have a real sense of humor, although often of the type which laughs frequently and loudly.

B *which reverses this and puts a curlicue on the end of the beginning-stroke* has pride which is apt to be more or less self-respect and not sensitiveness as to personal appearance and other trifling matters. The tendency is to have sound judgment and to be careful of detail.

The printed B is to be read like other printed capitals.

C *is chiefly important in considering angular and rounded writing.* In trying to determine whether writing is extremely angular or not, the point can be settled by considering whether *C* is or is not angular. If *C* is, then the handwriting is extremely angular, for this letter is nearly always rounded even when the writing is chiefly angular.

D *which is narrow and which has the final-stroke brought over to "close" the letter, and in which there is no indentation at the base of the letter* shows a nature in which caution and timidity are extreme. There is no great determination or courage in the user of this letter.

D *which is narrow, but not squeezed in appearance, which has the final-stroke of the letter brought over, but which has a good indentation at the base,* is not the indication of great timidity, but does show caution and extreme conservatism. In business such writers can do well only as they follow recognized paths and only as they pursue eminently "safe and sane" lines. The women using this formation are never expansive socially and often are sticklers for conventions.

When the final-stroke of D *is brought over and swirled or is ornamented in any way,* the writer has an assertive vanity. The instinct to play for applause and to all but demand admiration may be expected of those who make this letter habitually.

All forms of D *which are "open"—i.e., have the final-stroke of the letter not brought over at all*—are variants on the generous and open-hearted *D*. No matter what other disagreeable qualities may be discovered in a writer's "hand," this *D* is a mitigating note, for generosity and open-heartedness will always be shown.

E *which is made with an inflated upper-stroke conforms to the rule for inflated loops.* It is sometimes found in writing where there are few other inflated loops and shows a mild sort of egotism: sometimes a harmless and amusing one, as when a man who might well be proud of his position in the literary world is proud, instead, of his golf record and indifferent to the other. It is sometimes used by people who are vain of their personal appearance.

E *which is printed* is not only expressive of what the other printed capitals are, but shows a special severity toward personal adornment, in reverse meaning to the previous formation.

E *which begins with a stroke starting midway of the letter*—a perfectly superfluous stroke which is a remainder of archaic forms—very naturally expresses what we are accustomed to call rather vaguely as "an old-fashioned character." Reactionaries; the people who do not keep up with their own times; too conservative persons; those who are apt to get into a rut and stay there—often use this formation.

F *which is severely plain* is the normal F. Very few people ornament F, even when they do ornament other letters. It is more or less the touchstone of innate good taste.

F *which is something of a combination of two flourishes,* even if rather graceful and unobtrusive, is less indicative of good taste than the plain *F.* Any ornamentation of this letter seems to show a corresponding elaboration of taste which is not good. The makers of the flourished *F* usually slightly overdress, have manners which are a little too elaborate, like a bit too much of a high light on all art which attracts their attention.

F *which is greatly and vulgarly ornamented* is the acme of the indication of bad taste. It is rarely found, but when found, it is by no means always in the handwriting of an ignorant person. It is really astounding to see where this most unpleasant *F* will sometimes be used. On the other hand, the vulgar taste of which it is the evidence may not be conspicuous in the person of the writer. Education and training may have taught caution and self-control in the expression of taste. Many a person raves about the opera who is tone-deaf! When found and fully seen, the particular bad taste of which this *F* is an exponent will be not difficult to classify, for it will be blatant.

When any other capitals are printed, F *will be sure to be also.* This would be so, since the printed *F* is the very best expression of the severe good taste which causes the making of the printed capital.

When G *is made, according to the copybook model, with the entirely superfluous beginning-stroke,* there is the indication of a cool, practical and very matter-of-fact nature. This formation is often used by those who also use the *old-fashioned E,* but frequently they are dissociated; and they are really quite distinct in meaning. The *E* gives reserve, timidity and mildness, while this form of *G* is much more apt to express confidence in self which is not fully justified. It is not the true vanity indication, however; the people who use this *G,* with commonplace writing, are those who overestimate the small place in the world which they hold. *If* the writing is not commonplace, then this *G* should not be found in it, and is evidence that the nature still needs a good deal of developing.

The G *which has eliminated the initial-stroke* has made a big progress toward higher development of mentality and toward good taste and refinement of feeling.

G *is occasionally made reversed.* It is really a formation like the "8" *g* of the smaller letters, but with a little more feeling for form and design. Only those who use the disconnected letter of words, showing intuition, use this formation. It is nearly always written, as is the rest of the writing, with light pressure. Ideality, a cultured mind, together with keen sensibilities, are all shown by this formation.

H is one of the capital letters which has the least individuality.

An H *made with the very elaborated formation which is in itself a complete capital* S, *and with a curved bar, and a half-flourish on the final-stroke,* presents a perfect picture of the unnecessary. It is needless to say that the people making this capital will not use many formations showing elimination! An indication which is not very constant, but which is frequent enough to cause graphologists to speculate, is that the user of this form is a person to whom elaborate social customs seem natural, and to whom "talkative" can well be applied.

An H *with a slight curve on each perpendicular stroke* is the conventional *H* of conventional good taste. This is used by the average person.

H *which is printed* is, like *F,* more or less a touch stone for good taste. In the hands of those who regularly print their capitals, it is more definite and well formed than when printed by those who do not print the rest of their capitals.

The capital I *which is modest and inconspicuous* shows a personality free from personal vanity. This letter expresses a great deal as to the personal attitude which the writer takes toward the world. The antecedents of this letter, which takes us far into the mists of antiquity, show us that the present capital *I* is but the symbol which has grown out of the primitive drawing of a man. The fact that it now expresses the ego is something which is in line, therefore, with its history.

The capital *I* and the signature often disclose what the handwriting otherwise would not. We must not refuse to take the testimony of this capital as to the real amount of egoism which is possessed by the writer. A rather boastful man once said, when told that his capital *I* did not indicate a boastful nature: "I put that on. If I did not, I'd be afraid to talk to anybody!" It is impossible to find a really vain person who uses the small and unobtrusive capital *I*.

All inflations of the upper loop of the capital I *conform to the rules for inflation of upper loops, with the addition that the meaning is transferred from the character to the personality.*

Until we stop to reflect seriously, we may think that this is a distinction without a difference; but it is really an important distinction for those to bear in mind who would discuss the human creature.

We may liken the personality to the upper layer of the nature, and character to the inmost elements. Thus, the inflated upper loop of the capital *I* may show that a man is pompous in manner and very complacent about everything which has to do with himself, but that very man, under the stress of emotion or high stimulation, may throw all that aside and become one of nature's simple noblemen. Out of all this consideration we get a rule for deductions:

If the inflated capital I *is to be taken as the evidence of real vanity, such as is more than personality-deep, it must be confirmed by other inflated upper loops in the writing.* Otherwise it is the indication of vanity which well might disappear under the pressure of hard work, competition, suffering or other contributing causes.

When the upper loop of I *is inflated, but is round and not elongated,* it is the expression of gay self-confidence, and of that amusing self-assurance which is not unpleasant to meet. Note that the curly ending-strokes of letters and the elongated or curved *i* dot will nearly always be found associated with this formation. If neither one of them *is,* then the indication is far more unpleasant and the good-humor of the writer will be far less.

When the lower loop of I *is inflated,* the pride or vanity is transferred from the expression of this quality in blatant ways, to pride which is more or less pride in fulfilling one's own ideals, in meeting the demands of one's own nature or life.

When the I *is angular* the mentality is one of less graciousness and more severity than is usual, and the mentality is in the ascendent. It is sometimes possible to find the angular *I* when the writing is rather rounded, in which case the writer appears more severe than he or she really is.

The capital I *which terminates abruptly, without suggestion of a loop on the lower-stroke,* has checked pride and vanity and even self-consciousness. It is possible to find this in the writing of many people who are not wonders, nor anything exceptional, save as they have pleasant and genuinely *good* characters. When, therefore, this formation is found in writing which is individual and exceptional, especially as to mentality, we may be sure that the processes of mind and soul which have placed it there have not been simple. In other words, this simple and unpretentious *I*, in writing which shows high pride and self-confidence and assertiveness as natural, has not crept slowly into the writing save as the struggles of the writer to attain a fine character have put it there.

The printed I is the most often found of all the printed letters, for it is frequently used by people who write, otherwise, a straggling and incoherent hand—in that case, the printed capital letter is a very delightful formation, since it assures us that, although the character is still in the process of formation, the ego is being steadily beaten into the modesty and moderation which are so fine. When found in the writing of those who print *all* capitals, the meaning of this formation may not be good; it may express, rather the cool assertiveness of the personality which is so often possessed by those who print their capitals.

The capital I *which is not really printed but which is just an upright stroke* is used, frequently, by those who use the leftward inclinations, and in that case seems to be an expression of the exceedingly uncommunicative personality which is so frequently associated with this writing. This form of the capital *I,* no matter what the type of writing in which it is found, expresses a certain simplicity which is not the simplicity of ignorance and unsophistication, but that of the very opposite pole of complexity of character and mind.

Occasionally we find the capital I *which has become squatty and which looks almost like a certain form of* Q or the figure 2. The *E* which is "old-fashioned" is apt to be used by those who make this formation, and both of these letters show certain reactionary qualities. Progressiveness, self-reliance, determination and foresight are elements of character not apt to be possessed by the makers of this formation.

The capital J *is to be read solely according to the rule for loops.* (See the chapter on "Loops.")

Capital K, *when started with the formation which*

is a sort of S, is precisely of the same indication as that shown by an *H* similarly begun.

The K, *when this formation is much simplified and the upper- and lower-strokes which make the rightward side of the letter are short,* is the modest *K* which shows a personality that is not too assertive.

A very awkward and straggling K shows the mind as not well developed, and the tastes not yet under the control of culture.

When the upper-stroke on the right-hand side of capital K *is elongated* the mentality of the writer is one of unusual individuality. This does not mean, necessarily, eccentricity, although it does at times *if* the other letter formations are indicative of this quality to any extent. These people are apt to be more than usually irritated by conventionality and cannot be coerced: they are usually foes of set religious and political ideas. As this formation is apt to be developed in adolescence, here is a valuable means by which the inborn rebel may be estimated in extreme youth.

When the capital K *is made by one upright stroke and one stroke which "ties into" the upright one,* there is the indication of a certain bright and active mind which is chiefly focused on detail—on the affairs of the moment, as it were. Such a writer will be little interested in philosophy or anything which is outside the circle of immediate interests, but, within that circle, is likely to be both intelligent and active.

The printed K is especially indicative of what the printed capitals stand for, since even those who print many of them will often write *K.* When it is printed, therefore, there is the strong confirmation of the printed indications of individuality and good taste.

Capital L, *when flowing, rightwardly inclined and made with a strong pressure,* is indicative of that all-embracing characteristic known as *personality*. However, it must be confirmed by other indications, of course; otherwise, this formation of the *L* is a promise and not a mirror of a fact.

A cramped, awkwardly made, and otherwise unimpressive capital L shows the lack of expression of personality.

An L *which is written almost upright, when the rest of the writing is more rightward,* shows a personality which does not do justice to the nature.

An L *which is written very rightward when the body of the writing is upright or only slightly rightward* expresses the more or less artificially developed personality which is often "made" by stage training, training in elocution, social training, and so on.

The inflation of the upper loop of the capital L expresses pride in personal achievements. Desire to rule, too, and dislike of subordinate positions, are shown by this inflated upper loop.

The inflation of the lower loop of the L drags this pride of achievement and the desire to be worthy of high places, to the lower levels, where to be *admired* for the achievement is the paramount desire.

When the capital L *has a very small upper loop and practically none where the stroke turns on the basic line,* there is the indication of either freedom from desire for personality development or total lack of that development. These people are never good employers and are unsuccessful in public positions, though often greatly beloved by all those who come into contact with them in their private capacity.

The old way in which the capital M *was made was with the beginning-stroke on the basic line*—there or thereabouts, the exact place being doubtful, since a large, involved flourish often started with that stroke! We still see this style of *M* made, largely without the flourish. It is always the indication of a more conservative nature than the one which instinctively turns to the other form.

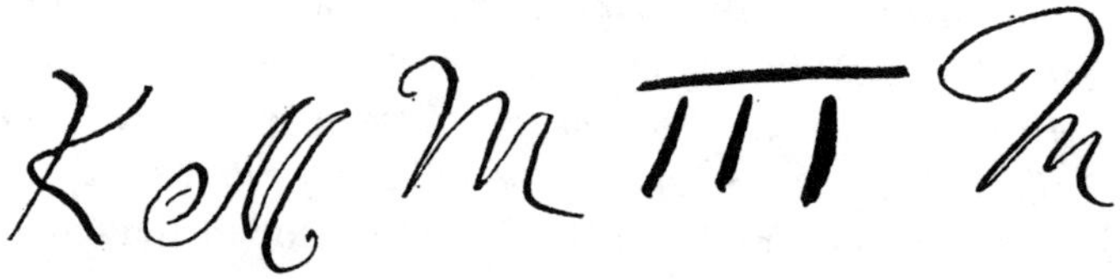

An M *made of three upright and one horizontal is indicative of cool efficiency.* This is one of the favorite formations of the younger generation of to-day.

The modern M *has the beginning-stroke in the air after which the first down-stroke of the letter is made.* This is the instinctive formation of the average intelligent person who is actively interested in his own times and who is not too conservative.

In the modern M *we frequently find the beginning-stroke complicated by the incurve,* which means that the stroke is not outward flung, but is turned in on itself. All the various forms of incurves, wherever found, but of which the best exponents are in *M* and *N*, show possessiveness and clannishness: *i.e.*, the instinct to hold what is once gained and to give intensive interest and attention only to those who are in the close circle where possessiveness is a natural feeling. Thus, the users of the incurves are never humanitarians, in the wider sense of the word, and are ardent partisans. With them it is "My country, right or wrong," *my* friend, *my* beloved. It is needless to say that these incurve users are almost incapable of looking impartially at any one or anything that may be antagonistic to the interests and possessions of the incurve user.

The adherence to class which is characteristic of the clannish people brings them heavily into both the aristocratic and laboring classes, the two extremes of humanity who do not see well outside their own class affiliations.

These people make good parents and teachers for quite small children, but do not do so well for the older ones, who do not take kindly to the restrictions which are sure to be the ideals of the clannish instructor.

The angular incurve, on M *or any letter,* accentuates the clannishness and takes away some of the protectiveness and good temper which is given when the incurve is rounded. These people have the element of possessiveness more strongly developed than the rounded incurved writers and are aggressive in showing it. They are very hard to get along with, as a rule, too, unless surrounded by people who are stronger and more efficient than themselves, in which case their respect keeps them from showing irritation. Such people as these make good police, rulers of high-grade workers, and administrators, when the ideal of the administration is to bring the administrated up to the very highest degree of efficiency and intensive loyalty. Jealousy of the cool and rather unemotional sort is sure to be part of the composition of these writers, which is due, of course, to their extreme feeling for possessiveness.

Curved, outward-flung beginning-strokes on the capital M express love of pleasure and a certain defiance of conventionality. This is often found associated with the *i* dot which shows humor, and usually is used by people who have a happy disposition.

When the first stroke, or "point," of the capital letter M *is higher than the one or two others which follow,* the writer has the kind of pride which dislikes to admit failure and which wishes to be liked and admired. These are the people who are fighters for advancement and success and who are not easily discouraged.

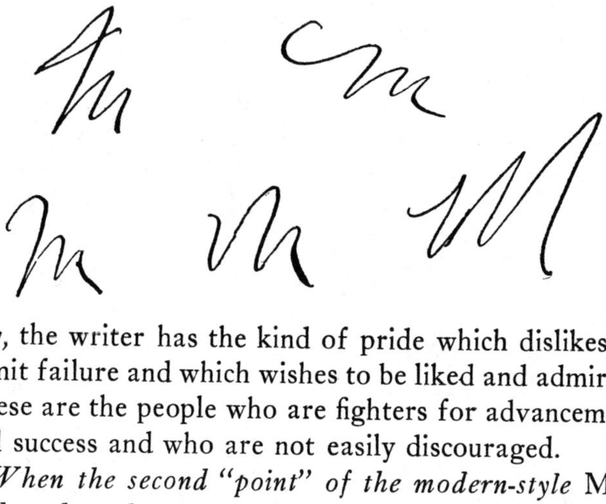

When the second "point" of the modern-style M *is higher than the one preceding or following it,* there is eccentricity of some kind in both the mind and the nature. Sometimes this formation is used by people of mild genius and by those who are really talented and exceptional, but more often it is used by the "characters" of a town or section of the country; and in both cases it shows odd reactions, mostly centered in the personality.

When the second "point" of the old-style capital M, *or the third "point" of the modern* M *is higher than the one preceding it,* the indication is a very odd one and will merit the careful attention of the graphologist. This is often interpreted by the untrained graphologist to mean a nature which is humble and unassertive; but quite the contrary is actually the case. The appearance and manner of such writers may, indeed, support that view; but that, like the seeming retiring formation of this *M,* is far from being what they are. The fact is that the people who use this formation are stubborn and assertive, at heart, and that they have a tenacity and aggressiveness which is unsurpassed by any type. Intolerance, in some form or other, is sure to be characteristic, despite the probable fact that the writer of this form will urgently represent intolerance as intensely hated. Such people are exceedingly hard to understand and hardly ever have much popularity, but they are sometimes people of sterling worth and in rare cases have oddly fascinating though perplexing personalities. Their personalities are never easy to read, and they are distinctly people of few, though often fine, intimacies.

All formations of capital N *are to be read according to the rules for capital* M.

Capital O has not a great deal to tell us, except for one thing, which is concerned with whether the oval is made from right to left or from left to right. This can usually be determined by observing the force with which the instrument of writing is held as it is put to the paper. From right-to-left, the pressure will be slightly heavier at the point within the letter; from left-to-right, the pressure will be slightly heavier at the point outside the letter. A little experimentation with the pencil will soon make this clear.

The capital *O* which is made from left-to-right is, of course, the most common. That from right-to-left is exceedingly uncommon; it is never quite as smooth or graceful as that one made from left-to-right and yet usually succeeds in having a little more individuality. Therefore, the writer of the right-to-left capital *O* will be the more interesting individuality and probably the more interesting personality, too, with a probable difficulty in getting that personality "across," as the expression is.

Capital P is governed by the same rules which apply to capital *R*.

Capital Q is to be read in the same manner as the right and left formations of capital *O*.

When capital Q *is made like the figure* 2, the nature is less aggressive than when the *Q* is made like *O*, with the small curved line at the base which differentiates it.

Capital R when made with the large half-circle before the main body of the letter is expressive of that pride which is interested in appearances. The makers of this formation are apt to be rather envious; they have to struggle hard to be fair and impartial in their judgments. The ability to talk fluently is often possessed by the makers of this formation.

Cutting off this half-circle and making the upright-stroke of the letter quite separate from the curved formations to the right gives us the capital letter *R* which expresses moderation and good taste without any distinct individuality. That is to say, of course, without any distinct individuality in the letter itself. It is often true that those who use this formation show individuality, perhaps in other capital formations, and frequently in the small letters.

The printed capital R, more than any other of the printed capitals, expresses the development of mental assurance and self-understanding, showing the user to be sure of his or her opinions, exact in stating the pleading for them, apt to be somewhat argumentative in exploiting them.

The capital R *which is made in one continuous formation, in which all superfluous strokes are eliminated,* is the indication of extreme rapidity of thought. The makers of this *R* are usually also intuitional, their reasoning processes being hard to follow with equal speed and accuracy. The accuracy of the mind which is behind this capital *R,* however, is a different accuracy from that which is behind the printed *R.* The writer of the continuous *R* is accurate about matters, for instance, which would not even seem to be important to the printed *R* user. The printed *R* writer is accurate about concrete things, about the details of statements and about material facts. The continuous *R* writer is accurate about ideas, thoughts, conceptions and philosophies. Unless of exceptional caliber neither of these types will ever be able to understand the nature of the other, nor to admire sufficiently the mentality of the other.

The capital S *which is printed* is apt to be used by even the ordinary-mind-development person, for the reason that it is a primitive formation and therefore one which is exceedingly easy for the human hand to make.

When capital S *is made with the superfluous stroke which precedes the simpler formation* we may be sure that the writer is conventional and is apt to be stamped with the fairly ordinary thought of his or her times and of his or her class and station in life. This formation is very frequently found in association with the capital letter *E* which shows conventionality.

Capital T *printed,* in a hand which does not contain all printed capitals, expresses some instinct for constructive thought, probably along the lines of social relations, morals, government and so on; possibly along the line of literary or general art criticism. When all the capital letters are printed, the *T* then falls into the regular classification and is not so specially expressive.

Capital T, *made with two separate flourishes,* is to be read as is *F* when similarly made.

Capital T *made with one action of the writing-instrument, with a short horizontal-stroke, a perpen-*

dicular- or slanting-stroke and an upturned ending-stroke, is the ordinary capital *T* of the ordinary person and the rather exceptional person. It is the greatest common denominator, as it were, of humanity, for it will be found used by "all sorts and conditions of men." It is common to even the rare, distinctive hands. The fact that utter lack of culture characterizes a writer does not prevent that writer from using it; nor does the fact that the writer is a person of rare culture. It is not, therefore, a letter which will be especially revealing to the graphologist, even though it is curiously interesting to reflect on the universality of this formation in the writings which have come out of the Latin tradition.

Capitals U, V, W, X, Y, Z are to be read for legibility, pressure, width, rounded and angular formations, and so on, through all the general graphological indications.

Capitals Y and *Z* are to be read also in accordance with the rules governing loops.

SIGNATURES

The signature is the expression of the personality, to a greater extent than is the body of the writing. In fact, without the habitual signature to study we are often in doubt as to the personality, for the handwriting, *per se,* does not give us the information on this point that is to be read in the signature. This is quite logical, for in the repeated writing of the name the self-consciousness must find an easy channel into which to flow. The familiarity of the formations enables the writer to make them almost automatically and thus releases the hand from too intent observation of the mind, a condition which always tends to the production of writing which is expressive of the personality rather than the mind and character.

It is not uncommon to find people with two signatures—one of them more or less manufactured, as with those whose name may be a temptation to the forger, or whose signature must be accepted by banks and stand guaranty for something. In that case, it is nearly always true that the manufactured signature will be of narrower letters, closer formation, shorter connecting-strokes and more precise, or else far less, legible letter formations. All of this, besides achieving the result which is desired, the making of a forgery difficult, also expresses the very elements of feeling which have caused that signature to be manufactured: caution, fear, reserve, carefulness and secretiveness. Thus, no matter how the signature is made, it is expressive of what impels the making of it.

When we see that the signature is of this cautious formation, with possibly involved flourishes which make it difficult to read, we may be sure that some aspect of the writer's character corresponds to this, no matter whether there are aspects which do not so correspond or not.

Sometimes this cautious signature is balanced by one which is frank and open and unreserved, which is used as soon as the writer feels that the urge for caution is lost. This duality of signature is never observed except in the writing of people who have very unusual temperaments, for the signature is the one thing which usually is almost impossible for the writer to change materially, even by direct and continued effort.

When the habitual signature is composed of narrow letters, short connecting-strokes and angular formations, and the writing is of more rounded formations, wider letters and longer connecting strokes, we have a personality which has been more or less made to order and has probably been affected by pressing conditions of life, in some way or other.

These are the people who lack personal magnetism, seem to be unresponsive, and often fail to win strangers and acquaintances to liking, but whose real nature—shown by the body of the writing—is affectionate and warm-hearted. They therefore hold the affection of those who burst through the barriers reared by the unresponsive personality, and find there the nature which has such an ill representation.

Forward-leaning, flowing, attractive-looking signa-

tures, with rather large capitals which are not really plain, and with long connecting-strokes, show a very magnetic personality if the writing also agrees with this.

People of this temperament are sure to be gracious in manner, rather talkative and often clever of speech, quick to see what others like, not argumentative or aggressive, quick to smile, and always interested in social life. Imitativeness is developed and the mind, sometimes exceedingly active, is facile and receptive.

When the signature is of the type described in the previous paragraph and when the writing is composed of narrower letters, of more restrained letter forms, of smaller capitals, and of greater constraint, all through, we have the indication of the personality which is more frank, charming and friendly in appearance than is really warranted by the nature.

Such people are usually rather disappointing to those who rely upon the indications given by these personalities, and are often accused of being false and "two-faced," but that is far from being the fact in all cases. Whether it is the fact at all, can be determined by looking in the body of the writing for the indications of deceit, treachery and selfishness. Selfishness will usually be found, but not in large measure. If in large measure, then it is safe to say that the personality is something of a deliberate fraud and that the writer is inclined to use it and its charm for purely selfish ends.

When the signature is wholly at one with the body of the writing, so that there are no signature peculiarities, then the personality is the exact replica of the character.

When the signature is turned to the leftward angle of inclination and the writing is less leftwardly inclined, or is inclined to the right, we may assume that the personality seems much more reserved and unemotional than is the fact of the nature.

Such people often disguise their ardent dispositions with a cool and reserved manner.

When the signature is composed of small unostentatious writing, and the capitals used in the body of the writing are far larger than in the signature and much more flowing or ornamented or elaborate in any way, we have the nature which, with a meek and forbearing personality, conceals towering ambition and a great deal of egotism.

This word "conceals," however, must not be interpreted as meaning that the deception is always intentional or is even known to the writer. A great many people who honestly believe that they are mild and gentle and meek thus reveal the real facts of the case, but are totally unconscious of them. Very often this extra-small and unpretentious signature shows one of these phases of involved feeling which we seem to have agreed to call "an inferiority complex."

The underscoring of the signature is always an indication that the writer has gained some assertiveness and that the personality is one which has more or less force and distinction.

The underscore is the graphological sign of the assertiveness which wishes to make the individuality something concrete and positive. As against the underscored signature, the signature without underscore expresses a nature which will more easily be shoved out of recognition among others, will accept "the back seat," will make less brilliant an effect in society.

It is seldom that the actor or the orator or the statesman fails to underscore his signature, and an odd and interesting experiment, conducted among rather a large circle of people, will soon show that the underscored signature is the signature of the people whose personalities shine; take the writings of, say, forty people who are at an evening party, having first observed who are the outstanding figures—the natural leaders and "high lights" of the occasion. You will find that these are the most heavily underscored signatures, and that the wall-flowers will have the most inconspicuous signatures. This rule would not apply, of course, to a gathering of very young people, for the underscored signature is the sign of maturity.

The short, straight underscore, medium pressure, is assertive of rights and of possession.

Such people are eager "to have and to hold" and are apt to be clannish, wanting everything for the few for whom they care and having little real humanitarianism. They are usually without tact, but have keen good judgment about practical things, and are not bad-tempered.

The long, straight and rather heavy to very heavy underscore is the expression of a nature which is aggressive where the previous type is merely assertive and possessive.

Such people are indifferent to many of the finer issues of life and are quick to feel that living for others and working for posterity is not worth while. The

SIGNATURES

disposition is sure to be determined in all sorts of ways. Physical courage is to be expected, but spiritual development is never high.

The long, straight underscore of a delicate pressure transfers the possessiveness and aggression of the same underscore which is of heavy pressure, to a higher plane.

The disposition is one of interest toward the world, and of assertiveness which does not descend to too great personal possessiveness. Many of the elements of the heavier pressure underscore exist here, but softened and lightened by the transfer of the emphasis to less materialistic grounds.

Curved underscores accentuate indications of the personal charm of the writer. The smoother and more graceful the curve, the more is the personality gracious, assured and magnetic.

It is not surprising to find the emotional actress and the romantic actor and the musician with the exceptional personality using the curved underscore. Should the writing be disorderly and chaotic in arrangement and the letter forms without distinction, then we may rest assured that the personality is more or less composed of tricks and that there is little real or lasting charm. Should the writing be graceful and interesting we may accept the information given by the underscore as wholly authentic.

Angular underscores show temper, force, ambition and an overbearing personality.

It is impossible to deny charm and magnetism to even these people. Witness the well-known underscore of Napoleon and the angular underscore of very heavy pressure of Zola.

The underscore which takes on a very eccentric form is the indication of a personality which is eccentric.

There is no deviation from this rule.

Signatures which are not underscored are not, necessarily, indicative of undistinguished personalities.

If the handwriting is very distinctive and the capitals decisively made we may presume a personality which does not belie itself. However, no personality is ever quite as able to put itself "over," as the descriptive expression is, when the signature is not underscored. This, however, leaves out of consideration the fact that a great many natures are not in the least concerned with the effect which the personality makes on the world. Ralph Waldo Emerson had one of the most unpretentious of signatures, the capitals conveying the impression of aristocratic simplicity, while his small letters expressed the extraordinary clarity of his mind.

The signature which is not underscored must have some exceptional letter formations to compensate for the lack, if we are to attribute any unusual elements of personality to the writer.

An element in life which deters many people from using underscores to their signatures is that they have never been so placed that the personality has had an opportunity to find expression. Women whose whole lives have been passed, closely confined to their homes, hardly ever use an underscore, yet those same women forced out into the world, even at middle age, and frequently finding success in that world which they never would have attempted to get, unless obliged to do so, quite often develop interesting underscores to their signatures, in proportion as their individualities expand and their consciousness of their personalities gains. Men who have been salesmen for years usually develop the underscore—if they are good salesmen!

In short, the underscore keeps pace with the personality and with the ability to set out the personality attractively.

Children sometimes start in early to underscore their signatures. It will be found that they are precocious, easy talkers and often more matured than their years in knowledge of the world. A change in the signature and in the underscore, either or both, after thirty, does not usually occur, but when it does we may be assured that the writer is quite out of the ordinary, and, if the life is spared, will be an outstanding figure, in time. I say "in time" for when handwriting changes, at all, after thirty, we have the interesting person who is the slow maturer but the sure arriver; and when the signature changes—it frequently remains the same even though the writing be changed—we have the very exceptional person who will have a long career with ever-increasing success, unless very untoward conditions are encountered or death arrives prematurely.

The signature which is underscored with a straight or curved line, crossed by two perpendicular strokes, is indicative of business ability.

We sometimes find only one stroke, sometimes three; sometimes small circles, or rightward or leftward inclined strokes; sometimes the ends of the underscore are brought around to make the small strokes. Occasionally the underscore is double and the perpendicular strokes are four. Whatever is the variation, the indication is of something which is akin to the merchandising spirit and the excellent merchandising judgment.

Signatures underscored with a great many flourishes show bad taste, of course, but there is often a crude sort of power and genius about such writers.

Hypocrisy is sometimes shown (when the accentuation of the "diplomat's hand" is marked in the body of the writing attached to this signature).

Signatures which bring the underscore or the flourish of the underscore up over the top of the signature, are indications of eccentricity at some point of the character and of marked individuality throughout, of the kind which is apt to ignore the conventions.

Many of the signatures which seem so much more interesting and individual than the body of the writing are mere, and sheer, imitations. These are the people who laugh like one person, smile like another, wear clothes like another, and so on.

It is a safe thing to say that if the signature is very interesting and individual, *more or less* the same letter forms will appear in the body of the writing.

WHAT HANDWRITING TELLS OF VOCATIONS

It is quite possible to select the work for which a writer is especially fitted, *if* the writer is a special worker by mind and temperament.

There are a great many, of course, who are general workers. They can turn here and there, adapting themselves to a number of different pieces of work along certain lines; while others have sharply marked powers.

The graphologist may estimate vocational possibilities largely through the type of writing used, which is, of itself, an indication; but there are some other points which it may be well to consider.

Mechanical Ability: This manifests itself in all sorts of ways. From the man who is "handy with tools" to the expert in radio or the building of automobiles, the type of talent is the same. The *degree* is all that distinguishes the putterer from the efficient expert.

In proportion as the handwriting shows clipped beginning- and ending-strokes, small letter formations which are very exact, and a tendency to angular formations, in that proportion do we have an expertness and a higher and higher degree of mentality accompanying it. Edison's handwriting does not conform to this, but Edison was never a mechanical expert *with his hands*. It is the *idea* for the experiment which he furnishes. And in the fact that his handwriting is a good deal like that of Emerson, the philosopher, we may see how true handwriting, is, since Edison, without even knowing all the mechanical principles of mechanics, can bring a philosophy to bear on them which is thoroughly worth while and which is a help to those who *do* know the mechanics. Just as Emerson, who never bothered himself about the actual facts of history yet presented to us almost the only sane philosophies of history.

It is interesting, in view of woman's traditional helplessness in the face of a hammer and nails, to record the fact that the mechanical ability type is by no means small in amount in women's writing.

Literary Ability: The refinement, originality and sureness of the letter formations make the *rule* by which we go, in this case; but it is to be noted that there are many variations, most of which can be easily and correctly estimated.

Large writing, in which the small letters are not so distinctive and the capitals more assertive, usually belongs to editors and editorial writers, writers of advertising copy, good orators, and writers of articles.

Flowing writing is apt to show the writer of emotional fiction. These people usually have gracious and beautiful capitals.

Constrained writing shows the scientific writer and the writer of heavy articles. Those interested in civics and government and politics—who are more direct students than writers—use this.

Almost-printed formations show a keen sense of form. Many poets use this. The writers who care greatly for style have closely formed, sometimes printed, and usually letter-separated writing—while the true story-teller almost always has the forward-leaning angle, even though with this printing tendency.

Artistic Ability: This is not always the simple thing that it would seem, and there are a great many subdivisions of it.

A feeling for color is nearly always expressed with the forward-leaning, flowing writing which is gracious and suave, and which has a fine rhythm. Margins are used by the people who are constructively artistic—sculptors and architects, makers of fine and original jewelry, and so on.

The circle *i* dot shows the adaptive form of art. Such people make up any material well, from silk to stone. They adapt the creativeness of others to the everyday needs of the world. They are usually clever with their hands and quick to invent small and beautiful objects. They may be said to be the trade artists. The circle *i* dot, with rather commonplace letter forms and either upright or moderately right or leftward writing shows the very ordinary sense of art. Dressmakers, milliners, painters of lamp-shades, people who can color drawings and so on, will show this type.

Executive Ability: The flowing rhythm is usually possessed by the best executives, especially by those who deal in large quantities of humanity. The large writing of this type shows the person who succeeds by physical activity, by personally directing others, by being, more or less, the super-salesman. Small writing, forward leaning, the *t* bars long and the type Material-Vital, is usually the very unusual executive, whose mentality is unusual. The very highest types of executives approach the Mental type and are often constructive and original, with a strong and dominant personality which is shown in the signature.

Teaching Ability: The forward-leaning writing, with moderate capitals, easy pressure and rounded letter forms gives us the average good teacher of ordinary themes. The more that the capitals increase in individuality, the greater is the ability of the teacher to handle difficult subjects. High school teachers and college professors usually have an upright or leftward hand, with precise and fine letter forms, approaching the Constructive.

Research, Scientific: Those who undertake work of this kind should write a small, fine hand, of the Constructive type, with almost upright writing, and with small, close capitals.

The Lawyer: What the handwriting of the practitioner of the law should be depends on the type of work undertaken. The "pleader" or "courtroom lawyer" has to have all the qualities of the popular actor and the successful preacher, and should, therefore, belong to the same subdivision of the Vital type. The lawyer who is actually the delver into the mysteries of the law should have almost the same handwriting as that of the research worker in science. His terminals should be clipped, his connecting-strokes very short, every letter connected with a stroke, and his pressure medium heavy.

The Musician: A musician must have, of course, the flowing rhythm which speaks of a sense of harmony. The loops are often softly rounded and somewhat fattish-looking. The pressure is hardly ever heavy. Evidences of sensuousness are usually present. The signature is nearly always that of the forward or very backward-leaning, with an underscore.

The singing voice does not show in the handwriting, because it is a thing quite apart from the actual power either to make or to feel music. Many a person with a fine natural voice has been unable to learn to control it and has been totally indifferent to its possession.

The Actor: Actors, good salesmen, magnetic preachers, are all part of the same human type—the Vital. They usually have the flowing rhythm which speaks of ardor and the ability to express it, of interest in and with humanity, of suavity, tact, graciousness and fluency. Small, clipped letter forms and the absence of connecting-strokes take away from the commonness of these types, and exceptional capitals add still more to the indication of a high plane on which the individual functions.

Engineers, Teachers of Exact Sciences: They are apt to print both small and large letters, presenting a very beautiful page, but one in which the prevailing impression is that of coldness.

Salesmanship: This is, as has been pointed out in a preceding paragraph of this section, part of the great classification which gives us actors, orators, fluent clergymen, and so on. The salesman, however, is a very well-marked subdivision of the type. His handwriting, on lower mental levels, is flowing, moderate pressure, rounded capitals and even basic line, the letter formations not especially individualistic. A good many bookkeepers use this hand, but it will usually be found that they will be far more successful as salesmen, once they get a little training in that line of work. The ability to talk, not necessarily with ease, but at least with conviction, is shown by this type. It is expressive of a wholesome interest in the out-of-doors, and without direct and self-conscious egotism, has self-confidence and good-natured assurance.

This subdivision of the type is found very frequently in the American gallery of typical "hands."

Welfare Work, in All Its Branches: Those who are preëminently successful in anything which demands the humanitarian viewpoint should use a more or less rounded writing, with some suggestion, at least, of the *protective A* and kindred formations, with a moderate *t* bar and with a signature which is not too individualistic. Being required by the very nature of the work to sink the individuality, the signature in these hands should be no more distinctive than the body of the writing. Eccentricities, even if showing interesting mental tendencies, should disqualify a writer for welfare work; too often, as handwriting will show, it is a case of the blind leading the blind, when people who are themselves slightly abnormal or subnormal are allowed to take up the care of others, who are only accentuated versions of themselves. It is to be rememberd, too, that even highly interesting people are less well fitted for this work than those who have the instinct to subordinate their personalities to others and to the work in hand.

Explorers, Adventurers and Outdoor People: These are almost invariably of the Vital type, with large admixtures of the Material and with partial development in the Mental. The man who explores is a scientist, writes well, and is a good outdoor man—has, in fact, a dash of almost all the types, except the Nervous; and in some cases, he has that. There is no set way in which we can show that the man or woman is actually *doing* these things, of course, but the *ability* is not difficult to deduce.

The Wife and Mother: Graphologists are continually asked by women, "Am I the type to be a good wife and mother?" To reply to this is not a simple matter. In the first place, wives and mothers do not function alike and, paradoxical as it may seem, belong to fundamentally different types. On the other hand, a great many women succeed in making a man a perfect mate, in bringing up children with entire success, in running a house and running a business and being a useful member of society generally—who are not of the types which especially are marked out as either wives or mothers.

Then there is the fact that the woman with rounded writing, almost upright, light pressure, is a wonderful mother for very young children and not so good for them after they have passed into their 'teens, when the woman with more individuality in the writing, the woman who is more apt to be a better mate than an innate mother, will be a more successful mother for these later years.

Therefore, the question as to whether a woman can be a good wife and mother, or not, can only be answered by another: *Whose wife and mother?*

These remarks also apply to the anxiety of men, who wonder if they are "of the temperament to marry." The answer is, of course, *"It depends on what kind of woman you marry.*" For every Jack there is a Jill! Taking the angle of inclination as a partial guide and carefully estimating the two characters, it is quite possible for the graphologist to point out the kind of person a writer should marry; or, being married, the way in which the other person can best be dealt with.

DISEASES AS INDICATED IN HANDWRITING

The cooperation of physicians in all parts of the world will, in time, bring us complete data on which to make a detailed diagnosis as to the physical conditions of writers. At present, there are not many very definite statements which can be made as to this very interesting matter of diseases as shown by handwriting.

The basic line of writing is especially indicative of the flux in the spirit which is occasioned by physical causes. Contrary to the usual belief, the moods have really very little influence on the handwriting. Extreme and long-continued depression, great melancholy, suicidal intent, are all shown in the writing, but only when they have so long been felt that they have, as it were, worn a groove in the consciousness.

Thus, we come to the first law as to the way in which disease and its attendant disturbances may be charted:

The persistent droop of the basic line, causing it to run downhill, is never totally dissociated from serious physical conditions.

It is true that it is often the expression of disappointment with life, of sorrows and discouragements; but the downward inclination is never persistent until some of the physical powers have been sapped.

Any sharp change in the basic line is an alarming sign.

When the basic line has been firm and straight, and

begins to break into something which is wavering, or which is canted sharply upward or very much downward, this is the sign that there are very revolutionary changes taking place in the physical being of the writer. It is, as so many eminent physicians have pointed out, very difficult to say where we may draw the line between the mind influencing the health and the health influencing the mind.

When, to any sudden change in the basic line, we add tremulousness, or *unnatural force*—due to the subject's holding the writing-implement tightly and bearing down with it, in the effort to control the unsteadiness of the hand—we have the indication of acute disturbances.

When the basic line remains firm, although there has been a great deal of illness, and when neither tremulousness nor unnatural force is present, we may be sure that the vitality of the writer has remained almost unimpaired.

The wavering and disorderly basic line which is an indication of a weak character will usually betray itself by the wavering and weak *t* bar and by the insipidity of the letter forms. Therefore:

The wavering and disorderly basic line which does not have the accompanying indications of weak character, is an indication of nervous disorders.

The tendency of the basic line to sag in the middle of each line, like a disconsolate clothesline, to slip down suddenly at odd places, then to right itself, only to slip again, and to perform other eccentric tricks, is always to be looked at with the utmost care. This may be nothing more than the unsteadiness of a youthful hand, whose equilibrium is not yet established, or it may be the uncertainty of old age; should it be neither of these, we may be sure it is the indication of extreme disorder of the mind and spirit which has invaded and influenced the physical self. The serious nervous "breakdown" which is impending often registers in this way.

The increased or lessened pressure, contrary to the custom of the writer, added to the variability, also unaccustomed, of the basic line, is a danger-signal, showing serious mental disturbance.

A change in pressure is the most drastic change that a writer can effect. Such a change usually and normally takes place over a long period of time. Showing as it does, profound changes in the depths of the being, such as the development of spirituality or of its dark twin, sensuality, the change creeps on so slowly that it is not perceived.

When, therefore, we have the sudden change in pressure, the mental emphasis or the emotional emphasis has been unnaturally transferred, causing mental disturbance.

This does *not* mean that insanity in any degree is even threatening the writer. But it does mean that extreme care is needed for the writer and that both wisdom and kindness will be necessary if no bad after-effects are to be anticipated with the passing of the condition. Parents who find this change taking place in the writing of the adolescent should see that they have some professional advice; if possible, without the knowledge of the subject. Certain types of youth —notably those belonging to the Nervous, Mental and

Artistic—are especially prone to serious mental and emotional spasms before their twentieth year, spasms which are accurately recorded in their writing, in the variations of basic line and pressure. To ignore such conditions is a dangerous attitude to take. Sometimes, it is true, the subject makes the progression to mental and emotional balance, and incidentally to physical health, without assistance; but too often this is not the case.

Contrary to what may be thought to be a natural sequence, tubercular conditions, which drag down the vitality, do not lessen the pressure nor make the writing tremulous. The fierce fever of the disease drives the hand relentlessly, almost until the last, but there is something which can, with some reservations, be taken as an indication of the disease.

A sudden upward swing of the basic line of writing, which is extreme and is sometimes varied by the last three or four words on each line as suddenly dropping, probably indicates a well-developed tubercular condition.

But this applies only to a well-developed condition. The tendency toward the extreme upward slant of the basic line and the dropping of last words from the line, is not found in people who are merely slightly affected by tubercular conditions. So far as graphology knows, at the present time, there is no indication in handwriting of incipient tubercular conditions. The sharp upward swing of the basic line, in serious conditions, probably corresponds to the curious optimism which is one of the pronounced symptoms of this disease, the sharp downward droop of the last word or two on the line corresponding to the real state of mind, which, beneath the disease-engendered buoyancy, is really present. Another oddity is that, as the upward slant of the basic line increases, with the cheeriness of the patient, the *t* bar is apt to lessen in strength and in length, thus registering the weakening of the resistance of the will to the inroads of physical decay.

Persistent "breaks" in the connecting-strokes of letters, which are obviously not the breaks of the real disconnection which is the graphological sign of intuition, show serious nervous conditions which often end in the writer having some dangerous illness.

It is really seldom that pneumonia, kidney trouble, influenza, and other often fatal diseases seize upon individuals who are in perfect health. That they may *seem* to be in perfect health is no doubt true; but in very many cases, as much as six months and more before the seizure the characteristic broken appearance of the handwriting told of the weak power of resistance which the writer had.

The basic line which shows nervous-breaks in the connecting-strokes of letters, coupled with a persistent tendency to drop the last word or the last two words sharply downward, sometimes to such an extent that they actually hang down below the second line, and especially when some disorderliness of arrangement is shown, forms the picture of the typical "suicide note."

Here we have the nervous condition, long existing, with the consequent breakdown of physical resistance; and the sign, in this sharp break in the end of the basic line, of the complete letting-go of all courage, force and nerve-power. Hundreds of examples of suicide notes are to be found on file in various police departments of the large cities, where the prevalence of this combination of signs can be seen.

People often reach this stage, of course, and do not go on to actual suicide, but only because they have very superior will-power or circumstances are especially kind to them. The graphologist who finds handwriting exhibiting these characteristics should not be deterred from making the correct diagnosis by any statements of the writer, the writer's friends or family, as to the entire health and content of the writer.

Physicians understand very well that the conditions of the mind and of the body are often little understood by the very person who suffers from them, or by those who are close to the sufferer.

A sudden change in the size of writing is always intriguing to the graphologist.

It is sometimes deliberately affected by the writer, in which case the change will pass; and it is sometimes the expression of a change in the character or in the mental state of the writer, in which case there will be evident the difficulty of the hand in adjusting itself to this change, such as an occasional letter straggling out or back to the size formerly used. Suppose, however, that we have writing which is usually large and which precipitately reduces itself to extremely small size; or suppose that we have a very small and compact hand which branches out suddenly into much larger size. We have then the registration of a shock which the writer has suffered, either physical, emotional or mental. Sometimes all three centers will have been shocked. The change in the size of writing seen in shell-shocked soldiers, during the late War, was most noticeable.

The sudden change in the size of writing is sometimes seen in those whose minds are really affected, not as the result of shock, but as the result of steadily deteriorating mental states.

When the change in the size of writing has to do with real mental conditions and not with the after-effect of direct shock, there will be other evidences of the conditions. These evidences will consist of exaggerated capitals, of inverted letter forms and oddities of spelling, uneven and disorderly spacing, and so on.

The one indication of disease which is not to be confused with any other and which can readily be perceived, is the "heart tick" in the upper loops of h, l, *and* b; *sometimes seen in* d, *if looped, in* f, *and in* t; *very rare in* t *and* d; *often seen in* h *only.*

This little, ragged indentation in the upper loops of the small letters is the indication of a heart action which is strongly affected. It is no doubt caused by a very slight and totally unfelt unevenness in the heartbeat which registers in the hand, unknown to the writer. Just why it should find the letter *h* the best recipient is not quite clear. It may be that the consciousness—the reaction of the consciousness in the hand, and not in the mind of the writer—that the extra little stroke is to be added at the base of the letter, hastens this registration. When *l* also accepts the registration and when other loops show it faintly, then we have a pretty serious case.

It is to be noted that this does not tell the exact nature of the heart trouble. It may be valvular, but it may also be that odd affection called *angina pectoris,* which is not true heart disease, although so dangerous. This "heart tick" has often been found in the writing of people who laughed at the idea of their hearts being affected, but who later found such to be the fact, or who suddenly died from such a condition, without warning. People exhibiting this indication should at once have a proper examination by a heart specialist.

The shortening of the upper and lower loops of writing, with the effect of the loops practically disappearing, making the letters the size of those without loops, is the indication of a great lowering of the vitality and is often the sign of such disorders as epilepsy, tumors, cancerous growths and other malignant conditions.

Many women, who are the greatest sufferers from cancers and growths in the body, exhibit this sign toward the fortieth year of their age, or perhaps ten years later, the two periods when such disorders are most apt to make their appearance in their sex. It is always a sign that should warn the writer to have a thorough overhauling of all the organs, no matter whether the health seems good or not. Such an overhauling may disclose conditions which can easily be remedied, which, if allowed to continue, may become fatal. Children and young people, showing this characteristic in their writing, may be declared by medical diagnosis to be entirely healthy, but they will be found to be of delicate constitution and without that hearty and lusty interest in food and outdoor sports which marks the healthy child. Care and attention, at this period, will often do a great deal to remedy this condition and to build up the body against the dangers to which it is innately allied.

Paresis, softening of the brain, delusions, hallucinations, fear of persecution, belief in extreme bodily danger—are all shown in handwriting which is so disordered, so full of tremulousness, so eccentric and so indescribably unwholesome that people who have never given a thought to the meaning of handwriting, outside of the actual message to be read from it, are affected by the sight of specimens containing such indications.

The important thing to remember is that the handwriting begins to change before the unhappy change in the writer is apparent, and that many an incipient case might be caught and cured, were this matter of the handwriting to be considered. People threatened with any of the above mental conditions *always* begin by causing their friends and relatives a good deal of uneasiness, through their slightly peculiar and eccentric actions; actions which are discounted, and passed over, the relatives and friends hoping that they are transitory. They are, sometimes, transitory. Emotional conditions, love affairs, money troubles, psychological changes in the nature, may all affect the person; but in that case the handwriting will not convey the warning: it will remain more or less unchanged. When, therefore, an individual is seen to exhibit some peculiarities of manner and temperament, the handwriting should be carefully watched. It will reveal whether the matter is temporary or serious and dangerous.

"Delusions of grandeur"—which means that the writer believes himself to be the reincarnation of Napoleon, or the coming Messiah, or something equally grand and doubtful—are responsible for more murders than any other one "kink" in the human brain. The delusion that the person is too great to yield to human laws, that "I am different," that great power and place are due—all these, although classed by alienists as minor mental disturbances, create more havoc in the world than all the rest of the mental diseases put together.

The so-called "master minds" among criminals are, as a rule, suffering from delusions of grandeur.

Delusions of grandeur are shown by strangely made and involved letter forms, by the exaggerated ornamentation of the capitals and by their size, spread and pretentiousness. The more unusual cases of this kind run to the very small writing, in which there are eccentric formations and in which the capitals are scarcely larger than the small letters.

A mental condition which is apt to be permanent is shown by many eccentricities which are so pronounced that they cannot fail to draw the attention of even the most unobservant.

Quotation-marks, exclamation-marks, parentheses, capitals used in the middle of a word, double i *dots,* t *barred twice, writing a duplicate message—the complete letter in ink and then the same in pencil, each word over the other*—show that the mental conditions are wholly wrong and that there is little hope for betterment. Unfortunately, many persons who habitually write this way are now walking about the earth without even the suggestion of surveillance. They are the victims of delusions of a dangerous type and are often that most alarming of the insane, the religiously insane. There is no question as to this indication. No matter how sane a person may seem, if his writing conforms to this picture, the flower of insanity is in full bloom.

A great many people confined in insane asylums and institutions do not show any of these traits in their writing. As a matter of fact, we need entirely new ideas on the matter of mental complaints. A great many people are confined to such institutions who need a number of other things, not the incarceration. They need surgical operations, tonics, country life, freedom from unhappiness, education, proper marriages, the right kind of work—all sorts of things. On the other hand, we usually allow men and women who exhibit the most pronounced signs of derangement to run loose in our communities, so long as they do not transgress any of the standard statutes of sanity.

The inability to construct sentences or to spell words, when the education of the writer has been such as to make this a matter of course, is the indication of active insanity, which is not apt to express itself in violence, but in loss of memory and in inability to deal well with the problems of everyday.

Sometimes this feebleness of attention in the matter of handwriting is the first sign of the mental breakdown. Sometimes the omission of words and the failure to construct sentences accurately are indications that a nervous breakdown is imminent, but in that case this confusion will occur only in parts of the writing and will not be marked by persistence.

MORAL DISEASES

In estimating the more or less evil person, and the morally unsound, the graphologist must bear in mind the statement, previously made, that handwriting records only such elements of character as are really fundamental. For this reason, the young person who has "run wild" for a year or two may present as clean a bill of health, graphologically speaking, as the most sheltered youth. That this is so is encouraging, from every standpoint, for the reason is that it takes time for conduct to wear a groove in the consciousness; that evil which is a new thing to a writer makes little impression on the handwriting, which is the guarantee that it has not yet made any on the character either.

In estimating evil, we must take into consideration the fact that men are nearly always worse in action than their own natures. None of us live up to even such ideals as we have. All of us fail to reach the summit of that life which is really possible to us. The most "hardened" criminal will, if he can be won to confidence, confess that his life has not satisfied him.

Therefore, in looking at the lowest layers of humanity, in which we are apt to find the swindler and the thief and nearly always the brutal murderer, we may be sure that we shall find heavy pressure, brutal and coarse letter forms, ungainly capitals and muddy-looking handwriting.

These are the people who are on the lowest level of

the Material type. We sometimes find such handwriting among business men, and occasionally among women. Once in a long time, we shall even find examples of the Mental type and of the Artistic, in which, pushed up from the depths below, we see a section of the low-grade Material type, finding expression in muddy writing, in coarse letter forms, in brutal club-shaped *t* bars and so on.

Examples of the usual writing of average criminals, however, will not show us this low type, but, rather, moderate pressure, forward-leaning angle of inclination and quite normal letter formations. The one distinctive mark of nearly all the writing of those who transgress against the law is that it shows a *weak t bar,* variable pressure, lack of indications of character strength. So that we may be assured that those who bear the stigma of being criminals are really even as you and I. We can look at them and remember that perhaps it is only accident which has kept us from bearing them company.

A great many so-called criminals offend the law for two reasons: either they are too lazy to fight the world with honesty, or they are so soft-hearted that they offend because of their desire to do their family duty. A carcful investigation of nearly all the cases of defaulters, for instance, will show that they write the forward-leaning, moderate-pressure and rather rounded handwriting, in which the *t* bar and other evidences of strength are missing; and further investigation will show that nearly always the real desire to take care of a family or to give happiness to some beloved one lies at the root of their offense against the law. Then, too, in what are listed as "big" criminals, we will find endless examples of the *o, a, g,* and loops with the odd little opening at the bottom. (See "Small Letters.") These unfortunates would never be criminals if their type were well understood and if they were kept out of the line of their unique temptation of large sums of money.

Morally, the thief is a weakling, and this is shown in the vacillating, weak, uneven-pressure, and variable writing of the average petty thief, pickpocket and small swindler. The thief who burgles banks, counterfeits, and invents the large swindle is one of two types: he is either the aggressive, primitive Material type, with heavy pressure, long and brutal *t* bars, and close connecting-strokes or he is the man who is touched with the one disease of the criminal world, "delusions of personal grandeur." In the latter case, the abnormalities of his handwriting will show him to the graphologist. In this connection, it is well to estimate carefully the fact that abnormal size of writing is always a matter into which the graphologist must carefully look *if* the letter formations are not also exceptional. Thus, extreme expansion or contraction, in a writing which has nothing else to distinguish it, is the indication of some serious abnormality in the mind. *With* letter formations which accord with the size—as of clipped, disconnected and highly Mental formations in the very small writing and flowing rhythm and rounded writing in the very large, we have but an exaggerated case of the *type*—as of certain scientific workers in the first type mentioned and of the very vital salesman type in the second. But, leaving this matter of type out and finding the most ordinary letter forms and an entire lack of distinction in the capitals, and *then* finding an exaggeration of size—or, finding writing very small, when the letter forms do not tell us of that unusual mental development which usually reduces size, we may be sure that, whether the writer is at large or not, we have here the "delusions of personal grandeur" which will lead to criminality.

A careful study of the handwriting of many so-called famous criminals will show the truth of this statement. It is also true of a great many of those whom the world has agreed to call great! The graphologist, who must be free of prejudices and phobias and childish concepts, will not be surprised to find that many military chiefs show this delusion, that statesmen and many politicians are the victims of it, and that the criminal classes are by no means confined to those publicly branded as such. Nor is it true that a writer is not what his handwriting shows him to be, because his actions do not seem to agree with it. The graphologist can often take up the handwriting of a man who has astounded the world by turning to criminal paths, late in life, and see that that man was always a criminal. Circumstances of some kind or other held him in check.

It is a good deal of a shock, of course, to find that your banker is a potential swindler, that your pastor is grossly material, that the woman who teaches your children is too highly sexed, that the man you think of marrying is a liar. Knowledge is power, but it is not peace! The graphologist needs, therefore, to apply the most rigid self-discipline to himself and herself, making sure that a calm and philosophic attitude is maintained, no matter what are the discoveries made. It is of the utmost need that the graphologist should not be narrow-minded, and should have no phobias, inhibitions or extravagances of thought or feeling. This is especially necessary in dealing with moral perverts, who will once in a while be found in any assortment of handwritings.

The moral pervert is nearly always of light pressure, for the reason that heavy pressure shows us the normal heavy material appetites, and it is precisely the failure of these heavy appetites which brings us the pervert. This word has been used by a good many writers to express only one thing, which is that of sex perversion, but the proper use of it tells us that it covers a great many perversions.

In perversion we will find that the pressure is moderately light, at least, and often very light, and that the letter formations have a curious "broken-backed" effect. That is, every perpendicular stroke is slightly bowed to the right and sometimes very oddly to the left. The capitals are frequently oddly ornamented. The *t* bar is usually unwholesome, in that it is too light and too long, or that it has eccentricities.

It is needless to say that the extreme angles of the leftward angle of inclination are much more apt to exhibit the indication of perversion than the rightward, since perversion of any kind is the result of repression. We get all sorts of variation in this perverted "hand." Many a specimen has only suggestions of it, as in an occasional broken-backed formation. Some specimens are so indicative that people who know nothing of graphology will exclaim at their "queerness."

A personal reaction against which the graphologist must guard is the tendency to give the makers of these perverse writings such a shuddering distaste that justice cannot be done them. In handling quantities of handwriting, and in becoming more and more cognizant of what each specimen means, as to real character, the graphologist will be assailed with personal problems which are peculiar to the profession. I confess that the handwriting of perverts of any description affects me to that degree that I do not even touch the paper with my hands, if I can help it; but I have taught my mind to ignore this distaste and to do justice to these unfortunates, many of them brilliant of mind and even not without the capacity for affection and for enjoyment of normal things. A well-known writer, internationally famous, now dead, was undoubtedly a pervert of the most exaggerated type, and yet his claim that the discovery of his perversion, which lost him his wife and children, "broke my heart" was literally true. What was more, before he died, his nature, literally broken from its egotism by suffering and trouble, lost its evil and became directly spiritual.

In estimating the pervert, of whatever kind, we must estimate the fact that a certain form of egotism is at the base of it. The pervert is not satisfied with normal pleasures, normal gratifications. He believes that he ought to have more and different—especially different, and this last is due to his secret belief that he is not as other men. The odd thing is that there is a certain amount of truth in this. The pervert is rarely stupid and usually has real mental brilliance. Drug-takers are usually clever and shrewd, to begin with—high-powered people who chafe at the routine of life. Perverts in foods (even going down as low as the "chalk eaters" of the Carolina hills) are often talented and have exceptional personalities. The sex perverts are nearly always people of brilliant intellect. What really goes wrong with them is that the old crime of Lucifer runs riot in them. They refuse the common lot of man. They forget that a man is great only as he lives for others. They exalt the puny individuality and forget the grandeur of humanity.

To explain the fact that from perverts we often get marvelous music, great poetry and other forms of beauty, we must estimate that their perversion is a perverted form of a quest for beauty. This one fact will set the barrier for us, and serve as a classification, between the Materialist, whose excesses are those of a hoggish appetite, and the pervert, who is most often of the Artistic and Nervous types and sometimes of the strictly Mental, and whose appetites are not gross but exotic.

In dealing with the question of criminals, the graphologist must not be led into deductions which are wrong because of any public hysteria concerning them. To explain even the most atrocious of murders we must accept the fact that the *thoughts which we entertain are the really potent factors of our lives.* Circumstances may press us, but thought is the lever by which they are controlled. The true story of any murderer will show us that his handwriting does not lie. The writing may show only a weak and cold nature, and when weak and cold natures allow the mental bars to be let down there is even more danger than when this is allowed by the ardent and the imaginative; for the imaginative can, at least, more or less foresee what is going to happen and how matters are going to turn out. The unimaginative cannot do this. And they are, therefore, the more apt to be found among the people who commit atrocious crimes.

The writing which cannot find an angle of inclination at which to stick, which cannot find a solid basic line, which persists in uneven pressure, which has a wavering *t* bar, is the usual writing found in the records of the police departments. Outside of this classification, which gives us the lower strata of criminality, there is, practically, no such thing as a real criminal type of writing.

Moral diseases exist and we have many ways in which they can be identified in the handwriting, but this is not direct criminality. The graphologist is forced to take the attitude of many philosophers and students of humanity, in the belief that a great many of the criminal acts of individuals are but explosions of energy which are disastrous only in that they are misdirected.

GRAPHOLOGICAL DEDUCTIONS CONCERNING THE CARE AND EDUCATION OF CHILDREN

It is impossible to set an age at which the character begins to show in the handwriting. Unusual children sometimes have very definite letter formations at an unbelievably early age. I have seen a little girl of five express the chief traits in her character with a fairly well formed handwriting, and I have seen young people of twenty—quite well educated—whose writing was no more expressive of character than if they had been ten.

Of course, a great deal of this has reference to the fact, referred to in the statement about age as indicated in handwriting, that age, *by years,* means less than nothing. We ought to have some new way in which to measure maturity and immaturity, for the count of the years is totally inadequate. If this were not so, guessing ages would not be the incessant sport that it is.

Out of this fact, however, we may deduce something which is of vital importance in dealing with children: we may answer the question, *Is this child going to mature early or late?*

If the child is to mature early, the handwriting will be what the writing-mistress will call "good." That is to say, the letter formations will be set; the capitals will have fallen into their permanent classification; the pressure will be regular; the rhythm will be established. If the child is to mature late, the handwriting will remain straggling and uncertain for a long time. The children who are the despair of their writing-teachers are far more apt to be of real importance to the world, later on, than those who have commendations for their copybooks.

Bearing out this deduction, we can observe that the precocious child is apt to have a very mature-looking writing and in the case of the musical genius (who is the only genius really to come to flower in what is practically childhood) the handwriting is wonderfully mature at an early age. The handwriting of the little Josef Hofmann, for instance, could easily have been taken for that of a grown man.

Temperamental children, whose nerves need quieting, and who are too excitable to endure well even the usual pleasures of childhood, find great trouble in keeping a smooth rhythm. Their hands will jerk, jump and cramp. They are apt to have heavy writing, because of this difficulty: they grasp the instrument too tightly and bear down too heavily.

Such children need placid lives, outdoor associations which are not exciting, quiet companions, and love and understanding, which overlooks a good deal.

The child who innately writes well, on the other hand, should not be excused for failure to be punctual, for failure to perform practical duties, for failure to be good-tempered. He is well able to take a practical, matter-of-fact and sane attitude toward the world and his life, and any tendency to excuse him from this attitude will weaken his character. On the other hand, he is not the child who can endure too great indulgence in self-gratification, as he is of the Material type or the ordinary grades of the Vital. Nor can he be spurred too greatly to mental effort. He is the boy who ought to have practical training, either for the trades or business and who should not be especially encouraged, and surely not forced, to go to college. If he wishes to go, that is a different matter.

Erratic-looking writing, which the child and the growing adolescent cannot seem to remedy, is the indication, it is true, of considerable lack of poise and balance, but it is also the indication of that deferred maturity which may blossom into something very fine late in life.

When children and young people have writing which constantly changes, we have the perfectly normal evidence of a perfectly normal progression of character.

When the handwriting of young people is too individual—presenting us with the picture of an intricate mind and a subtle temperament, we may be sure that the writer is a hothouse product. A number of specimens of writing, which were recently shown me, came from the hands of very young people who had either committed suicide or been charged with serious crimes. In almost every case, these unfortunate children were born into wealth and were both allowed and encouraged to mature, by every device known to civilization. At twenty some of these writers were actually decadent. Therefore, the handwriting which is more than mature, produced by the hand less than thirty years old, is a danger-signal of the most serious import.

In looking through such archives as contain the writing of famous men and women when they were children, any graphologist will be struck with the immaturity of it, at ages when many children write fairly well.

This ought to be a consolation to parents who have suffered from worry about the handwriting of their children. It is well to remember, too, that neither "good" nor "bad" handwriting means a thing as to moral character, in the child, any more than it does in the adult.

The handwriting of children changes after their twelfth year, as a rule, and at that time a great many who have written quite well will begin to have difficulty with writing, due to the fact that they are really beginning to mature, while the incoherent writer, who has never done well with the writing-instrument, will gather a little betterment. This is the time at which some small estimation of the emerging character can be made, the rules as herein given being used, as in more mature writing.

Young people are greatly and rightly occupied with the question of the kind of work which they should do, and are frequently impatient because the character analyst cannot fit them with vocations, instantly and completely. The fact is, of course, that there are few people who start out in life with some one bent so strong that that alone is the only one which ought to be or can be cultivated, and when this is true, *there is never any doubt about it.* Thus, the musician is one of the first to show talent early. Mozart was a prodigy when he was six, and there are many other instances of this early and complete development of musical talent. Painting, dancing, talent for the stage, talent for drawing—are all sure to show themselves pretty early, if they are going to be anything with which the world will be set on fire. An exception may be taken to this rule, occasionally, as when talent, early showing for one art, later turns to another.

The one and sole exception to this rule—and a most glaring one—is the talent for writing, which is not only the latest of the talents to develop but is late for even an aptitude to show itself. Out of the young people, then, whose writing continues to change far on in life are we the most apt to have the writer. The reason for this is entirely logical. All the other arts and talents are those which are more or less aptitudes—inborn—instincts—but the writer has to mature and to mature in the *Mental* type, before work can be produced and the Mental type is the slowest of all the types to mature.

The person who is interested in graphology, observes the rules which govern the science and takes careful heed of the development of a child's writing, will see recorded there all the big steps which are taken in the gaining of character and maturity.

THE TYPES OF HUMANITY

Obviously, it is necessary for the graphologist to have some classification of humanity; for by carefully estimating the type first, in making a delineation of character, the difficulties of the operation are greatly simplified and our own perceptions much clarified.

The first, or fundamental, type is:

The Material Type

The Writing: This is usually heavy in pressure, although there are exceptions in which the pressure is either variable or lighter than would be expected from the Material type; in this case, the letter formations give the clue, being without the flowing quality that characterizes the Vital type, and showing, in lack of imagination and in lack of individuality of letter formations, their attachment to the purely material side of existence. Generally, however, the heavy pressure alone will indicate the Materialist, and the capitals are rarely individualistic.

It is to be remembered, though, that there are various levels on which each type of humanity operates. Thus, the intellectually material person may be a teacher or a writer—the materialism being shown by pressure that is too heavy for letter forms of such individuality. In the Material type there is frequently found a branch of it known as the Philoprogenitive type, which has the very fine *protective A*.

Too often the word "materialistic" is used as a term of reproach, as being gross or selfish. mean or low in aim—which is manifestly false.

The writing of the Materialist, therefore, must be most carefully estimated, using every one of the many points of characterization by which to make the estimation. The pressure tells a great deal, but with that must be considered *all* the letter forms, in order to check and determine the definition.

The Personality: As a rule the materialistic person is not conspicuous for tact and suavity. The tendency is to be rather solid and positive, often brusque, in manner and to have the voice which is somewhat lacking in the lilting qualities of the Ideal and Mental and also lacking in the persuasive qualities of the Vital. Taciturnity is sometimes marked. The body may be very loose-jointed, but often is thickset, stocky and with heavy limbs, a short neck, and a very full face.

The Health: This is not a nervous type and not especially sensitive and for that reason such persons often have serious diseases without knowing it. This is the type from which we have one-third of our sudden deaths from heart disease, this disease being unsuspected by the victim. Diseases of the bowels and kidneys and stomach are more frequent in this type than in any other because of the temptation to overeat and overdrink. On the other hand, immunity from fevers, infection and epidemics is greater than with any other type. But once the Materialist is really ill, he is more apt to die than some of the other types, for being a worshiper of health he feels acutely the danger of ill health. He is easily depressed by ill health; especially prone to apoplexy and gout, to overweight and to rapid decline in health after middle age.

The Dominant Traits: Love of money and of physical ease and comfort are strong. Ardor is apt to be turned into either emotional coldness or into sensuality. Absolute selfishness is to be found in this type to a greater degree than is found in any other, *when* it is found at all. Actual evil is not strong, as a *type* indication; but it is oftener found in this group than in any other, since the lowest criminals, as well as many excellent and useful citizens belong to the Material type.

Physical courage is often found, but high moral courage and the finest kind of bravery are rarer. The subtleties of the emotional and the intellectual are not to be found; the Materialist is apt to have either a sort of matter-of-fact goodness, which does not lift its eyes very far toward real spirituality, or a cool, rather selfish, attitude toward the world, or downright selfishness.

The affections are always possessive, but may or may not be selfish and may or may not be constant. The ideal love is not possible to this type, which will never be able to imagine any love which does not bring self-gratification, in some form or other. As lovers, they are sensual, but often do not know that this is so, and would earnestly deny the fact.

Obedience to orders is something which the Material type understands, and for this reason soldiers of all grades are apt to be Materialists, sometimes, to be sure, of the finer levels. The very idea of the aggressiveness of war is antagonistic to all the other types; and for this reason only Materialists rise, as a general rule, to high rank in armies. Other types lack the instinct for it.

Temper is often strong and deep; resentfulness is positive; and aggressiveness is not concealed. Love of action is one of the predominating factors of all Material types, on whatsoever plane they function.

The Talents: Some very fine and high-level workers are found in this division of humanity. A great many musicians belong to it. A great many artistic workers are partly of it. Sections and portions of materialism may be found in all the types, with the exception of that offshoot of the Ideal which is the Spiritual. The great mass of the Material type, however, is formed by the handworker, and therefore we find that extreme skill with the hand is the real talent of this group.

The Work: Soldiers, as previously stated, are to be found largely represented in the materialistic group. Farmers of the unimaginative type are heavily represented. Carpenters, masons, plumbers, electricians, machinists and engineers, a great many housekeepers, many of the types found doing hotel work, a great number of inferior actors, many acrobats, a great many singers and painters, are included. (Note that these workers are never at the top of their profession, for if they are at the top there will be a large admixture of other types, such as the Constructive, the Mental, the Artistic, and so on.) We also find people at the lowest level of intellect and morals in the Material type. Low-class criminals, hoboes, the slackers of the world, the murderers and gross sensualists. Great care should be taken that the proper differentiations are made in the various handwritings of this type.

The Mate: This should be either the Materialist or the Vital-Materialist—the person who has a good deal less of the intensity of the bodily senses, but who is not too far away from them, either. It is a great mistake for a Materialist to marry in other types, unless there is a large admixture of materialism in the nature of the mate. The fatal attraction of opposites nowhere works greater harm than in this attraction of the Material for the Ideal, the Vital, the Constructive, and even for the Mental—an attraction which never lasts long and always ends disastrously. It is this attraction which allows the well-bred girl to run off with the chauffeur who is infinitely her inferior; which permits the highly educated man to take a wife from the ranks of the "chorus"; which draws the delicately reared woman to the man of the world who is a well-bred blackguard. The Material type cannot rise to the stimulations of the other types and therefore ought to marry its own kind; more than that, it should marry on its own level—which is far from necessary in many other type groups.

The Material type makes a good wife or husband to a mate who is not too exacting. The Materialist, either man or woman, is apt to lose patience and to go to extremes which they would otherwise not think of, if mated with types which demand ideality and imagination in the conduct. Many of the brutal murders of women by the gross-materialist husband would never have taken place if it had not been for the exasperation which fills the man at the attitude of a woman whose ideals he cannot meet and which, indeed, he resents, despite the fact that it is precisely that type of woman to whom he is constantly being attracted.

The Differences: In this type group the traditional difference between men and women is really slight, as to nature, but is greater, as to physical makeup, than in any other type, the men being very much heavier and the women a good deal lighter in build. The grossness of the men, on the lower levels of the type group, is greater in proportion to the women, than is found elsewhere; as are the brutality, blood lust and passions.

Men of the Material type, on the other hand, are often more ardent fathers than many on higher levels in other type groups. This is partly due to the strong feeling of possession and partly to paternal emotion being almost the only directly idealistic emotion apt to be felt. The mothers of the Material type, however, are less wise than mothers of other groups and are apt to be far less worth while as mothers for children of more than tender years.

The women of this type are fully as skilled as the men in the use of the hand, and sometimes far more so; their judgment is especially excellent in work which requires shrewd common sense.

The Vital Type

The Writing: The pressure is either very light, medium light or medium heavy. The angle of writing will be far to the rightward or leftward. The letter forms not awkward. The *t* bars not lighter than the body of the writing. The signature almost always a little more interesting and individualistic than the body of the writing. The writing always suggests *movement* which is graceful and assured—in other words, the rhythm is gracious and flowing. The capitals are vigorously made.

The Personality: These are the people who are always interested in life and all that goes with it. They live with vigor and ardor and are seldom either languid or brusque in manner. Courage is instinctive, despite the fact that they have a good deal of sensitiveness. The personality is usually tactful and ingratiating. Speech comes easily. They have temper and passion, but have a good many interests and so never become the monomaniacs that the Materialists so frequently do. They are not often religious extremists. They usually have blond and medium-dark hair, with sparkling eyes and either high color or a warm ivory complexion. The gestures are easy and the voice assured.

The Health: The heart disease which is most apt to attack this type is not the "leakage of the valves" which is so characteristic of the Material group, but disturbances which are partly nervous, such as extreme palpitation, and especially that strange condition known as angina pectoris. Fevers attack this type frequently. Troubles of the stomach are experienced, but not the drastic difficulties having to do with the bowels and kidneys which are so peculiar to the Materialist, for the Vitalist suffers from indigestion, not due to any fundamental trouble, but due to haste in eating, indifference to self-care, impatience with diets, and so on; the attention of this type group is always directed abroad and not to self, as is that of the Materialist, who, when he attends to his health at all, is apt to do so with far more skill than the Vitalist. The Vitalist is also apt to suffer from breakdowns, due to overwork and overconcentration on practical matters.

The Dominant Traits: Friendliness and a great liking for the world in general are main characteristics. Courage of a physical type is strong. Love of hunting, fishing and the outdoors is especially characteristic. The affections and friendship find frank and easy expression. The will is strong. This type likes to talk and argue and is not easily drawn into anything which is not really congenial. The Vitalist is a "joiner." It is his type from which most of the members of clubs and fraternities are drawn. Active church members, politicians, and popular preachers and orators are essentially the Vital type group. A fine sense of organization is possessed by many. These people are indifferent to the subtleties of life, have a broad sense of humor, like the theater and melodious music, and dislike gloom, and too great a straining at the unusual. As a rule, the Vital type is not heavily represented in the criminal classes nor in any of the degenerate individuals of the world, but a fair amount of it is the occasional criminal—especially the one-time forger and embezzler.

The Talents: Very many musicians who are composers are found in this type, as are exhibition dancers, stage managers and publicity men. A large proportion of those who succeed in vaudeville and burlesque belong to this type. Some of the bankers and financiers who have achieved world eminence belong to the Vital group, but it is by reason of their personal influence and not because of the coldly analytical mind and material nature which is characteristic of the banking and financial group as a rule.

The Work: The orator, the actor and the salesman are heavily represented in the Vital type group. The salesman and the saleswoman who are successful are almost, without exception, members of this group. The stage has a good many of the Artistic type and some of the Mental, but even in them there is a fair admixture of the Vital. It is the expansive type, the friendly type, the adaptive type. The better-grade farmer, horticulturist, forest ranger, stockman, and merchant belong to this type group. Whatever the work is, it should be something which is more or less materialistic and yet which adds the element of personal contact, without which this type cannot do anything well or with happiness.

The Mate: This is the type which can mate well with almost any of the type groups except the very Material and the very Spiritual. Among these groups, however, it is to be noted that the writers of the leftward and extreme or moderate angle of inclination are the least promising. The Vital type cannot endure great illness in the mate and has to have one who will have the same intense love of life as the Vital. Too great conservatism, lack of interest in the world in general, religious fanaticism and chronic invalidism are the special things abhorred by the Vital type. They are open and frank in their love, apt to be demonstrative and ardent in manner, and do not like a mate who is too shy, too reserved, or too self-conscious.

The Differences: The men are a good deal more aggressive than the women, and the women have a good deal more executive ability than the men. The men are better salesmen and the women are better organizers. The Vital man is more indifferent to deep and careful thought than the woman of his type. She makes a better parent, for the man of this type is essentially something of a wanderer and is not as deeply attached to his home as the woman is. The woman is more careful of detail and the man is more reckless of danger. Vital women are, like Vital men, splendid in the group and amalgamate well. The club woman, now becoming so strong a factor in life all over the world—even in countries where such a thing was unheard-of fifty years ago—is mostly of this type.

Motherhood, to the Vital type of woman, is quite important, but the type, *per se,* is not the woman type which is lost as to individuality when motherhood comes. That type is a combination of the Material, the Vital and a large admixture of the Philoprogenitive.

Both Vital men and women share their love of the out of doors, and are often people who are sport devotees. The health of the Vital woman is superb and her endurance the greatest of any type among women. Both men and women of this type, once mated, are capable of having real platonic friendships with members of the opposite sex—a thing which is all but impossible to the true Materialist.

The Vital type in both man and woman is long-lived.

The Constructive Type

The Writing: The outstanding element of the writing is the tendency of the letters to be clear-cut and the pressure firm but even, with absence of any sudden increase of pressure. In the finer types—the more perfect Constructive types—all the capitals are printed and so are many of the small letters, while the spacing and paragraphing of a letter or piece of writing is very definite and made with a due sense of proportion. The angle of inclination is often upright, but tends to other angles, save only the extreme right or left. The *t* bar is usually moderate in length, but is quite strong. The beginning- and ending-strokes are usually omitted.

The Personality: The tendency is to be a bit curt and often taciturn. The manners are good, but not effusive, and the speech tactful enough but not suave. The frame is apt to be loose-jointed and the bodily actions graceful, despite the fact that the flesh is frequently "knobby" and without beauty as to skin, which is often sandy, dusky or too pale. These people are apt to be good dancers and superb horsemen.

The Health: Endurance of physical hardship is marked. Fatigue, lack of food and water and physical comforts seem to have less disastrous effect on this type than on others. Good eyesight. Often wonderful teeth and hair. Usually good fighters, and take "punishment" well. Athletic by predisposition. The physical weakness is that routine, confinement and discouragement are almost fatal, and that long, hard work which is monotonous will bring about nervous breakdown, almost surely, no matter what the resistance. Subject to accidents more than the other types, owing to the fact that they are wanderers by nature and delight in danger and are quick of temper.

The Dominant Traits: Carefulness and constructiveness are the keys to the work to which this type is adapted. Conscientiousness in the doing of that work is usually shown, even when the same trait may be lacking in moral matters. To most of the Constructive type honor is something which is mainly concerned with the work—with promises to accomplish, with practical obligations. The honor which concerns itself with moral and spiritual obligations is present in a high degree in some individuals, but is not thoroughly characteristic of the type. Religious feeling does not usually run high. Confidence in self is pronounced. Independence of advice is marked, the instinct being to do what pleases the individual and suits the individual ideas. This type is cool under fire and brave in the face of physical danger, but "breaks" under subtle torture and mental stress. The nature is often sensuous, but interest in *action* is so great that that acts as a deadener of the sensory reactions. Instinct to wander, explore and travel is often insistent.

The Talents: At the apex of this type we have the world-famous architect and the sculptor. At the very bottom (in the matter of talents) we have the cabinet-maker and the very good carpenter. Some of the painters and illustrators belong to the Constructive type; and a good many interior decorators and designers do, too. The Constructive type is always skilful with the hand and always keen and accurate of eye.

The Work: Preeminently the constructor, of all

grades and sorts. The bridge builder, the engineer, architect, house builder, empire builder, maker of railroad and steamship systems, explorer, the type of salesman who builds up a large personal following over some set of objects which are, in themselves, constructive. In lesser men and lower levels—toy-makers, landscape-gardeners, and so on. They welcome danger, are reckless and often lose their lives needlessly in the enthusiasm of a pursuit. Most of the women of this type are less reckless than the men, but are physically fearless, and are able to endure loneliness better than other types of women. Both men and women can endure lonely work.

The Mate: This is the most "difficult" of all the types, so far as the attainment of happiness in mating is concerned. The men and women are both ardent and yet cold in personality and the tendency is to be very tenacious of personal liberty and action, and yet a bit possessive toward the other person! For the very best mating, the Constructive type should mate with itself, or with the Constructive-Mental type, but too often it is temporarily drawn to the Material or to the other far extreme, the Ideal, with neither of which can it be satisfied. The women who marry this type have to be of the type which is not set on having a home in some particular corner of the earth, as these men are always on the move, unless they are so successful that they can have a permanent home from which they can wander and to which they can return. The outdoor woman of the Vital type, who is also a bit Material, is usually the best mate.

The Differences: The women of the type are more

stable than the men; they endure steady routine better and are better-tempered. They are less daring in their work and less resourceful. The constructive type of man rules the world of to-day and has ruled the historic world of the past, where the actual monuments and the bridges and houses and temples have been the only real signs of development. Woman has always been the constructionist on another plane—that of thought, conservation, and the building up of human values. Therefore, it is not surprising that laws for child welfare, for the welfare of workers, laws protecting the young and the very old, regulating the conduct of the irresponsible, laws for sanitation and for housing and feeding—have been woman's contribution to the constructiveness of the world. It is probably along these lines that the Constructive woman will find expression.

All tradition to the contrary notwithstanding, the constructive woman is not always the builder of a home. She is not always a good mate. She is often a "lone wolf" in her business and professional work, to which she is always so attracted; and yet, she is very constructive, in the real sense of the word.

The Nervous Type

The Writing: This is uncertain of pressure, with the size of the letters variable. The capitals are sometimes graceful and the letter forms interesting, but lack of rhythm and bad arrangement of the space detracts from the appearance of the writing. The *t* bar is usually weak and the basic line wavering. The basic line frequently descends. The connecting-strokes are variable.

The Personality: Usually "raw-boned" and very often sandy-haired, or red to blond hair, with pale or deep blue eyes and light lashes and brows. They are apt to have ugly ankles and wrists, but pretty hands and feet. They are awkward in action, but not without attractiveness. They are talkative almost without exception. It is hard for them to sit still; they are fond of excitement and like to find life full of thrills. For this reason, a certain number of them are to be found in criminal circles. They are restless in mind and body and temperament and are the victims of a mentality which is keen and appreciative and yet not very "workable." They have a good deal of personal magnetism, but often offend by their tactless remarks and are not able to preserve the suavity which is needed in intercourse with the world.

The Health: The health of this type is a very curious matter. They are among the most long-lived of types and yet are always ailing; they have a certain queer endurance and yet cannot stand the ordinary stress of life. If a person of the Nervous type, for instance, were cast away on a desert island with others of different types, it is likely that the Nervous type would survive the hardships which would kill the others—and would then go insane from the recollection! They are subject to fevers, minor disturbances of the stomach and liver. They sleep badly, and often are excessive takers of medicine. They frequently are found in the ranks of the drug-addicts. Throat trouble is persistent with the type. They need outdoor life.

Motherhood is never easy for this type and fatherhood always brings unreasonable worry.

The Dominant Traits: They have strong likes and dislikes, and are sensitive to physical things. They are either too conscientious or very callous; impatient and not good judges of anything, but intuitive and quick to say what they think. Very often religious. Sulky and sly when they feel they are being treated badly. Either very disorderly or fussily neat. Carry responsibilities badly. They have a queer courage which comes to the surface when they are pressed. Their minds are keen; they learn very well, but cannot use what they learn. They are very aggressive in some ways, but usually are unable to force their lives through to success. Efficient in one thing and very inefficient in another. As young people, they have to have teachers who understand their type. They are usually sincere and honest, but are unable to judge other types of people and so not *able* to be just to them. They like good clothes and comfort. They are not able to express very well what they feel. It is a type which is greatly swayed by the forces of the world—easily affected by mob psychology—always in tune with the small thought of the day and the time—never able to look ahead.

The Talents: Many of the people who do well on the stage are of this type. This includes the playwright, occasionally. These people, however, are very seldom engineers or mechanical workers; they learn well under stress and often do well with the most surprising situations when it is clear that no one else can be secured for them, but fail in the ordinary jog-trot of ordinary life. They are natural linguists. They are sometimes musicians, but never very fine ones. If taught to control themselves and to work with definite ambition, they are interesting and unusually worth while people.

The Mate: Some modification of the same type ought to be the mate. A mate with more of the Vital, more of the Material, more of the Ideal, but *not* more of the Mental or the Constructive, with which this type does not easily amalgamate. They often do well with people who are affectionate but not too demanding. The Nervous type loves approval and appreciation and admiration; likes a pleasant and happy life of companionship in which sex does not play too great a part.

The Differences: The Nervous woman *seems* more nervous than the man of the same type, for the reason that she does not struggle so hard against showing the state of her nerves. The Nervous type of woman is said to be too "feminine," but the Nervous type of man shows the same characteristics and that in often greater degree. The Nervous woman is apt to become interesting to her children about the time that the Materialistic mother ceases to be. She is the mother who does well with the half-grown children and who—as also the well-poised Vital mother—is "wonderful" for the child from twelve to twenty.

The Artistic Type

The Writing: The range is all the way from the rather straggling and indifferently formed writing of the average commercial artist to the highly specialized writing of those who are high in artistic achievement. The writing varies a great deal, too, in the matter of expressing a union of the character and the artistic feeling. In some artists' writing, the character overpowers the indications of art and in some, art is to be perceived without much background of character. Individual letter forms, in the small letters, are not half so apt to be used as in the Mental type, but the capitals are pronounced and often most unusual. The disposal of the words on the page is often a clue. In the case of painters and singers the rhythm is long and swinging; and in the case of decorators and architects, constructiveness is predominant. The circle *i* dot points the way to the lesser folk of the artistic world.

As a rule, the writing which is so exceptional and out of the ordinary that it draws comment, is that of either the Artistic or the Mental types. The Constructive type will *always* be more or less the printed type of writing, and this is to be considered in making the estimation of the Artistic and the Mental. We often have the overlapping specimen, which combines all three, the Constructive, the Artistic and the Mental. The writing of the Artistic type, however, is more free and the rhythm more pronounced, as the type is more pure.

The Personality: Here we come to an *impasse.* It is not possible to give the outline of the personality which is most frequently found in this type, for the reason that it may be anything! On the other hand, it is possible to make a statement as to the misconception of the personality of the Artistic type, for the alleged "temperament" is a legend and nothing more.

Some of the highest grade artists, of all kinds, have had good practical ability and have had personalities which were anything but interesting. In fact, we may take it as a truth that extremely eccentric and unusual personalities, in those who are professors of some art or other, are the indications of either a very low level artist or a supremely great one; ordinarily they indicate mediocre artists, for the majority of the truly great artists are conspicuous for their humanness and ability to adapt themselves to ordinary life. We may take the testimony of history that Michelangelo, Rembrandt, Sargent, Corot, were good-natured and friendly men—so much so that those who knew them found it hard to believe that they had also outstanding genius.

On the matter of the personality of artists, then, we have to be very cautious, keeping ourselves alert for new impressions. It is worth noting, of course, that the Nervous type frequently impinges on the Artistic, and that the ungainly and awkward bodily formation of the Nervous type is repeated in the Artistic.

The beauty of some of the Artistic type will nearly always be found to conform to beauty in the forward-leaning or extreme leftward-leaning angle of inclination and to some grace and suavity in the writing; for it is true that while the majority of people do not show physical beauty in the writing, there seems to be, in the Artistic type, some light relationship between the bodily conformation and the writing.

The Health: The type, in all its variations, is apt to be attacked by fevers and by obscure internal diseases. Many of the Artistic type suffer from appendicitis, gall-stones and rheumatism. When the type impinges on the Nervous, they are inclined to be affected by tubercular conditions and by anemia. Mental disturbances are most frequently found in the type in which the Nervous is the stronger element and the Artistic the weaker. These people need serenity in their personal surroundings and do not bear well too great a strain on either the body or the mind.

The Dominant Traits: The Artistic type bears the onus, in popular estimation, of being more immoral and untrustworthy than any other, but this is not true of the mass. There is such a surface instability about the Artistic type that individuals of it *appear* less reliable than they really are. Thus, this type hardly knows the meaning of punctuality and is seldom a good fulfiller of social, domestic or financial obligations; it is impatient of the *forms* of reliability and apt to express that impatience with emphasis. Unreliability of speech is one of the really persistent traits of all the individuals of the Artistic type and of the Nervous-Artistic type.

Honor and sincerity often underlie the seemingly inconsequent surface of these characters. The will is strong along some lines, and weak along others. The mind is active, along strictly definite avenues, so highly specialized that some world-famous artists might be thought to be not quite "bright" if judged by ordinary standards. The love of home is apt to be the least strong in this type; but love of the opposite sex is very strong, and interest in nature, beautiful buildings, humanity and history is often keen. The type is almost invariably an inveterate wanderer, and is totally unadapted to routine work, to merchandising and to farming.

Good judgment in purely financial matters is usually lacking, although there are many who have the shrewdest estimation of their own value to the world and what it should be worth. A feeling for religion and for spiritual matters is not usually possessed, but if present, goes to the extreme and makes a fanatic out of the individual. The disposition is to dislike family life and not to feel too keenly the ties of family, except possibly that of the mother. These people do not fit in well with the big family group and cannot live in too close association with such a group, being far less of the group type than any other, except the Mental.

The Talents: Here we have little difficulty in deciding the general line to which the writer is adapted, but often find it difficult to determine exactly the right avenue: as, for instance, when there is equal talent for music and the stage.

Generally speaking, the true musician, who has sufficient talent to warrant his taking up that career, will have the rhythm which shows this. Writing which points to the stage will be more flamboyant than any of the writing of other lines and will usually show, in the capitals, that personal pride which is part of the equipment.

When the talent for the stage is of a very high order the writing runs over into the Mental type, and of course it is always true that actors of noble mental and temperamental caliber have always had literary talent as well.

The ordinary commercial artist gives us writing

which is apt to be disorderly and not very attractive-looking, in which our clue is in the capitals, almost wholly, which are usually printed.

The illustrators approach the Mental type, to which, indeed, they most truly belong, since their ability to seize the essence of the books, stories and articles which they are called on to illustrate partakes of the true literary ability. Their signatures, too, are usually rather more indicative of interesting personalities than many of the others which belong to the Artistic type.

Painters, on the contrary, who seem to concentrate all of their powers on the feeling for color and form, and sometimes even solely for color, have rather uninteresting writing, which would not show their trend were it not for the flowing and gracious rhythm which marks it. They rarely have the jerky, splashy writing of the commercial artist. Their signatures are often quite commonplace, as are their personalities.

The artists who are on the lower levels usually have pleasant writing and frequently have good-looking signatures. The employment of the circle *i* dot and of capitals which, while not distinctly fine, are yet worth attention, will characterize this group.

In making the estimation of talents, therefore, we have to bear in mind these facts as to the variations on the art tendencies of writers.

The Mate: The mate should most positively be of the same type or very close to it. With the one person of the mating extremely erratic and eccentric it is necessary, of course, for the other to be less so. It is also a good thing, when one of the persons to a mating is actively and creatively the artist, to have the other one of the less creative artistic type and more of the appreciatively artistic. Under no circumstances does a union with any person in which there is not at least a dash of the artistic promise happiness. As for the more Material and the less fluid and yielding of the Vital, in union with the Artistic types, the result is soon seen to be disastrous.

It is frequently urged that the Artistic ought to marry its opposite, as otherwise the marriage will be characterized by great extremes of feeling and therefore with clashes; but the fact is that the Artistic type is apt to have the clashes and the agitations of marriage anyway. The married life of the typical Artistic type is never as serene as the marriages of other types may be; but a great deal of happiness can be attained by this type, even so, since the type is not distressed by emotional upheavals to the degree that others are.

The one type of person which this distinct type ought not to marry is that of the "home body." The very woman whose virtues and character traits mark her out for the traditional "good wife and mother" brings disaster to the house of the Artist. Her very neatness, reliability, care for detail and strict attention to her own business will distract the other, to whom these qualities do not appeal. On the other hand, the half independent, half emotional, very individualistic woman, who often finds it hard to marry happily with other types will occasionally, in the Artistic, find a haven. The good, safe, sane and reliable business man, on the other hand, although the shelter of his home and his money may draw the Artistic type of woman, will never have her real love and must always live in the shadow of the possibility that the inevitable semi-art type man will arrive—who can really hold her affections and community of interest.

As for the Artistic mating with the Ideal-Spiritual, that is quite as out of the question as the mating with lower levels of the Material-Vital. The Artistic individuals who, themselves, present the anomaly of the upright and slightly inclined writing, can marry with good aspects only the rightward and leftward angles of inclination.

The Differences: Until a hundred years ago it was thought that women hardly belonged to the Art types at all. Women composers of music, even to-day, are so rare as to make the erudite and rather piffling Chaminade-Carbonel a great figure among them. Rosa Bonheur, with her big, lusty horses and great canvases, astonished the world, not by the greatness of her work alone, but because she was a woman. In fact, it is only in the past thirty years that we have begun to number women among the arts, in sufficient numbers really to count. Women sculptors, musicians and painters are steadily increasing, but it will be a few more years before women architects and monument builders become notable. Even hat and dress designing are only just coming into the hands of women; many men are still engaged in these fields. Yet the distinctly Artistic type is quite as frequently found in the writing of women as of men; in the course of time there will probably be no disproportion of sex in the Arts.

In matters of the heart, men of the Artistic type are apt to be somewhat less constant than the women;

on the other hand, women of this type are occasionally aggressively inconstant and even immoral. In business, the women are apt to show more responsibility for debt and more shrewdness in the gaining of an adequate return for their work. They use money better than the men. The men present rather more picturesque figures to the world and are apt to have somewhat more of personal magnetism—a quality which is often surprisingly absent in the various individuals of the various degrees of the type, except, of course, those who are drawn to the stage.

The man of the Artistic type is not so sensitive to the opinion of the ordinary world as other types. He is not ashamed to have others see him cry, is not foolishly boastful of mere physical strength, and will be indifferent to his appearance in a way impossible to other men, not sharing their morbid fear of being "different." He is usually extremely sensitive to things which other types of men affect to ignore, such as odors, flowers, perfume, and his surroundings generally. That the Artistic type of man does not lack bravery, however, is something which need not even be discussed. Many a man of the Artistic type who flew into a rage because his bedroom curtains were of the wrong color went right into the trenches, in the late unpleasantness in Europe, and ignored dirt, disease, danger, rats and vermin, as heroically did the more aggressive types.

Among the people who distinctly belong to the Artistic type are professional cooks. Indeed, many famous cooks are men of extreme intellectual development, whose reactions to other arts than their own are remarkable, the well-known chef who is also a real connoisseur of pictures being a case in point. The professional cook, the world-known chef, almost without exception, has been a man. There have rarely been famous women cooks, but there is a steady movement in this direction, and the professional woman chef will yet be evolved, perhaps.

The Ideal-Spiritual Type

While it is true that the idealistic person may not be rightly considered the spiritual person, yet the tendencies so intertwine that they cannot completely be separated. Generally speaking, there are idealistic people whose conscious thought is not spiritual; but fundamentally the character and its reactions remain the same, so that, in making this estimation of the types of humanity, it is better to consider the type a complex one.

The Writing: This is sure to have light pressure. There is no deviation from this rule. Graphologists will meet, in this one fundamental distinction as to the type, with all sorts of difficulties. The writing of famous clergymen and other supposedly spiritual leaders of the world may be offered in rebuttal. In these cases, and in others where the life of the character has undoubtedly been devoted to good works, the graphologist, by a little careful investigation, will see that the nature is really humanitarian, philoprogenitive, kindly, unselfish, and so on; but this does *not* assure us that the nature is on that high plane of development which belongs to the Ideal-Spiritual.

The pressure of the writing, then, is always light and the capitals delicately made and often almost without distinction. The signature is not assertive. The *t* bars are long or not, as may be, but are placed rather high over the letter, as is the fine, and unhumorous *i* dot. Disconnection of the strokes between letters is persistent. The incurve is never present in more than a barely rudimental form. Grace and charm may or may not be shown in the writing, but the air of refinement is very striking.

The Personality: This is usually marked by indeterminate coloring. Vivid blondes and striking brunettes do not seem to be able to attain the level of this type, not being as innately free of the shackles of the flesh and its attractions. The manner is seldom aggressive, save in the event of the temperament being turned into fanaticism. Mark, however, that the truly Ideal-Spiritual never becomes the unhappy or the aggressive fanatic and is *never* interested in forcing on the world ideals which are not well received. By this test we will see that the average so-called fanatic is not really of this type at all, but is much more apt to be either the Material or the Constructive, and the ensuing fanaticism nothing but a burning desire for the individual to have his or her own way with the world. The true Ideal-Spiritual is the least aggressive of all the types and is far more apt to retreat from contact with the world than to endeavor to reform it.

A sense of humor is either absent or much subordinated. When present in the type, it is a delicious and delicate thing which gives the personality a rare and wonderful charm. Physical timidity is very often present, but moral courage is so great that when there is real reason for it, this weakness is overcome. The love of children is sometimes strong, but is not of the possessive type found in the Philoprogenitive. The disposition is loving, kind and most unselfish; but strong attachment to individuals is not marked. Possessiveness, in fact, is largely out of this type, and therefore love for individuals has a certain lack of ardor. Demonstration, the expression of passions, quick movements, aggressive voices, love of clothes, food and pleasure, are all away below the level of interest. These people are often physically frail, due, in large part, to their indifference to food and to their reaction against almost all of the sensory pleasures of the body. Needless to say, that they are indifferent to sports. However, they do well in certain lines of outdoor life.

The Health: All the ailments of the Nervous type are suffered by this type, the Nervous type frequently impinging on the Ideal-Spiritual and sometimes the Nervous, Artistic and the Ideal-Spiritual are combined. Lafcadio Hearn was a perfect example of this compound, being marked by the ungainliness of the Nervous type, and its frequent inhibitions, having the poor eyesight characteristic of the Ideal-Spiritual, and being a really superb artist of a strictly limited *milieu.*

The body of the Ideal-Spiritual type is almost never robust and is seldom well filled out, even though tall. Disturbances of the stomach and bowels are never of the violent sort so common to the Material type; but chronic indigestion is almost a constant indication; and heart disease, of the strictly valvular type, is frequent. Like the Nervous type, though, this type will often outlive those who seem far more vigorous, *providing* there be an incentive of some kind—some loved person to care for, some Cause to further, and so forth.

The Dominant Traits: Reflection, intuition and idealism are the prevailing traits. The disposition is to be mild in likes and dislikes. Conscientiousness is high. Adherence to the letter of the law as well as to the spirit, is characteristic of this type; for to individuals of it "a white lie" is just as heinous as a black one. Understanding of human nature is usually weak, and ability to deal with people poor. Generosity is present, in intent, but the type will not be found to be generous with money and material things, for the simple reason that it cannot really visualize the *need* for material things.

The ability to forgive the grosser misdeeds of a rather gross world is small. Adherence to the dogmas of religion is apt to be strong, even when the mind is of such a caliber that a broader outlook is really preserved than this would seem to indicate. Courage is moral and not physical. Pride is never for self. Self-denial is easy and for that reason it is never properly estimated nor rewarded in others. This is one of the reasons why those belonging to this type do not make good employers. They are not ambitious and seldom make money; when they have it through inheritance they will seem mean and parsimonious. They are especially apt, if rich, to give heavily to libraries and other public institutions and totally to ignore the claims of individuals—such as relatives, and so on.

These people are not innately jealous, and in the finest examples of the type they are almost free of earthly faults. Descending the scale, they are jealous or possessive in odd ways in perhaps abnormal reactions. The higher examples are almost completely indifferent to what happens to them personally; but such examples are rare, indeed, to find. The greater the proportion of spiritual attainment and perception, the less earthly is the character, of course; and the greater the proportion of ideality, the more does the nature allow of an approximation to the more human reactions of fine humanity.

The Talents: It is not often that we will find actual talents in real examples of this type, except when there is a better approach to humanity than is usual, in which case we get the really "called" clergyman, priest, welfare worker, and so on. Unfortunately, there are few who combine a broad understanding of people and the finer development of this type, for without that understanding these people, although truly spiritual, are even less able to handle humanity than the Materialistic type which all too frequently is found in the sacred offices. The rare and unusual poet approaches this type, and occasionally the general literary workers do. The peak of the type, as to talent, is found in the great philosophers of the world, among whom we can cite Emerson as an almost perfect example; his handwriting is definitely expressive of the type.

The women are sometimes fine needle-workers, and both men and women do well with certain types of animals—dogs and cats and birds—but not with "stock." They are preeminently bee-keepers and successful growers of flowers, and in some cases turn to science along these lines, the world-renowned Henri Faber being a conspicuous example of this type. As naturalists they are superb. We need only select John Burroughs and

Luther Burbank as examples. It may be argued that Burbank disavowed belief in either God or immortality; but the utter unselfishness and purity of the lives of such men carry their own message, irrespective of what their lips may have to say.

The Mate: The ideal mate will have an approximation not only to the same type, but to the same level of mentality, the same reactions against or to the world of the flesh. To these people, far more than to any other type, mating is an uncertain matter, having as much, if not even more, chance of bringing unhappiness than happiness. The mate of this type, in short, ought to be the twin. The more that the physical make-up and the very mannerisms and voices are alike, the better. The more that the handwriting is almost a duplication of the other, the better; and this the graphologist should bear in mind. This type is sometimes attracted to the higher levels of the Material, but the attraction is never lasting, and the inability in the least to understand the Material assures the failure of the mating. Occasionally, the really Mental type can mate with the Ideal-Spiritual, but not often.

The Differences: The women of this type have great difficulty in finding happiness in marriage. The men get along for a time, especially when young, with women of other types, but soon tire of them. The women of this type are not especially good mothers, but have extreme conscientiousness about motherhood. The men are often cognizant of the needs of parenthood; but neither men nor women of the type are very successful parents except when, by chance, they have children of the same type as themselves.

The men of the Ideal-Spiritual type are slightly less adaptive to ordinary life than the women; and the women are somewhat more skilful with their hands than the men. The Ideal-Spiritual man is the least able of all men to make himself comfortable in a material and practical world and has little instinct for the making of money. If he makes it, as in the case of Burbank, it is because his talents are outstanding.

The Mental Type

Here we are in difficulties indeed, for it is all but impossible to describe that indefinable thing which marks the handwriting of this type, or even accurately to estimate the type itself. It is quite possible to define its outstanding characteristic: *i.e.*, the preponderance of the mental activities over other elements and the quality of those activities.

The Writing: This ranges all the way from the heavy pressure of the true Materialist to the light pressure and irregularity of Nervous formations. The Mental type is less frequently combined with the Vital than with the Material. Sometimes it is almost merged with the Constructive; almost never with the Ideal-Spiritual, save in such extreme examples as make literary landmarks of the centuries. The Mental type is *always* marked by letter formations which are very distinctive, though by no means always beautiful. No matter how ugly a man may be, nor what his state, his intelligence and even his education are somewhat to be guessed at by his appearance. This is as true of the Mental type in handwriting.

Probably the most consistent letter formation of this

type is the Greek *d*. The capitals are apt to be very simple and sincere; the small *g* frequently like the figure 8, or with the loop all but eliminated. Beginning- and ending-strokes are usually eliminated, and the writing is almost invariably small. Frequently there are wide margins. The signature may be quite commonplace, following the law that signatures express the personality rather than the mind or character.

The Personality: Here, more than in any other type, we are much at sea. However, there are a few laws which we may observe. If the signature expresses personality, we usually have a higher grade of the type than if the reverse is the case. Capitals which are larger than the rather small ones which are characteristic of the type will bring vanity to the personality as well as to the character. Long connecting-strokes between the letters will give greater ease of manner than otherwise. It is not quite safe to generalize about the coloring, but the weight of evidence seems to show that vivid coloring is rather more apt to give individuality to the Mental type and that pale coloring, such as that of indeterminate and ash blondes, will give subtlety.

The Mental type seldom has a really ugly hand. There is something both virile and graceful about the typical hand of this type—but of course we are discussing a "type," which is a very nebulous thing and which we have to apprehend more with our own mentalities and our intuitional perceptions than with the direct and concrete observation which is possible with the other types.

The Health: There is a wealth of evidence to show

us that heart disease is very frequent with this type and that nervous conditions are often bad. The type does not seem to be subject to apoplexy, unless it is combined also with the Materialistic type, as shown by pressure and other indications. Great development of physical powers, which used to be thought incompatible with mental development, is really found with it often; the Mental type is not often given to sports save in an amateurish way and as a direct means of health, but swimming, walking and dancing are greatly enjoyed, as a rule. True to type, the Mental depends largely upon the state of the mind for health; sorrow, trouble, shame and discouragement have killed more people belonging to the Mental type than all the other dangerous conditions possible to a human being. In examining writing of this type, then, we have to look sharply for evidences of depression and discouragement and disturbance, for this is the danger-point, both for the state of mind and the health, for these people.

The Dominant Traits: The Mental type has produced for us all sorts of people, from the saint to the confidence man and even to the murderer, but it has seldom produced a criminal who has persisted in crime. The Mental type is capable of murderous rage, of planning to swindle, and is rather more easily forced into theft through fear of disgrace than other types, but the true Mental type does not and in fact cannot remain in crime.

Another fallacious idea regarding the Mental type is that it is one with the Ideal-Spiritual—that a high development of the mentality brings a corresponding increase of spiritual perception. The truth is, of course, that it may or it may not. On the other hand, any really well-developed Mental type will turn in disgust from too great sordidness. Should any one bring up the case of a well-known criminal whose mentality was supposedly of a high order, it would be well to examine a specimen of the writing of such a man. He will not be found to belong in the Mental type, but in the high level of the Material, where mind has begun to function and where the subject is especially teachable and clever. It is this surface cleverness which the Mental type nearly always escapes. Perhaps no better illustration of the difference could be found than in the fact that the really intellectual person is often thought dull at school or college and that the after-dulness of the precocious child is a proverb.

Another common mistake as to the Mental type is that it is devoid of passions. It is true of about a third of those of the Mental type that their reactions to the pleasures of the body and to the delights of the senses have mostly been transferred to another level than that of ordinary existence. Men and women who are the gentle and unworldly scholars of literature are apt to exhibit this, but the great mass of the Mental type are vigorous and lusty creatures, whose reactions to life are distinctly on two planes: that of the mind wholly, and that of the body. There are others who fuse these, but the Mental is apt to keep them separate—being a cold and rather impersonal creature on the Mental plane and sometimes a creature of extreme emotionalism on the planes of feeling. Nothing so contributes to the subtle charm of this type as this combination.

The Talents: The creative writer, the philosopher, and the historian are the greatly talented people of this group. All grades of writers have to be at least somewhat of the type.

The Work: Among the Mental type we have preeminently, of course, the writers and the educators. Statesmen *should* be found in this classification. World-famed financiers usually *are* of the Mental type. The Mental type is often successful in cooking and in gardening, the creativeness of those occupations causing the success. As organizers of work which is merely detail the Mental type is not, in the mass, successful. This type is easily bored by routine and by work which makes no use of the mentality, but will cheerfully shoulder mental work which is staggering to other types. The type, if given the right kind of work, has superb endurance and usually a will-power which is unbreakable, *when* it is really focused. This does not mean, of course, that the will-power is always in operation.

The typical Mental type finds it hard to do any work which is not mental. But in going down the scale of scope and development of the Mental we may find all sorts of grades. The physician and the nurse, for instance, are usually marked with the Mental; the surgeon is usually of the Mental type, but he inclines to the Constructive also.

The Mate: Here we might as well stop and say that we cannot even attempt to classify. The Mental mates with all and sundry! The student of humanity will be confounded by finding a high type of the Mental mated to a very ordinary type of the Vital, or even the ordinary Material, as well as with the highest of its own type. It is safe to say that the totally uneducated will make a poor mate for even the ordinary Mental, and that the extremely nervous members of the Nervous type are almost sure to bring unhappiness to both; but otherwise the mating of the Mental type is very eclectic.

The Differences: The women of this type have, in the past quarter-century, made a very distinct advance over their brothers, in the field of the novel and in the field of fiction generally. On the other hand, medical research is so far almost exclusively in the hands of men. Statesmen have no feminine competition worth discussing. We have the names of no women, in past history, to place beside those of the great philosophers and religious teachers; but as teachers and educators women have come a long way indeed, and have practically supplanted the men teachers in this country.

Both men and women of the Mental type make pretty good parents. They are loving mates, but the women are, as a rule, slightly more inconstant than the men.

The Philoprogenitive Type

The Writing: This is some variation on the Material or the Vital. In fact, the Philoprogenitive can hardly be said to be a distinct type, in the sense of showing sharp differences from the Material and the Vital. It is a specialized type and that which will distinguish it are the letter formations which mark the essential features of it. The most prominent of these is the *protective A*. (See "Capitals.") Other formations, sometimes associated with the type, are the *lasso t* and the *credulous b.* The writing is usually rounded, about one degree off the upright or excessively forward-leaning, in the latter case sentimentality being even stronger than is usual in the type. A peculiar appearance of softness, due to the excessive roundness and the gentle formations of the capitals, is so easily perceived that little mistake need be made in estimating it. The *t* bars are sometimes short and sometimes medium, but are seldom long; the basic line is usually even. The *a, o,* and *g* are frequently so open as to be all but formless. (See "The Small Letters.") In such a type of writing it is almost never that we find the signature varying in one particular from the body of the writing. The lasso in either the *t* or other letters or used as a flourish over the signature or over two *t's,* shows persistent eccentricity, turned on the one element which marks this type. That one element is *protectiveness.*

The Personality: Since these people are chiefly interested in giving attention to others (for protectiveness is attention), they are apt to be rather colorless individuals, but are by no means lacking in assertiveness. It is in precisely such persons that we get illogical fanaticism, and the most intense reaction to mob psychology. The reason is plain. The protectiveness which is the strong element of the character is due to the feeling that no individual, however unimportant, should be without attention and care. Therefore, these are the "joiners"—the people who hasten to ally themselves with "movements," with organizations, with fraternal societies, with religious societies of extreme fraternal feeling. The manner, then, depends a good deal on how such people are met. The personality will be pleasant, friendly and warm so long as it is felt that sympathy with the peculiar ideas of the philoprogenitive one is felt. The personality is affected by a frequent lack of wholesome attractiveness. These are the people with moist and rolling eyes, with limp hands, with lank, too fine hair, with pale and unpleasant mouths, with undeveloped figures. If we put before our mind's eye the gentle-hearted, absent-minded, rather unworldly and yet sometimes bad-tempered and shrewish "old maid" of tradition (of whom there are so few!) we shall have something of the picture of the typically philoprogenitive type; but we shall have to transfer part of the picture to the masculine aspect, for there are fully as many men in the type as women.

Health: As the Philoprogenitive is less intense than either the Material or the Vital, from which types it mainly derives, it is apt to fall into the category of the Nervous, as to health; having, frequently, poor digestion, low vitality, a predisposition to throat- and eye-troubles and a good deal of weakness of the lungs. This type, like the Nervous, may seem, in some individuals, to be always ailing and yet those individuals may survive the greatest hardships. Such persons, fired with missionary zeal, astound the more vigorous by enduring privations in foreign lands, or by nursing starving people through plagues. The dominating element of the type will, in short, carry it onward in the almost superhuman way which is characteristic of all forms of fanaticism.

Dominant Traits: It is impossible to overestimate the instinct which this type has to succor and save, to retrieve, to salvage. It is needless to say that logic is not what we may expect from them. The reaction is not the thought of what is worth saving, but of what would wish to be saved. It is impossible, with a fine type of the Philoprogenitive, to show that there are cases in which a stern justice is better than mercy, *except* when mercy is to be shown the aggressive people who make no appeal. The Philoprogenitive saves stray dogs of no breed, malformed kittens, the lowest grades of humanity, the lame, the halt and the blind, but is not especially aroused to fervor by the gallant, the sternly upright and self-sufficient and the expertly efficient. It is not surprising to find that the adoration of the child, not as a potentiality, as the embryo of the full man, but as the child, *per se,* as the frail and helpless creature, is the main cult of this type and that its strongest reactions have to do with this.

Sincerity is nearly always characteristic of the type, but self-understanding or understanding of other types is not. The mind is accurate and painstaking. The affections are intense, for ties which concern children and often for ties which have to do with gentle and kindly affection. The temper is not high and often seems not to live at all, but in the gentlest individuals of this gentle type there slumbers the fanatic, especially those who belong to religious bodies whose attitude is fanatical. People who mistake prohibitions for temperance, who impose unjust laws on the strong, that the weak may profit, who cannot see that to demand special laws for women is to insult womanhood, who are ceaselessly occupied with *saving,* rather than in doing constructive work—they are the philoprogenitive type. The extreme usefulness of this type cannot be exaggerated, *if* it is really understood and allowances are made for its deficiencies.

Talents: We will not find many highly talented people in this type. Music, painting and writing are seldom done. A mild degree of talent for music is sometimes possessed, so that the writing of songs is successful. The writing of poetry is a frequent talent, in a mild way. Love of the beautiful in nature is sometimes strong. There is often an expertness of the hand which allows of beautiful and minute work being done, such as that of engraving, embroidering, and so on. High scholarship is almost never attained.

The Work: Here we have some very definite matters to consider. These people are splendid teachers, and while they seldom are the vital and magnetic lecturers needed in advanced institutions of learning, they have success even there, when their subjects are congenial. A good many of the very minor scientists, especially those who make little practical application of science, may be found in the type. In dealing with little children and with the sad and broken wrecks of humanity which fill the lower strata of life the Philoprogenitive is all but inspired. As missionaries to the uneducated and sunken, the evil and discouraged, they are supreme. As emissaries of Western knowledge and religion to intelligent Eastern races they are worse than useless; they are actually dangerous, since it is impossible for them to meet the intellectual subtleties of the East. The Philoprogenitive is interested, aside from the main matter of human salvage, in economic good sense; and in dealing with practical considerations this is often highly developed.

The Mate: This is one of the cases where marriage ought to be with a person of as near the self type as possible. Some of the mild people of the Nervous type can marry with the Philoprogenitive, and gentle, non-progressive Vital people do fairly well from their own standpoint, but not so well from the standpoint of the partner who is Philoprogenitive; for it is to be observed that the Philoprogenitive is not *really* mild. He or she may seem so, but that is only as long as their special subjects are not touched. The men of the Philoprogenitive type are fully as passionately interested in children as the women, if not more so; and the woman to whom the child is not wholly the end and aim of the mating, who is not a passionate adorer of childhood, will seem very unnatural to these men; while the man who is not the ardent father will deeply offend the woman of the Philoprogenitive type who cares to be beloved only in her children, present or potential. To such a woman, being a mother is the crown of existence and without that crown she either feels utterly useless or else turns to work which is that of the general mother. Those who marry this type without a thorough realization of the child cult (for it is really that in its extremity) which characterizes the type, will be surprised and will also find it very hard to make the proper adjustments, since childhood, as a cult, is not instinctive to any other type. These people are marked with a curious intensity of feeling, in youth. They mate early and if deprived of the mate by death or misfortune are apt to take another one soon.

The Differences: If there are any differences between the men and the women of this type, they accentuate the type in the man rather than in the woman. The Philoprogenitive woman is present in many women, to a very mild degree, but the Philoprogenitive man runs true to type and does not have the admixtures of the other types. The men of this type show less mercy to the eccentricities of genius and of high mental attainment than do the women. The women "mother" almost any one, even the individualistic Mental and Artistic types, toward which the average Philoprogenitive man feels utter aversion; an aversion which is strong enough to overcome his natural instincts for salvage. The instinct for mating, in the Philoprogenitive man, is intimately concerned with his desire to have a family of his own, and so we almost never find this type of man being influenced by the call of sex alone. He mates deliberately, usually with the wish to own his own home. He is frequently an excellent citizen, so far as he goes; being constructive only so far as laws concerning conservation are presented for his consideration.

The Philoprogenitive woman, on the contrary, although frequently entirely without mental activity in her earlier years, when, if possible, she occupies herself with the rearing of her own children, often turns into a woman of wide efficiency after her years in the care and training of children. To this type belongs the wife and mother who, without seeming to become the strong individualist that many women are, yet blossoms late in life into prominence in civic affairs. The Philoprogenitive man may become a high figure in philanthropy, but if he is going to do that he usually shows this early in life.

HOW TO MAKE A DELINEATION OF CHARACTER FROM GRAPHOLOGICAL DATA

Observe that in making a delineation of character from information afforded by the handwriting, we have to take the character piece by piece and mold it into something that lives. Thus, we do the same thing that the portrait painter or the sculptor does, and, like those artists, we must have some conception of the various types of human beings and of how our subject will fit into a certain type.

The painter, asked to produce a study of a miser, an ardent lover, a merchant, a mother, will have the type so clearly in mind that he can give us a portrait in which the salient features will be characteristically limned. The graphologist should understand that humanity can be divided into types, and that every one can be classified according to those types. Some are just one type; some may be a combination of two or more than two.

In making a delineation, the first step is to decide what type or what proportion of several types, may be assigned to the writer. The next step is to go through the various points, in the order in which they appear in this volume, making an estimation of the result. It is to be remembered, always, that to find the evidence of some trait missing is not to be sure that that trait is missing from the character. If the direct evidence for that trait is not shown, look for it in the indirect evidence. Suppose that the *protective A,* which indicates kindliness, pity for the suffering, and the instinct to help the young and old, is not found. This does not mean that the qualities shown by the *protective A* are lacking from the character. It merely means that the qualities shown by the use of the *protective A* are not the outstanding ones.

This brings us to a law of graphology which must not be forgotten in the actual making of delineations of character:

The strongest traits of character in a writer are always shown by formations which are the most conspicuous in the specimen.

Thus, it may be found that the will-power is fairly strong, as shown in the *t* bar, but other indications do not confirm this, and this takes away the force of the evidence. But where the *t* bar is long and strong, no other indication of the character in the writing can take away the fact of this outstanding evidence.

Having started out by determining the type to which the writer belongs, study separately the various indications in the writing, taking it up point by point, and write out your findings. If one characteristic contradicts another, the balance will be somewhere between the two.

Look at the signature for light on the personality.

Now call on all that you know of life and try to place your subject against a background. Try to estimate the degree of education, the probable line of development, the possible experience in social and business and professional life. What kind of interests?

What kind of friends? What type of person beloved? Good taste? And so on.

With your sketches made, as it were, and with your proportions all blocked out, you now take your brushes and try to put on canvas that which you see.

This is neither simple nor easy, for first you must make the delineation so definite that you, yourself, have a clear idea of the character. A certain amount of literary ability is needed and the instinct for the colorful and descriptive word. There are people who can delineate the character of a writer for themselves with great accuracy, but who seem unable to find the words wherewith to paint their conception of the character they have visioned. And there are others, with the trick of the ready word, who can paint an interesting portrait with which we can find no fault except that it is not like the sitter!

A careful study of the words used in describing human beings and human actions will assist in the making of intelligent and interesting delineations. The persistent misunderstanding of ordinary terms of this nature is something with which every professional graphologist is painfully familiar. A few hints on this point will show the pitfalls along this line.

Will-power is neither good nor bad. Most people consider it a compliment to be told that they have it, but will-power may be applied to the most nefarious uses. The tyrant has will-power. And so has the saint. Will-power is not the possession of weaklings, of course, and really stupid people rarely have much of it.

Persistence implies continuity of purpose. It does

not imply tremendous will-power, in the sense of the pushing, positive, bludgeon sort of thing which will-power really is.

Patience is not a virtue, despite the old saw. It may be, when it enables a human being to survive hardship and to endure sorrows, wrongs and troubles, but the venomous man-killer has patience and may nurse his vicious purpose for years, waiting for the right moment in which to strike.

Temper, good and bad, is something for which we need better descriptive names. Good temper may be, and often is, downright laziness. The person is too indolent to "show fight." So-called bad temper is something which is very elastic. It may be evoked through a person's being continually placed in trying positions; it may be the outcry of the nerves, worn by friction to extra-sensitiveness.

Sensuality and *sensuousness* are different. Sensuality gives us gross appetites unrefined by art, culture, love of beauty and refinement of feeling. Sensuousness gives us delight in perfume, color, light and movement; takes away the ability to enjoy anything which is gross, gives the ability to rise above the material plane in enjoyments.

Intuition: A peculiar and wholly unwarranted meaning is attached to this word by some people, who believe that intuition means a form of psychic perception—if there be such a thing. Intuition, on the contrary, when studied, will be shown to be rather the higher logic, the only trouble being that we are not yet familiar with its laws. No doubt that swift and accurate deduction which we call intuition and which does not seem to be based on anything tangible, is really and actually based on observations which we have made in the recesses of our being; which we call by the name of the subconscious self. A great many outdoor people think that they are intuitive about the weather, about where water can be found, and so on, when they are really remarkably observant and their so-called intuition is based on observations so minute, so painstaking and so prolonged, that they have been lost to perception, but have left their impress on the retentive mind. The fact that intuition is shown by the disconnection of the connecting-strokes between the letters of words expresses this action, exactly, in which the mind forgets the connection, although it really exists and needs only real recollection to bring it to light—just as it needs only a little stroke by which to bridge the gap left between the letters of a word, when the words are formed of disconnected letters.

Ideality: This is not spirituality. It will give high ideals of conduct and of thought and feeling—but many an idealist has been constitutionally incapable of any spiritual attainment.

Spirituality: This is a direct and conscious effort to be at one with the sources of goodness, be those sources thought to be what they may. It is the aspiration for Godliness and the possession of an innate leaning toward it.

In making a delineation, one must be careful to weigh each word. The instances given will show what mistakes can be made.

It should be remembered, too, that it is one thing to tell a person something face to face, and quite another thing to write it in cold type. The smile, the glance, the friendly hand, the intonations of the voice, all soften and illumine what we say, but the written word must convey its message unequivocally. Harsh and censorious statements need not be made. Tact and moderation should characterize each statement.

On the other hand, the habit of hedging is to be deplored. It is possible to make frank, exact statements and yet so to couch them that they shall not unnecessarily offend. It is so easy to let our personal reactions to a specimen of writing creep into what we have to write about it or say about it. Lazy, "good-for-nothing" dreamers are apt to irritate the aggressive type, and if the graphologist is aggressive, every new trait which he turns up and adds to the portrait of this good-for-nothing will exasperate him the more. Puritanic people find the pagan temperament trying to delineate, and it is quite safe to say that the pagan temperament finds the Puritan equally difficult!

If, however, the statements are made coolly and without animus and with moderation, few will ever take offense. But if the resentment, anger or distaste of the delineator slips into so much as a word or a tone, the subject will instantly feel, and rightly, that prejudice is speaking and not scientific estimation.

The graphologist must, indeed, endeavor to look on humanity with a detached eye, but with a kind and tolerant heart and an understanding mind.

The mere classification of certain elements of the writer, the mere giving of names to character traits, will not be worth much. Serious mistakes are made by those who believe that honesty is honesty, without modifications, and that dishonesty can have no gradations.

Let us look at the matter, first, from the standpoint of the types of humanity. Before we have considered how such types are registered in the handwriting, we ought to have studied them carefully in the flesh. The real student will attempt to classify more or less all those persons who are known with any degree of intimacy, and soon the instinct to do this will be so ingrained that any casual stroll down a street will result in an almost automatic observation of bony structure, coloring of skin, eyes and hair, shapes of mouths and so on.

On the other hand, the student will remember that the bodily presence is not always really indicative of the type, on the *extreme upper and lower levels of mental development.* Thus, the ill educated and ill born may have characters and even minds which are either high or low in scale. The handwriting will reveal this when the body will not. And the highly educated and well born (in the sense of normal conditions surrounding birth) may be fitted with bodies which do not adequately reveal their best selves. The handwriting on this higher level will, of course, show the facts with minute fidelity.

It is also of great importance for the graphologist to realize that no one type is the possessor of a surplus of either faults or virtues. The Ideal-Spiritual is the one in which actual faults are the least and the Material type and its many variations are the ones in which we find the greatest amount of actual faults, but it is to be remembered that many a fault is but a virtue pushed to an extreme.

We may, in trying to make the estimation of the actual workings of character, make a diagram such as is given here, in which different levels of human development are shown by horizontal lines and certain traits of character are shown by perpendicular formations. Thus, honesty, beginning on the lowest level

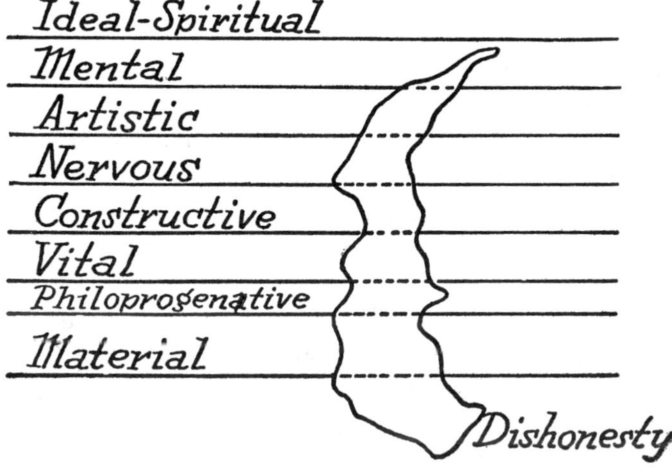

—that of Materialism—gives us the honesty which will not take an object belonging to another, but which is unable to understand that there are extensions of this virtue. On the Vital level we get a better understanding of this, possibly a general feeling that fulfilling moral obligations is even more important than practical fulfilments. The Mental level will give us a wider horizon for honesty. On that level we begin to perceive the still extending horizon of honesty of opinion and honesty with ourselves—the most difficult use to be made of the virtue. The Ideal-Spiritual type will give us a comprehension of honesty which far outstrips all the comprehensions of that virtue by any of the other types. In the Artistic and Nervous types we may or may not have any perception of honesty, since both these types are so concerned with what is indifferent to that which we know as honesty. (See observations on this point in the chapter on "Types of Humanity.") The Philoprogenitive may possibly take an attitude toward honesty which will be different from that of all the other types.

Another thing to think of is that race makes some difference in human reactions. What would be cruelty in one race—as shown in the individual—is about the norm in another. What would be extravagant and abnormality for the average Englishman is about the norm for some other races.

Social strata make a difference. As the mind becomes more and more trained and as refinement of taste becomes greater, we may expect the individual to advance—or to be found in higher levels of social strata. The graphologist who, in taking up a specimen of writing, has not, in his or her mind's eye, a vision of the various strata of society, as well as a pretty good understanding of racial characteristics, will have some difficulty in envisioning the background against which the character portrait is to be set.

It is important to estimate the fact that:

There are often cases in which the presence of a certain trait must be inferred from the presence or absence of others.

Take the case of the open *a* and *o,* for instance. If we find these two letters "closed" that is not the indication that generosity and frankness are lacking; it is just the indication that generosity and frankness are to be looked for elsewhere. Say that in the instance where *a* and *o* are closed we find rounded handwriting, the *protective A* or formations close to it, the open capital *D* and a well-proportioned connecting-stroke. It is impossible that with these indications we shall be facing a character in which there is a lack of generosity and frankness. On the other hand, it is obvious that, as we have not the "high light" on the formations thrown on this trait, it is one which, existing, yet is subordinated in action by other elements. If *o* and *a* are closed, therefore, and the other points of writing are as just mentioned, then we have the people in whom generosity and frankness are strong but not dominating. Out of this we get the following rule:

Character elements are highly developed and in actual use, in proportion to the degree of prominence which they occupy in the handwriting.

A combination of several indications, taken in their combined effect, may tell us of the existence of another indication not positively shown. We may call these indications: "submerged indications."

The graphologist may resort to various mechanical aids to the making of delineations of character from handwriting. The effort, however, to use any mathematical formulas will be found to be very hampering, for the reason that human character is not a one-dimension matter. It is not on one plane. If we try to reduce this statement to a picture, we may do it somewhat as follows:

In mathematics the statement is a one-plane statement. That is to say, if we say "two and two are four" there is no possible modification of it, no addition possible, no shading admissible. Two elephants and two other elephants, or two elephants and two matches—it makes no difference, the result is four.

If human nature were a one-plane matter we could take a certain combination of traits and absolutely get the same result out of them, but human nature is not only more than a one-plane matter; it is multiple and that to a degree which as yet can have not even an approximate estimate. Thus, in one human being there is a dominating part of one type, but we may have portions of other types, not only occupying sections of the nature, but darting up and down in the different levels. So that, faith, hope and honor, we'll say, are not matters which we can deal with by any hard and fast *one-plane* formulas. The effort, then, to set up the traditional number of one hundred or—ten—and then to portion out the character traits in numbers which shall complete the traditional "completion" number, is perfectly futile.

The graphologist who is at least something of a writer will have to his hand the best possible medium by which to work—which is the semi-fictional mode of writing. Those who have even attempted to train themselves in the writing of character sketches will perceive both the difficulties and the possibilities of graphological work more quickly than those who have never tried to set down, in words, what is a mingled matter of vision and perception. To make the character portrait, seen in the handwriting, to live in the written word, has a great many analogies to the effort of the painter who tries to put on canvas the living embodiment before him.

The character portrait must be expressed, not only in exact formulas, but also must have what the painter calls *depth, air, light and perspective.* It must have *background, proportion, faithful drawing, true color.*

The painter, it will be remembered, fixes the *bony structure* first. The man who produces for us the fine flesh tones, the perfect semblance of the softly rounded woman's body, has drawn in, before that, the strong, well articulated skeleton. He must know, besides paints and canvas and brushes, bones, muscles, sinews, joints. The graphological worker may liken the knowledge of words and their use to his paint, his canvas and his brushes, and then the simile will be exact.

In applying this demand to character delineations we approach the difficulties of the literary worker, and while the good graphologist is sometimes good despite his inability to express well what he sees, the really good graphologist will have at least enough of the literary temperament and of mental training to give the life to his portraits which we see and feel in those who create wholly fictional characters for us.

As in the matter of painting, then, and as in the matter of creating character in fiction, we proceed to fix the type first.

The angle of inclination is what will set this for us, to a large extent. We may start by remembering that, roughly speaking, the extreme forward angles of inclination lean *toward* people and that the leftward extreme angles lean *away* from people. Thus we have a graphological diagram for what some students of humanity have called the introverts and the extraverts. The rightward angles are the extroverts—the exhibitionists—those who like to touch the world, to make contacts. The leftward angles are the introverts, who hate to be with crowds, who not only do not seek contacts but more or less avoid them, who are "difficult" for others.

To this definition we then add the degree of pressure and we have pretty well set the temperament. To those who believe that such simple and uncomplicated indications are insufficient for the determination of temperament, I offer a very limited table of deductions, which may be made as follows:

Upright writing, light pressure: Slightly inclined to the introvert or repressed type, without expansiveness.

Upright writing, medium pressure: More emphasis put on demand for appreciation and emotional satisfaction of a sensuous nature.

Upright writing, very heavy pressure: Real inclination to sensuality, without the ideality which lifts and refines it. The person without much that will tend to future betterment; what he is—he is!

Moderately rightward inclination, light pressure: Opening of the temperament to greater expansiveness in matters other than sex attraction, which remains repressed.

Moderately rightward inclination, medium pressure:

More expansiveness in all relations than the former and less repression in sex feeling.

Moderately rightward inclination, heavy pressure: Not necessarily more expansion but great indulgence in sensuous gratification and probably a more dominating will.

Forward, rightward inclination, with light pressure: Frank and ready expression of friendship and of emotions generally. Liking for people. Interest in expression. Ready talkers.

Very forward leaning rightward inclination, medium pressure: Those with vibrant personalities, who impress themselves and their desires on others by persuasion, by magnetic impulse. Quick to show feeling. Warm and unabashed lovers.

Extremely forward leaning, rightward inclination, heavy pressure: These are the leaders, the orators, the successful politicians, the heads of movements and so on. Talkative and eloquent, persuasive and dynamic.

Leftward leaning inclination, at a slight degree away from the upright, light pressure: Somewhat like the upright light pressure, but with a little more intensity of feeling and therefore—since we are now coming to the introverts—*less* expressive of emotion than the upright. Friendly and interested in people in general. (Very few heavy pressures.)

Leftward leaning inclination, at a greater degree away from the upright, light pressure: Extremely sensitive people who often seem sullen.

The same inclination, heavier pressure: Sensuous

and often hot-tempered. Irritable. Not interested in people.

Extreme leftward leaning inclination, light pressure: These are the people who appear cold and unemotional, often affecting cynicism and adopting a repellent attitude toward almost every one. They are just the same, save for inhibitions, as their own angle on the rightward side!

Extreme leftward leaning inclination, with heavier to heavy pressure: Sensual, impassioned, ardent, and exceedingly complex.

The graphological student can go on and add more detail to such classifications as this. Observe that we have used nothing but the angle of inclination and pressure. Add size and rhythm, and there is, as it were, another great section of the natures revealed.

Robert Saudek ("The Psychology of Writing") says: "If ever our Creator or Nature produced a model example of a man in whom it was as clear as the light of day that his powers of reasoning prevailed over his capacity for sentiment, this model was Immanuel Kant—and Kant wrote at an angle varying between 40 and 50 degrees—that is, with an extraordinary slant."

Mr. Saudek quotes this as a "refractory case," *i.e.*, a contradictory one, to the rule that the forward-leaning writing expresses capacity for feeling sentiments. It seems to me that the difficulty is not in a proper deduction giving a contradiction but in a wrong one being made. I do not believe that logic, reason or any extreme power of the mind can do anything to put out of existence, or to restrain from expression, the emotions. The two are parts of a man. In fact, the more extreme is the high level of the mind, the more ardent, flaming and intense are apt to be the reactions of the feelings. I do not blame Mr. Saudek for this mistake. It is constantly iterated and reiterated, not only by generally educated people, but by educators and those whose jobs are intimately connected with the expert appraisal of human nature.

Kant, as Mr. Saudek immediately afterward remarks, was the man who said "space and time are within us." So far from believing that "cold reason" was the level on which Kant thought, I believe that the clarity of his mind was due to the fact shown in his handwriting: that within him there was the most exquisite capacity for feeling. "Cold reason" in the sense of reason divorced from feeling, is a one-dimension operation. A limited operation. To prove this, and that in the simplest way, we have only to remember that the great and grand concepts which have raised the level of man from that of the beasts were those produced by natures in which mentality and human feeling were both intense. Confucius, Buddha, Krishna, Mohammed, the Christ, were essentially natures of many dimensions. Their concepts transcended anything ever originated by "cold reason" and equaled them on the cold reason plane, too.

Returning to the matter of the forward-leaning angle, then, it is not surprising to find that so many of the great ones of the earth have used it.

Crepieux-Jamin tried to place, at the beginning of his classifications of humanity, the mental test. "Superior" and "inferior" mentality was the start of this classification. Such a classification cannot be accurate, for we can have superior mentality sunk low in the Material type, or raised to its highest point in the Ideal-Spiritual. In the classification which I suggest we are working on the assumption of temperament being a better classification, and reckoning the "Mental Type" by the temperamental differentiations. This classification, as we have seen, can be chiefly settled by the angle of inclination and pressure combined. This seems a better classification and one which more broadly embraces human types than any classification which includes mentality only.

However, there are all sorts of ways in which we can begin heaping up piles of writing specimens, so that we may classify them. It is possible to separate the sheep and the goats, intellectually speaking, with almost as much ease as we separate red and black ribbons.

It is possible to separate the same mass of specimens into two piles: one the extraverts and the other the introverts. Intellectually, we can sort out the expansive and generalized minds and the concentrated and specialized ones. But unless we have a general classification which will allow us to construct the whole picture on the basis of that classification, up and down the scale, we will soon be in difficulties.

The classification of humanity is so complex a subject in itself, and the possibilities of being led off into this and that bypath are so great, that we have to keep ourselves keenly exact in the simplest of graphological work. We must resist the temptation to fall into traditional attitudes, to make "cut-and-dried" classifications.

Temperament in the Material, the Vital, the Constructive, the Artistic, the Nervous, the Mental and the Ideal-Spiritual—with the Philoprogenitive fitting in as a companion to the Material or the Vital—will be found to endure the test of constant classification use in heavy graphological practise. I make this statement after using it for over twenty years in a practise which has seldom fallen below fifty delineations a day, and which, for the greater part of that time, has run far into excess of that figure. I make the statement after having offered the classification to pupils for ten years and having had it received with growing approval as those pupils used it in their own practise.

Objection may be made that character, in the sense of honesty and dishonesty, sincerity and insincerity, reliability and unreliability, is really the bony structure, the foundation, by which we should classify. My reply is that honesty and dishonesty, sincerity and insincerity, reliability and unreliability, are elements of character which may be found running through all the types, as I have outlined them, and that the dishonesty which is found in the Material type is a different thing from the dishonesty of the Mental type. Fundamentally, we are this and that temperament. Every good fiction writer knows it. The better they know it, the better fiction writers they are. Our best portrait painters know it, and the better they know it the greater their fame. This innate classification of humanity is *practised* extensively by the world, although it is hardly ever preached.

Delineation of Character

Number One. Upright, heavy pressure, disorderly, somewhat "muddy"—undoubtedly of the Material type. This is a specimen which would be exceedingly difficult for a delineator who had not had a great deal of experience. On the face of it, we have the materialistic person with little tenderness and no imagination, and with a decided slant toward the sensual. The mentality, following the arrangement of words, would seem to be disorderly and confused. All this is true. But, to contradict it, what do we have? We have one of the finest indications of character development possible to be seen. Note the bow, with the ends turned down, which is the indication of faults conquered, passions fought with, aspirations encouraged! It is seldom, indeed, that we will find the conjunction of this extreme materialistic temperament, this mind which is still uncleared, and this very wonderful sign.

Here is a person with aspiration breaking through the attractions and passions of the flesh. The will-power is growing. Note the tendency of the *t* bar to lengthen occasionally. The mind has yet to justify the individuality of the letters. When it does we will have wider spaces between the words and wider and neater spaces between the basic lines. With the force which produces this pressure there will be temper, of course; courage; power and vitality.

Number Two. Short connecting-strokes, spaces between the words wide in comparison to the connecting-strokes, pressure medium-heavy and very consistent, *t* bar placed low, *a* and *o* closed, *and* the altruistic loop on the small *g*. Again, we have the Material type with which to deal, but what a difference between Number One and Number Two! Pressure here, so firm and consistent, gives us interest in the practical world rather than in the world of theories. The moderation of the capitals expresses exactly that quality, a deduction confirmed by the simple and unostentatious capital *I*. The moderate angle of inclination gives us kindliness, and when we unite to this the angularity of the letter forms we have a strong sense of justice. Adding to this the altruistic *g* formation, (which has partial confirmations in the *p* and *f*) we have the philanthropic individual who is not easily drawn into mere sentimentality and who is essentially well poised and sane. The will-power as shown in the *t* bar is marked. Note that everything—the pressure, the distance of the words apart, the distance of the basic lines apart, the distance of the letters of words, the size of the capitals in reference to the small letters—are all in perfect proportion.

My dear Miss Rice,—
I have never
for which I paid $1.0
at the Astor last
be very glad to ha
for further reading

From such a writer we will have, not the extravagant individuality of number one, and not the potentiality of genius, either—but preeminent good sense and self-control and especially good judgment.

Number Three. It is not often that we find a specimen of writing in which the persistent desire of the hand to reverse the action from left to right is seen. This is one. Observe that frequently, as in a final *o,* the letter is closed by an action which is the reverse of the ordinary one.

We have here, in addition to this, a great many eccentricities of the hand. The letters are either very rounded at the bottom and very angular at the top or *vice versa.* The small letter *e* is persistently enlarged. The *i* is dotted with the circle. The upper loops have almost disappeared and the lower ones are very ineffective. The pressure is light. Width between the words is more than ordinary. A good margin was used.

my handwriting
like to hear the
about your specia
complete readin
Trusting that
pleasure of hearin
in the near futu

In this specimen we have an almost perfect example of that rule, laid down in the consideration of the Artistic type, that the lesser artists exhibit greater personal peculiarities than the great ones. The use of the circle *i* dot, the margin and the leftward inclination of the hand are all distinctive. On the other hand, the shortening of the upper loops and the enlargement of a small letter are alarming signs. It is unfortunately true that it is precisely this type which needs to have the utmost care and understanding, encouragement and congenial surroundings. Encouragement for the development of the artistic talent is urgently needed, as a counterbalance to the moodiness, inhibitions and mental difficulties which are shown by these inhibited formations.

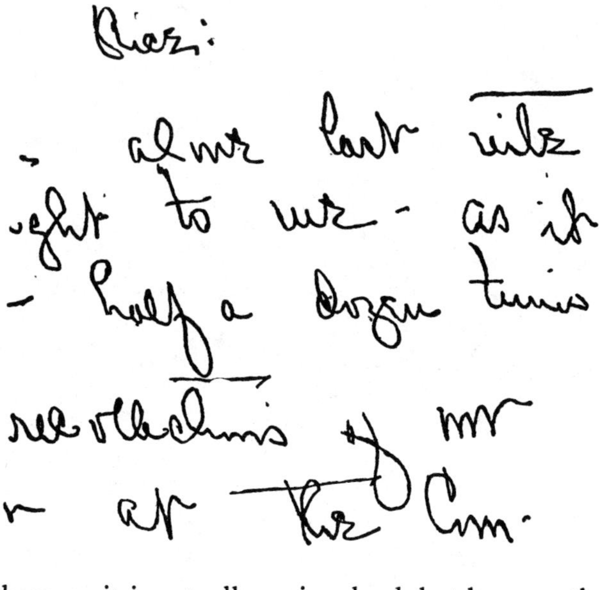

Number Four. This is one of the most interesting of specimens. It is a difficult subject for delineation, not because it is actually so involved, but because there are so many points involved. Thus, we have the medium pressure, the backward and pronounced angle of inclination, the long *t* bars with their marked hooks, the looped *d,* the large lower loops, the broken connecting-strokes, the open *o* and *a,* the conservative "old-fashioned" *c,* the rounded and small upper loops, the occasional broken-backed *t,* the stroke which is tremulous—and the extraordinary width between the words.

The type is more or less the Artistic, of course, and belongs to the inhibited "introvert" classification because of the lack of easy rhythm in the writing. The broken-backed formation, as in the *t* in "times," allied to the tremor, gives us the assurance that the nervous condition will always be a matter of danger to the writer and also that moods seize and hold to an unusual degree.

The effect of beauty which is attained by this specimen is delightful and we may be sure that it is not without meaning. Music and literature, the latter possibly fantastic, poetic and imaginative, ought to be open to this person as fields of endeavor. There is a distinct rhythm in this handwriting, although it is a stiff and constrained one. Intuition is keen; accented by the general sensitiveness, a matter which is to be deduced from the general exotic formations and from those which show love of music, as in the rounded upper loops. It is clear that until the rhythm is more flowing this person will have a great deal of trouble in finding self-expression. We may also infer that there is not complete health indicated. The hope and promise of the nature is given in the *t* bars and their hooks, for here we have the evidence of a will that never lets go, that outlives all, endures all, struggles, fights and is gallantly brave.

Number Five. The rhythm here is consistent and rather easy, despite the fact that the angle of inclination is extreme, and when we inquire into the particulars of the specimen we shall see that this is not a mere impression. The formations are mainly rounded, which is an exception in this extreme leftward angle of inclination. The *t* bars are upward and not downward inclined. The space between the basic lines is perfectly regular. The pressure is moderate, not heavy or light. The high first strokes on letters, repeated in many forms, tell us of pride and courage. The small *d* is a variation on the Greek *d,* with a leaning toward the formation which means love of pleasure and gaiety of disposition. We find, however, that the straddle *t* is well marked, and as this is unusual to find combined with the gay *d,* we may be sure that we have that rare thing—a gay and optimistic nature which is also *able*

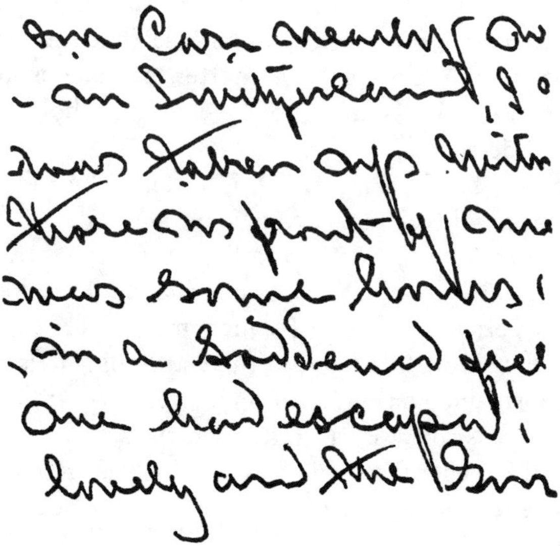

to be secretive. Note that secretiveness is not an instinct in the nature, as it would be with angular formations, this angle of inclination *and* the straddle *t*. The altruistic *y* is here to add to the beauty of the character. As for the angle of inclination, with its indication of reserve and introverted instinct, that is greatly lessened by the roundness of the writing and the flowing rhythm.

Number Six. This is the handwriting of a young woman. It is the expression of a nature which has

Dear Madam,

in Hearst's In
about hidden s.
and I should
would tell m
Also I should
interesting illust

been most unusually hedged about with conventionality, social distinctions and constraint. The social life is that of a generation or two before ours.

It would be difficult to find a better example showing how the conditions of life, affecting the individual, are reflected in the individual's writing; for the writing is not an imitation of any form which has been observed and is not the result of a certain form of taught penmanship.

Number Seven. A fine example of the gentle, moderate and idealistic Philoprogenitive type.

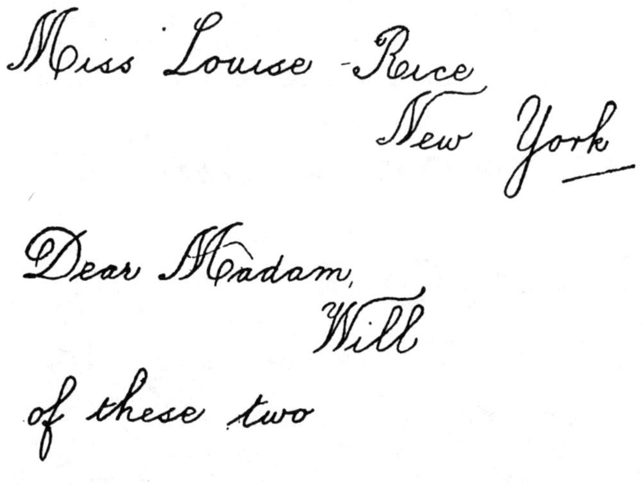

Miss Louise Rice
New York

Dear Madam,
Will
of these two

Number Eight. Rounded formations, hurried and yet flowing rhythm, an *i* which is dotted curiously close to the letter, considering the type of writing in which we find it, *t* bars which approach the spear shape, and closed *o, a,* and *g,* the latter not at all in character, give us the assurance that this is a most contradictory character. The closeness of the *i* dot to the letter and the closed formations tell us that this is a person of mingled enthusiasms, ardors, coldness and "closeness."

It would be quite impossible to rely on this writer's reactions in either practical or emotional matters. The intensity of feeling will drive the action into spontaneity and the caution and reserve will instantly check such tendencies. People with this rounded writing and hurried and yet flowing rhythm are always possessed of personalities which are fascinating.

Number Nine. A most extraordinary specimen, in which there is a union of the utmost eccentricity with extreme and even peevish conservatism. The peculiarities of the writing are mainly those of a certain curved formation, which is added to almost every stroke. Such a person may go on for a whole lifetime, living most conventionally, but the erotic and exotic underlies this surface and may break out. On the other hand, this specimen gives us the characteristic circle *i* dot of the semi-artistic and if such a writer has that outlet, then extreme and prim conservatism might pervade the life. The passions and appetites are not strictly materialistic, despite the pressure, for the in-

New York City
Dear Madame:—
Please send to the following address, full details about your special offer for a complete personal and confidential reading of handwriting.
Thanking you sincerely,
I am,

verted tastes and the very double consciousness would prevent that.

Madam.
Please send me full
your Private Reading

Number Ten. A variation, of more alarming character, of Number Nine.

Number Eleven. In even such a large and extensive collection of handwritings as mine, this specimen is quite unique. Note that the small letters are very small and that it is only the capitals and the loops which are

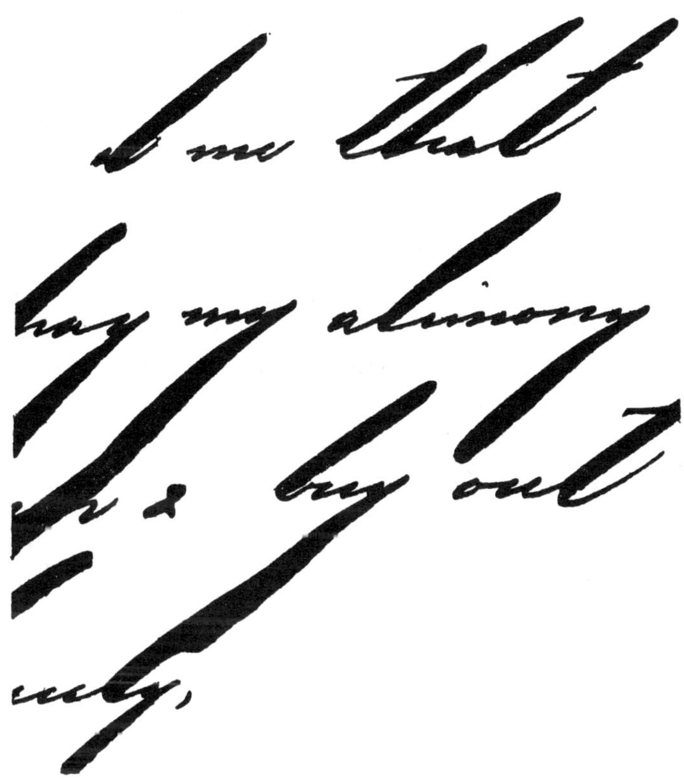

so extraordinary. Here is an instance of that rule for unusual specimens which tells us that eccentricity which does not run through all the writing is more or less an affectation. However, let us not shrug and put this by as a mere theatrical gesture in handwriting. Let us, rather, remember that the instinct for affectation may be either foolish or else an indication of abortive genius. The writer of the specimen is unknown to me, but I would strongly suspect that his life has been difficult, either in the possession of too great or too little money. Too little would make of such a person a bitter rebel and too much would lead to the gratification of that unquestioned sensuality which inspired these brutally thick strokes. *But*—a measure of strange and fantastic beauty has been attained by the use of these strokes. There is the same weird element in this writing that we find in some of the Cubistic and modernist paintings—unlike anything real, and lit with sinister fires, but enthralling. Therefore the graphologist may be sure that no ordinary nature produced this specimen and that potentialities, for good and ill, and for art in some form, are indicated. Also, a most unusual temperament.

Number Twelve. This is a fine sample of the Constructive type in which the rounded formations tell of

Sirs
I submit
reading with
chief failing
if I have

a gentler disposition than the Constructive usually have.

Number Thirteen. The broken-backed formation is seen, well marked, here. The heavy pressure and the uncalled-for use of quotation-marks, and the fact that a form of the gullible *b* is found, tell us that temper, aggressiveness, unreasonableness, assumed shrewdness and real credulity are strongly developed, and that eccentricity is dangerously near to being extreme.

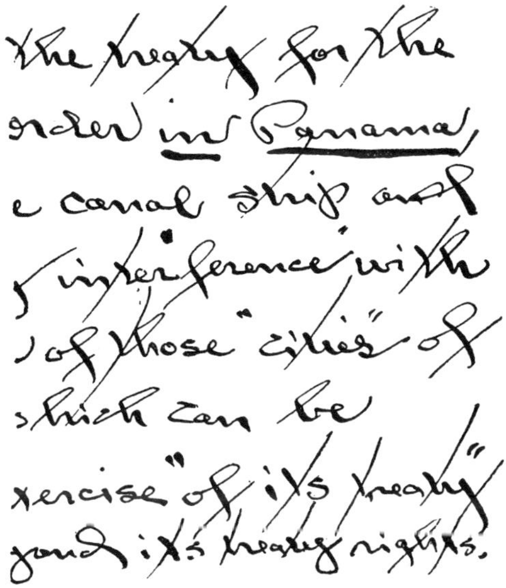

Number Fourteen. The introvert, strongly marked, but with a rhythm which is persistent and with the beautiful broken connections which tell of intuition and refinement of feeling. The large *r* shows sensitiveness to personal appearance and the desire to be appreciated and admired, but there are no indications of real vanity. Although with marks of inhibitions, this writing is really a very fine indication of character. The rounded loops and the looped *d* with the peculiar *t*

Cheque for one dollar
a character reading
my hand-writing

give us, however, little promise of real strength of character.

Number Fifteen. The *t's* in this specimen are exceedingly interesting as showing a character in the

I read me a copy
Interesting Illustrated
fascinating secrets
ing and Private Reading

processes of self-development. One instance of the fine bow *t* with the ends turned down is seen and in the whole specimen there were a good many more. There is a straight, positive *t* and several which try to be the bowed form, but end in being the weak and easy-going waved formation. The inflation of loops is the indication of pride. Possibly, as the character development proceeds, this inflation will subside. The odd form of the *d,* which leans a little toward the Greek formation, tells us that the rather graceful letter formations are not without meaning: the writer, although not trained, is an innate lover of beauty.

THE HISTORY OF HANDWRITING

THE HISTORY OF HANDWRITING

"Who first invented the alphabet?

"The Phœnicians.

"When did culture and education begin?

"Culture and education began on the banks of the Nile, about five thousand years before Christ."

Some such statements as these begin the standard school books on history in every civilized tongue. Even those brought out in the last few years continue the legend, which is absolutely wrong and misleading.

Fifty years ago these two statements were honestly thought to be true. Even the discovery of the Rosetta stone in the year 1799 did not do very much to clear up the history of the world prior to the sixth century, B.C. But with the discovery and translation of the Moabite stone in 1868, a great flood of light was thrown on the matter of the alphabet, and the beginnings of many things, and from that day to this the researches conducted by colleges and various archeological expeditions have brought up from the vasty deep of the B.C. years such information as has made an enormous panorama, alive and concrete, of the dim and veiled vista which we used to call "ancient history."

In no one particular have we learned so much as about this very matter of the beginning of culture and education, but the lower and deeper we dive, the more do we find that "beginning" pushed farther and farther away.

On the banks of the Nile, five thousand years before Christ, there was not a beginning, but an ending. An old, effete civilization, borne down with the weight of custom, learning, theological dogma, decaying historical monuments, caste and political complexity, was continuing to exist by sheer force of being the supreme cultural influence in the world of that day.

Behind that country on the banks of the Nile, behind that strip of land cumbered with buildings so ancient that all history of them had been lost, there were other countries, other civilizations. There were other tongues, other modes of writing, other social systems, all stretching back into tens of thousands of years.

Somewhere back of all civilizations and back of more primitive civilizations and back of men who at least had a semblance of clothes and weapons and organization, there lie the uncounted years of man, in his slow climb upward from the primitive, where, indeed, "education and culture" *did* have their beginning.

Each time that one attempts to set some general period that scientists agree upon as the time when man —conscious of being such—first can be counted as really on the earth, each time do scientists again push back this period, proving that even the hundreds of thousands of years already allotted to man's time on the earth has again been added to; another record has been made, by excavation in Egypt—in Crete—in Mesopotamia—in China—in Mongolia—in Yucatan—in Africa.

Therefore, one cannot state that the primitive man, who knew fire and had weapons, but who was somewhat too simian in his face and figure to be especially cultured, did or did not live in the period, however many hundreds of thousands of years ago, to which scientists now assign him, for next year it is likely to be proved that another fifty thousand years or so have casually been added to the record.

It can be said, though, that the time when the primitive man existed was so far back of recognized human history that it is hard even to conceive of that time; and that five, ten, twenty, forty thousand years before "education and culture began on the banks of the Nile" man had begun to conceive of the idea of putting his thoughts into visible shape and had already laid the ground-plans for all the edifice of civilization which has been slowly built through all the centuries since.

To conceive of the *actual* beginning of education and culture, we have to conceive of the *first attempt to write.*

Until that attempt was at least germinating in the mind of prehistoric man, he really had not much to mark him out from the more intelligent of the beasts, who, like him, lived in caves, where they often managed to get together a good bed of leaves, took more or less effective care of their families, played in the pleasant spring weather, hunted when it was cold, drank when they were thirsty and knew every wile and trick of their world; licked their wounds to heal them and kept a certain rough good-nature among the members of their own clan.

To reconstruct this world of the primitive man we have to picture a creature whose back was a good deal longer than man's, whose feet were more like hands, whose powerful and protruding jaws could crunch the bones of the great beasts which he slew, and whose body was decidedly hairy. We have to remember that he must have had speech of some kind, but that it could not have been very sharply articulated. Even to-day, among individuals of any civilized race, there is a great difference in the distinctness of enunciation between the thin and the thick-lipped, and as between the languages of the mobile-jawed and thin-lipped European and the heavy-jawed and thick-lipped African, there is this striking difference of the sharpness of the sounds produced.

This primitive man never does have the idea that such thoughts as wander in the darkness of his sleeping brain may be projected by anything save speech and it is even with difficulty that he manages that; but he has eyes, keen and accurate, even as are the eyes of the ani-

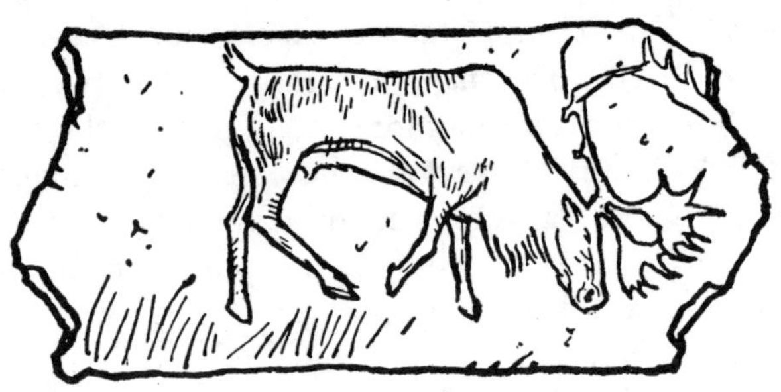

PREHISTORIC DRAWING OF DEER

mals whom he stalks and who stalk him. He knows their shapes, the very manner of their standing and running. He knows the texture of their hides and the angle at which their eyes are set.

The one weapon which he has is a piece of sharpened stone. He has long since discovered that rubbing stone on stone makes the sharpness more acute. He has, of course, the club, too. Probably the club was the first weapon, on which the sharp stone is a great refinement.

Some day, home from the chase, lolling on the pile of half-decomposed skins which is his only luxury, this man finds that there remains, painted on the backdrop of his consciousness, the picture of the animal whom he

PREHISTORIC DRAWING OF MAMMOTH

has just killed. The graceful, antlered head of a reindeer or the half roguish "old man" look of the hairy mammoth. Idly then, with the accustomed sharp stone cuddling in his hand, he turns to the wall of his cave, or to a bit of tusk at his feet and scratches something which is an astonishing piece of art.

To-day, hundreds of thousands of years away from those early men, our artists look with respectful attention at these figures.

Along with these pictures, made for sheer amusement, just as the child who can hardly talk will often draw quite cleverly on his slate, there were occasionally confused, meaningless lines, curves, dots, circles, awkward squares. Mere "graffiti," as science calls them, but the evidence of man's deepest mental instinct, the instinct to use the hand in *writing.*

These almost less than human men did not know what they were doing when they made these graffiti. They knew what they were doing when they made pictures. *That* was their conscious selves. That was almost an automatic thing, like their imitation of the sounds that animals made—their extraordinarily good imitations. The bushmen in Africa can mock the cries of the animals there as no white man can ever do, their mimicry not affected by the conscious effort. Prehistoric man drew pictures like that. As soon as he became the conscious and thinking man he lost the truth of the art and had to wait for untold æons to get it back again.

The graffiti was a different thing. It was the subconscious-self forcing the conscious-self to give it voice. It was the real writing instinct, although writing, itself, was to come long, long afterward and that as a conscious effort of the mind.

This same process can be seen in many of us to-day. Sit down at a telephone—wait for a cab—talk at a table—sit and muse—anywhere and at any time, let your aggressively conscious-self slip into the background and if your hand is within reach of a pencil and paper or any writing material whatever, your hand, so long civilized and trained, so delicate and fine, such a marvelously beautiful instrument, will repeat the action of the great, hairy paw which, untold centuries ago, must have reached out to the sharpened stone with exactly the same unconscious impulse.

These modern graffiti are to be found everywhere. Everybody makes them. It is a perfectly amazing fact that up to the present time neither any interpretation of them nor the fact of their relation to the ancient habit has ever been commented on.

Somewhere on the upward road of intelligence, somewhere along these many centuries that scientists now so casually mention, there came another man, who, from

CRO-MAGNON MAN

the place where fossil remains of him have been found, is called the Cro-Magnon man.

He had lost much of his jaw by that time, and his back had shortened and he really stood upright and that with ease, and his feet and hands had differentiated themselves. He probably still used caves for shelter, but now had long straight lances of hard wood, the points of which were sharpened and hardened in the fire; he wore the well-dressed skins of the beasts which he hunted, and his facial angle had come into the true human one. He still had big teeth and a big jaw and enormous shoulders and a good deal of hair, but for all of his small and too-bright eyes and beetling brow and snarling mouth, there was real intelligence in him and he was as far away from the Neanderthal man as we are from him.

The Cro-Magnon man had been drawing pictures for ages and was quite a dabster at it. He made life comfortable for himself and his family, had a stronger sense of the ties of the clan, no longer actively tried to kill the young males as soon as they were out of childhood, and was beginning to have some vague sense of matters in the universe outside of himself.

He probably, by that time, had named the Greater and the Lesser Lights, and the little-bits of lights which hung beside the Lesser in the dark; knew, roughly, the time consumed by the day and the night (although he could not count) and was now getting to be something of an epicure in his food, cooking it nearly always and having discovered the charms of shellfish as an article of diet.

Language was still rather a mouthy affair, and the vocabulary was scanty, but of ideas there had become a great number, many of them so important that it was to take many, many generations of men to work them out.

Suppose, now, that we relate for ourselves the story of the exact moment when the Great Idea—the Greatest Idea—of all the world, suddenly found expression. It is, of course, a purely hypothetical story, like all historical stories which are told, to show a time, a period, a certain place in the world's movement onward; but, making sure that we have all the setting correct—the setting that has been carefully painted for us, in detail, by the patient labors of generations of scientists and researchers in various fields—we will try to make this moment clear to ourselves. Let us call the story:

Beginning With Oog

His name was Oog. All the speech of his day was more or less in single syllables and with rather open and undetermined enunciation. He could really have spoken a little better if he had tried, but language was a heritage from forebears who had had not only a big-toothed and snarling mouth, but bigger teeth, and more protuberant, as well as more snarling mouths. He and his generation had perhaps added a sound or two to express things which the other generations had not thought of nor perceived.

In all the world of Mr. Oog there was not a road, not a habitation, not a manufactured article, not a piece of foot-covering, not a walled place, not a domestic animal, not a thing for the help of wounded men, or women in childbirth, not a vehicle, not a bridge, not so much as a hamlet—anywhere in all the round world, anywhere.

There was nothing to tell Mr. Oog that he and his fellows—housed in caves miles apart and always more or less at war with one another (except when they met in the strange times in spring when the young males and females mated)—were not the first men to be on the earth, except the dim memory of the oldest men that they, likewise, had had men and women about them, in their youth, who had gone in the Terrible Way, that way which left them lying motionless and which soon reduced them to things of horror. Where these old ones had fallen they had been left, those with them flying the place and never returning.

Mr. Oog, starting out for the day's business from the cave high up over the roaring water, where none might approach save at the risk of having stones rolled on his head, made a wide detour to avoid the place where one of his own Old Ones had taken the Terrible Way, the place where he had never looked since he had run from it long before, not knowing why there was a strange pain somewhere inside of him, nor understanding that he grieved for the death of his mother.

Although the steaming, moist, pestiferous earth reeked with miasma, and although danger and death lurked at every curve of the dim path that Mr. Oog's feet had beat out, he went jauntily on, not in the least troubled and knowing very well what he was about. No doubt, to him, there was the same sense of contempt-breeding-familiarity in the situation that there is in the modern pedestrian who frantically leaps from curb to curb among the deathly dangerous motors of a fashionable street, and thinks nothing of the fact that he has escaped damage or destruction by the breadth of an inch and the exercise of the utmost agility.

Like any man of the world, holding an assured position, Mr. Oog had definite affairs to which to attend and he knew exactly how to go about them. For one thing, he wished to purchase food for the crowd of lusty children at home and a bit of personal adornment for himself and a new fur coat for Mrs. Oog, she having that very morning declared that she felt the chill of autumn in the air and that she positively would not wear the old black bearskin another season.

The fact that Oog had to pit his life against the seller of these commodities did not trouble him in the least. It was all in the day's business. All of his shopping tours were delicately balanced on the point of life and death. Like a good family man, Mr. Oog was out to do his best for the folks at home.

As a substitute for streets he had the dim trail, rocky and difficult, and for shops of all descriptions, the dank woods on either side and the stark shapes which flitted there.

On this particular morning, Mr. Oog was in search of a saber-toothed tiger, whose body would provision the larder for several days, whose skin would give Mrs. Oog the coveted coat, and whose teeth and claws, tastily arranged on tough vine tendrils, would provide Oog himself with the sartorial effect popular that season.

He had promised to meet Mrs. Oog at a sort of trysting-place which they had, which was also the family clock. That is to say, just when the middle of the day occurred, the glory from the Greater Light slithered down through the great trees and touched the surface of a big, upstanding rock at the side of the trail. It was there that Mrs. Oog, herself a huntress of no mean ability and well able to take care of herself on that sinisterly crowded thoroughfare, was to meet her husband. He was to be there when the Light came.

Knowing Mrs. Oog, Ogg took pains not to go too far in his hunting, confidently expecting to find the desired animal and wanting to be punctual. However, within the time when the Light could be seen, through the mists, creeping higher, Mr. Ogg had totally failed to secure his purchases and in much dejection he got to the rock, a little in advance of his time, wondering what he should say to Mrs. Oog; and then, as he thus mused, what should he see, slowly slinking off down the trail, but the very thing he wanted—the saber-toothed tiger.

The tiger had eaten. His gait proclaimed it. He would go not far before he lay down to sleep. Oog could impale him with the spear without the least trouble—only, there is that matter of meeting Mrs. Oog.

What to do? We can vision him there, the Light almost upon him, scratching his matted head in perplexity. And then the great, the stupendous idea burst upon him. How great and how stupendous neither he nor men for long stretches of time were even dimly to perceive.

From the vine-tendril which belted his skin garment he plucked the sharp stone which was his accustomed companion and weapon, and also the instrument with which he had often drawn pictures on the wall of his cave to amuse himself no less than his children, pictures which had never meant anything.

The stupendous idea which burst dazzlingly on Mr. Oog was that he could make a picture which *would* mean something, which would convey a message. He had often amused himself by making conventionalized figures of men, those very selfsame "toothpick" men which our children instinctively draw as soon as they can hold a pencil, and of the saber-toothed tiger he knew every sinuous curve.

On the rock, therefore, Mr. Oog drew the tiger, repletion in his sagging belly and slouching walk, to the very life; and then he drew himself, spear poised, ready for the deed; and he added a sun which was declining, to show that he would be home by dinner-time.

The imagination staggers at the spectacle of Mrs. Oog, arriving at the rock, finding the picture and slowly

OOG AND THE TIGER

taking in its meaning—stunned, perhaps, by this new evidence of her husband's genius, after the fashion of all good wives, and reckoning little of the cosmic significance of it.

Whether other men at once discovered the new thing; whether men in various places made the same discovery at approximately the same time, as they have been making discoveries simultaneously through all the ages; whether the thing spread like wildfire and the intelligence of man suddenly hurdled great spaces and rose to new heights—we have, *as yet,* no means of knowing.

Between our hypothetical Mr. Oog and another man, generations away from him, who took the next great step, there is a void in our knowledge. But we know that both men existed.

As to the evidence of how he used the story idea, concocted by our Mr. Oog, we need go no farther than the North American Indians, who never got beyond that stage until the white man came to bridge the enormous chasm between their prehistoric stage of being, and modern life.

Indians were able to keep records with fair accuracy, so long as the original story had been told to somebody who would understand how to interpret the story symbol, and so long as the knowledge of that interpretation could be handed down from one generation to another.

Schoolcraft's *Archives of Aboriginal Knowledge* gives many instances of this picture-story method. One of the most famous was found, cut and drawn, on a large tree-trunk on the bank of the Muskingum River in 1780 and the copy of it is now used everywhere when Indian "writing" is discussed. It represents the successful foray of Wengenund, chief of the Delawares of the Muskingum against two of the white man's forts. The forts are easily identified. The ten lines under the sun represent two expeditions, as the break in their continuity shows. The figures on the left are men and women killed and captive. The oblique lines at the bottom of the drawing are the warriors engaged in the foray. The tortoise was the *totem* of Wenge-

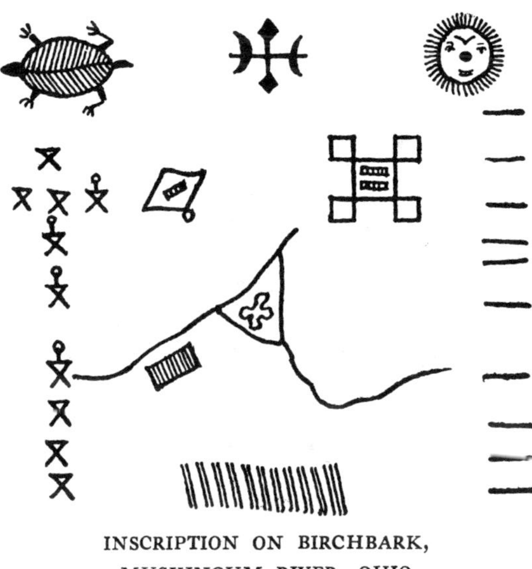

INSCRIPTION ON BIRCHBARK,
MUSKINGUM RIVER, OHIO

nund and the geometrical figure at the top was the family crest of the chief.

The drawings made by Bushmen are far less clear and logical than this, but they, also, represent the groping mind of man, seeking to convey a message. To see how far we must be, of necessity, from such gropings, let us look at a characteristic drawing of theirs. This is evidently the record of a feast, in which the animal provided the cause and in which children and presumably monkeys are seen at their sports, while a creature, somewhat caricatured, either addresses or blesses or adjures a woman and two men. When we remember that the crude marriages of this lowest race of humanity have some rites in which a headman, wearing a mask, participates, and if we vision the children as

DRAWING BY BUSHMEN

dancing about in the immemorable style of childhood and playful monkeys swinging from the trees of the arboreal wedding-room, we shall see that in this seemingly meaningless picture we have the marriage certificate of some dusky belle!

The drawing on the submerged rock in the river near Taunton, Massachusetts, approaches more nearly the mere scribbling which is called graffiti. It is likely that it was made by various persons, at different times, who, idly leaning against the rock, which was then on a trail and not along the steep banks of a river, cut into the stone, occasionally with some vague idea of telling something, but something which could not afterward even be guessed at. The drawing was far more readily seen in 1680, when Dr. Danforth made the first copy of it. Dr. Baylies and Mr. Goodwin, in 1790, made a copy of the drawing, which has been used for reproduction ever since, as it was made with the utmost fidelity. The rock is now in the bed of the

DRAWING ON ROCK NEAR TAUNTON, MASS.

river and is only partly uncovered at low-tide. In another fifty years it will be practically lost. Its age is very great, long antedating any history that the Indians had of it when the white man first came.

These instances show that next great step after the mere telling of a story, and how it came about, for—*after a time man realized that he was now fitted with a number of standard figures which meant a number of different things.*

Hence, the story did not need to be pictured in detail. The "toothpick" men were used for untold generations, for one thing. (We have seen that this conventionalized figure lives, to-day, in our own alphabet!) Two of them running, with twenty straight marks beside them, meant "Twenty men had to run away." Two of them fighting with ten straight marks beside them meant "Ten men fought."

As in Wengenund's drawing, the sun, coupled with numerical marks, would mean that many days; the

EARLY IDEOGRAPHS

same sign, with the full moon over it, meaning that many nights of the full moon. The quarter and half moon and the full moon could be used roughly to map out the months, of the passage of which man soon came to have a misty perception, aided by the changing face of the heavens at night.

The progression of the stars in their orbits early drew the awed attention of man, but he was not too awed to see that he could count time by it. One of the most interesting records of very ancient times is found in Yucatan, where the progress of the evening star, Venus, is accurately recorded on a large stone, for a period of *five years.*

Fire, a faithful representation of the flames being the picture, and the sign of water which we still use in the waved lines that we draw on maps to show its presence; mountains, rain, rivers, trees, the club, the sling, animals—all became standardized. Many of our figures of speech hark back to this period, far, far behind anything that we can even faintly know of history. Thus, our "brave as a lion" grows out of the fear with which the roar of the lion affected prehistoric man, whose psychology was exactly that of the primitive peoples that we have to-day: *i.e.,* the more noise you make, the more dangerous you are and the least afraid.

As Light was the first thing that prehistoric man worshiped, and as the great Arch above him awed him, even as it does us, the very first conception that dragged him on to make more than a story or standardize a story, was the deification of the sun and the horizon, the latter represented by a half-circle.

"Heaven," with its many meanings, is undoubtedly the oldest concept in the world of something which transcends material things. Long before there was the slightest approach to the projection of ideas, without reference to objects, in writing, the idea of the sun and the horizon as prototypes of some great Source was pregnant in the soul of man.

Ancient Chinese signs meaning "The Source of All Life" depict the sun with mysterious drops falling from it upon man.

With this clue, the student can see how the extraordinary religious system of the ancient Egyptians and of many other religions grew out of this great concept. It is also a good illustration of the slow movement of man, when it comes to using ideas, for no one can even venture, as yet, at computing the stretches of time which must have intervened between the first conception of "Heaven" as the Arch and also as the prototype of God's throne.

While the standardization of these very primitive figures was going on the standard of living was steadily changing. The use of wild fruits and edible grasses and roots improved the health and began to prolong the life of man. He learned to fish, and to paddle a log on the water and about that time found that the club which was weightier at one end than at the other could be used as a weapon of deadly accuracy. He learned to throw the wooden lance, too; and women started to make rough pots, so that meat was no longer always broiled over the fire or roasted, wrapped in leaves, in the ashes, but could be boiled. This matter of pottery did two things which made an immense difference in the history of man. It started the two arts of cooking and of sculpture.

Now came the very first movement toward real civilization in actual truth. Like all of such movements, it started in a strictly utilitarian idea.

Man had continued to get his steaks and chops by pitting his life against the animals from which he rived them. Now, however, he was less inclined to eat the carnivorous beasts, and many of the more ferocious of them, along with the saber-toothed tiger, were extinct. With the passing of the great number of carnivora, grazing, herbaceous beasts had multiplied, so that vast herds of the antecedents of our own cattle and deer roamed the plains, which bloomed with healthy grass, now that the early mists of the primitive world had rolled away.

Now, then, there came about something, the importance of which it would not be possible to exaggerate. Some way or other, a man or a woman had the thought to catch some young of the herds, to pen them up, to tame them and to keep their progeny.

Possibly it was the woman, pitying some bleating little calf, deprived of its mother by the throwing-stick of her man. Whatever was the process, the acquisition of flocks and herds, of cattle and goats, which were domesticated, meant an enormous change in the life of man. He was no longer the hunter, obliged to risk life and limb every day. Leaning comfortably on the stockade he could get beef or goat-meat or venison. Not having to drag the carcass the long distance to his home, better use could be made of it. The hides began to be beautifully worked by the women, with salt and water and hand labor, until they were as white and pliable as cloth. The horns became drinking vessels and the first beginnings of brass bands! The sticky substance in the hoofs made the first glue, the tails became adornments and the whitened skulls served for soup-plates.

A tremendous change was effected, too, by the use of the milk of the females of these herds and by the ultimate discovery of butter, the first refinement of animal grease that the world became acquainted with, and an exceedingly valuable food.

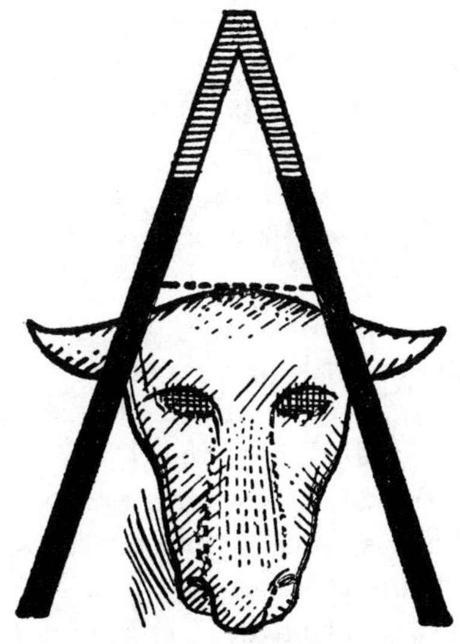

ORIGIN OF THE LETTER A

Infant mortality, which must have been great before anything but human milk was available, was lessened and women were less dependent on the hunter for food, and in households deserted of the male or deprived of him by death, where the woman had little children to care for, there was the possibility that they might all survive. Thus, the herd became also the first form of insurance.

Man, in short, had ceased to be the hunter, on the level of the beasts. He was rich. Like all of us, he liked the sensation of riches and was vain of it. He sought a symbol by which he might mark himself as a person of possessions.

What could be more appropriate than the outline of the head of his possessions? Therefore, this one symbol of the ox's head came into use so long ago and was so early standardized that there is, as yet, no written character made by man in which that form is not found, *already standardized.*

It is the first or very important sign in all the picturized writing that we have ever found. It was just as standardized in Babylonian writing, when Nebuchadnezzar reigned, and when his forebears of a thousand years before that, reigned, as it is to-day! It was *alpu* in the Babylonian writing, *aleph* in the Phœnician, *alpha* in the Greek and is *a* in every Occidental language under the sun.

It is really the first dollar-mark.

In all languages, where it has a *name,* as against the mere sound, that name means "the ox."

The degree to which it had already been standardized in prehistoric Babylonian times may be seen by the illustration in which this sign, with that for "man" and "king," "forest" and "orchard" are shown. The forest is marked by the wide heavens above it, the orchard by the wall, and the king is a man with a crown on his head, but *alpu* has already lost the features of the animal and needs only a little shifting to become the letter that we know so well.

The process by which man developed one phase of

his existence is easily seen in the second letter of all Occidental alphabets, which is *B*. This epitomizes the next great step that man took after that of becoming a herdsman, and its standardization, like that of *alpu,* far antedates any slightest suggestion of actual writing by man.

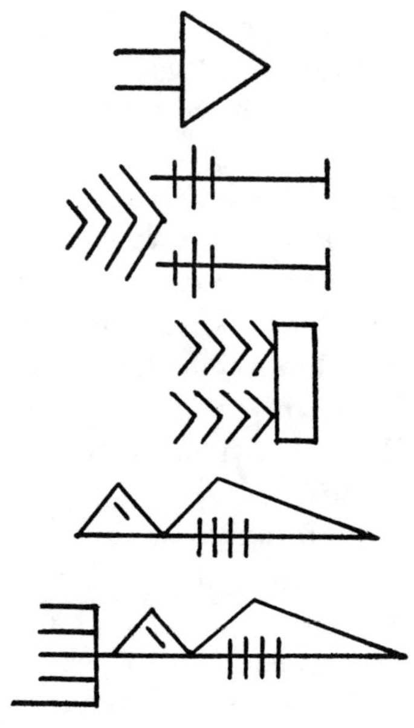

BABYLONIAN. OX, FOREST, ORCHARD, MAN, KING

The letter *B* in Hebrew means "house" and this is also its meaning elsewhere, and in its form it is the actual picture of the first dwelling which man made for himself, and which was the beginning of all architecture.

The story of what happened to change man from his

cave to a habitation of his own is authenticated, because we have seen the same thing happen with the Bushmen and with American Indians, and many times in the herdsmen tribes of Asia and Mongolia. The change from the cave to another mode of living was inevitable as soon as the herds of man began to grow large. It was not possible to find grazing ground in one section for the animals; therefore there had to be some arrangement for living *en route* to various pasturages. The actual thing in process of development can be seen, now, among the savages of the Patagonian highlands, by far the lowest in development of any humans now on earth. They have the skins of the animals they kill, which they roughly tie on, back or front, according to which way the wind is blowing! And when it blows too hard, in that windy and cold part of the world, they bend some bushes together at the top, tie them with vine tendrils, and lash these skin garments of theirs over them, squatting beneath the rude shelter until the storm is over, when the skins again become garments.

Something like this happened, as man straggled out with his already domesticated herds, seeking for grass. So he found that he could cut down small saplings, and with them make the supporting framework over which skins could be tightly pulled, and thus have a perfectly weatherproof dwelling which could be moved about at a moment's notice and yet give all the comfort of the ancestral cave.

The tepee of the Plain Indians, to this day, is precisely that form of tent, and it is worth noting that such a structure, when the support is deeply sunk in the ground, will resist a wind-storm which will easily demolish well-built houses. The tents of the Bedouin, which have not changed form since time immemorable, are also constructed on this principle.

With the Indian, the Bedouin, and the pure-bred Romany, there have always been two tents, side by side. The one for the man and his mate and the other for the children and frequently, as in the case of the Bedouins, for the young pet animals.

All you have to do to see the picture of those two tents, is to *lay B down to the left.*

Three other letters in our alphabet are also relics of the very earliest awakenings of man's mind.

CHINESE AND EGYPTIAN ORIGIN OF "MAN"

The capital *I*—the personal pronoun—is but the conventionalized figure of a man.

Observe, in the illustration, that in both archaic Egyptian and Chinese the drawing of the man has progressed little from the original "toothpick" man. Then observe what some fifty thousand years or so did to those drawings. To prove that this is not accident, but has proceeded through all letter forms we have ample evidence, even when the letter forms are far indeed from the original, as in the drawing of the vase

CHINESE AND EGYPTIAN ORIGIN OF "VASE"

in archaic Egyptian and Chinese and the corresponding forms into which they were eventually twisted.

The capital letter *I* in Latin form and the capital *I*

ORIGIN OF I

as written to-day are mere extensions of this ancient formation.

The letter *L*—"lem" and "lamdos" and all sorts of names beginning with the letter—has a most curious history. It, too, antedates history and its origin is in the recumbent figure of the lion, by far the most outstanding one in the world, found everywhere, and the source of endless art forms, as the traditional dragon of China, the sphinx, and so on.

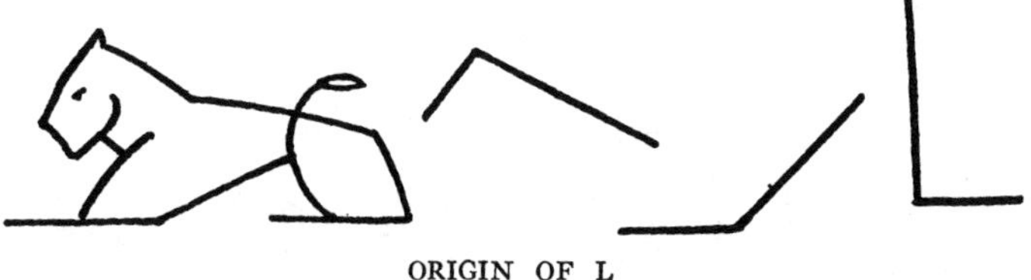

ORIGIN OF L

Now, the name of the lion in all languages has begun with the *sound* which we mark as *l* and which has always had some such sound. In ancient Egyptian the name of the lion was *labo* and to this day all the African tribes use some variation on this name.

When the next great step in writing took place, the lion's figure was chosen to represent the position in the chart of sounds which began with this sound of *l*. In the course of time, due to the processes which have always gone on in making the forms of letters, the figure of the lion was cut down and pieces of him were the pictorial symbol, or, rather, angles of him.

Observe that several angles of the figure will make an L, *in some position or other.*

ORIGIN OF S

The letter S *is the ancient figure of "water."*

Now let us see what happened when some of these

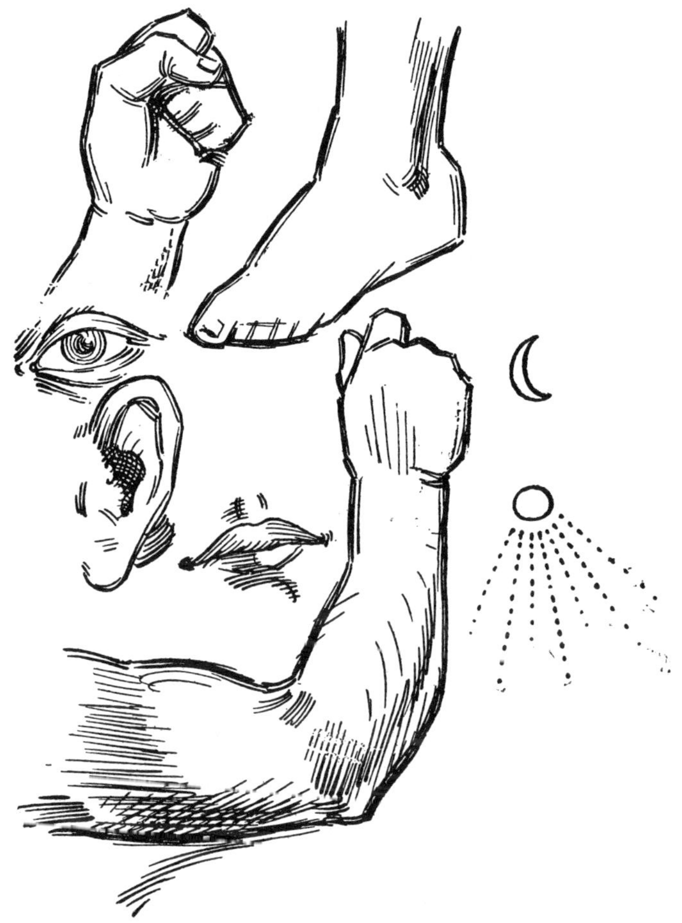

FIGURES FOR GENERAL IDEAS

standardized figures had come into such use that more or less general ideas could be read from them. We find a closed fist meaning domination; an arm meaning power; a foot meaning fleetness and "to go"; an eye meaning sight and the general idea of "seeing" in the sense of "perception"; the mouth meaning speech; the ear hearing and also "understanding"—and so on. Thus, if we have the figure of a woman, with some of the signs meaning that she is a mother, and with a mouth, an eye and an ear added, we may read it, roughly, "a mature woman, the mother of children, who sees and understands many things."

CHINESE
WORD "WOMAN"

In the Chinese characters we may see this process in actuality. Take the character for "woman." The first part of the sign, that to the reader's left, is the figure of a woman, or, as now used, the sign for "female." The figure at the top of the rightward part of the character is that of a broom and the figure beneath that represents a storm. Who says that the Chinese have no sense of humor? All of Chinese is similar. There is no character for a sound, as with us, the language and the characters having none of the interrelation to which we are so accustomed. Thus their "man" is still the representation of his two legs. Their characters for "fish," "boat," "heart," "tear," are actual pictures. "Peace" is shown by a woman under a roof. "Home" by a pig under a roof. "To marry a husband" by a woman and a pig under a roof! And the idea of "closed" is conveyed by a gate.

These pictures are still so recognizable that they are very amusing, but it is needless to say that to read and write Chinese is one of the most colossal feats of memorizing, since there are thousands of these signs, and even when they are all known—and remembered—reading is largely a matter of deduction, just as it was so long ago when man had gotten only to the period when he had these conventionalized and more or less

CHINESE
WORD "GATE"

standardized characters by which to send his message.

The Babylonians, Sumarians and other ancient peoples had in no sense a true alphabet, but they had progressed so far that they could spell out proper names, for instance, in much the way that we would with a rebus. Thus, a picture of a jar, an ax, a leaf and a hand might make the name of a king, by putting the names of those objects together, in the way which is familiar to every one who has ever tried the pastime of deciphering the rebus.

By the time that we come to the full flower and glory of the Egyptian civilization—and the reader must remember that the very oldest monuments of the valley of the Nile, whose age is so great that archeologists hesitate to give their conclusions, show this flower of civilization as not only blooming but already silvered with hoary age—we shall see that while the Egyptians kept their pictures, they had started on the track of the true alphabet.

The outgrowth of this was, like all other upward steps taken by man, an outgrowth of other steps. The Egyptian genius took the rebus form of writing, which had come, already, through at least fifty thousand years of development, and used the idea differently.

Instead of making the full names of objects spell out the name of one object, they made the names of certain objects stand for the sounds of which their language was already composed. A single instance will show this.

The name of "heaven" in Egyptian was *pet* and the sign for it was various forms of the sun-and-horizon figure, which started away back, somewhere, the same sign having served the men who used this as their first standardization.

This word *pet,* besides being a word of itself, was also parts of other words, which is a state of things true of every language. The Egyptians, therefore, when that syllable which was also a word and which, as a pictorial sign, was part of another word, *would write the picture.*

Look at the drawing of the Egyptian "alphabet" and you will see how this worked out. The two *a's* in this list represent our broad and short forms of the letter. The ox-head had, by the time that the Egyptian started on their system, been superseded by the eagle.

This alphabet, to be sure, was greatly complicated by the fact that the Egyptian scribe, wishing to make the meaning of the text clear, added various kinds of

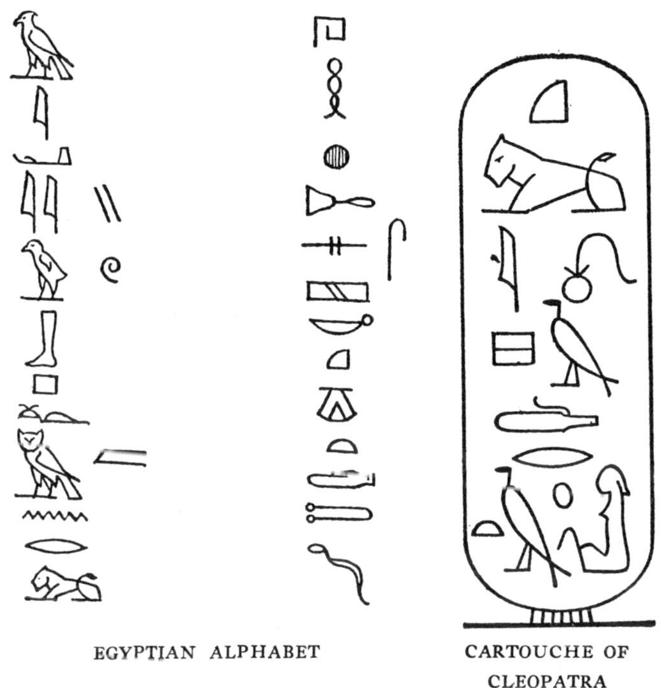

EGYPTIAN ALPHABET

CARTOUCHE OF CLEOPATRA

pictures, to help in this. The cartouche of Cleopatra will show this very clearly.

The quadrant is *K;* the lion is *L;* the reed is *I,* which we write *E;* the cord with the knot on the end of it is *O;* the shutter is *P;* the eagle is *A;* the hand is *T;* the mouth is *R;* and the eagle, again, is *A.* The eggs show that the name is a feminine one and the figure shows that it is a royal and hence divine person whose name is herein written.

In the great pyramid there are a couple of very interesting bits of writing, both of them the name of the king who put up the edifice. They were made, not by intent of the architect, or through the work of some artist, but by an inspector of the quarrymen, who, brush in hand, and perhaps discussing some detail of the work, or checking up on his records during an idle noon-hour, turned to the rock beside him and wrote the king's name. He wrote easily and gracefully and assuredly. We may be positive that writing such as that was not only common to the man, but had been common to man for untold generations, for the ease with which we perform this most delicate of operations speaks of our ancestry as well as of ourselves.

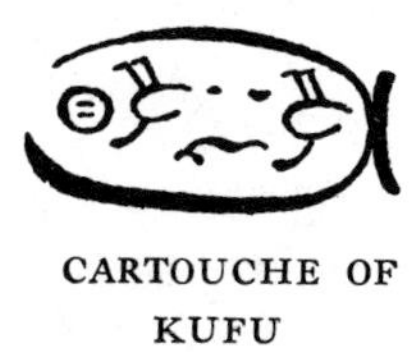

CARTOUCHE OF KUFU

In this cartouche (as the names of royalties were called, because they were always enclosed in an oval ring) and, as usual in Oriental writing, reading from right to left, we find the odd sign which had already lost its pictorial form, and which stood for *K*—note that in Cleopatra's time this sign had changed, written, as it was, four thousand years after this one—then there is the chicken, which stands for *U,* and a snail which stands for *F,* and again the chicken for *U*—

thus spelling *Kufu,* which the interesting but always inaccurate Herodotus was to hand down to us, later, as *Cheops.*

The Egyptians never got past this point. There they stuck. But even with this incomplete idea they contrived to produce some of the finest literature ever written.

Let us now turn backward and see what the valley of the Euphrates has to tell us of the matter of writing. This valley, the Mesopotamia of classic times as well as of our own, stretches from the Caucasus Mountains to the sea and lies between the Euphrates and the Tigris, which is what its name means—"the valley between the rivers." The two cities of Mosul and Bagdad cannot be traced as to their birth, so ancient are they. At the date 4500 B.C., civilization was roaring through them and through the valley, a civilization which had poured down from the slopes of the Caucasus Mountains, where it is likely that a warm climate had prevailed even during the glacial period which covered Europe with ice and for a long period wiped man off the face of it. During that time protected tribes, faring better, would have a chance to get that start of the world which the Caucasian has, more or less, kept ever since.

However, before the Caucasians came down from their mountain home, the plain had been overrun with Mongolians and they, leaving us the record on terra-cotta tablets and on stone, state that they drove out "the dark-skinned" peoples whom they found there; "they and theirs and destroyed their cities." This is a lost trail, so far. We do not know who those dark people were, but we have the evidence that they were already city builders, which takes them about fifty thousand years, anyway, away from even the patriarchial herdsman's condition of civilization.

One branch of this Mongolian family settled in the northern part of the valley, in the "Akkad" or mountains, from which they took their names Akkadians. Another branch settled in the southern part of the valley, in the river valley, which was "Sumer" in their language. This gives us, included in this settlement of the valley, the famous Chaldeans, known to this day for their discoveries in astronomy and for their extraordinary philosophical and spiritual researches. Far to the north of the great stretch of country lay the Semites, of whom, at this period, we know almost nothing, save that they were in existence. There was one great Semitic figure which one day, far in advance of the time of which we are treating, was to emigrate from the country of the Chaldees, from that "Ur" which has so recently been found and in which excavations are now going forward, and become the "Moses" of the Bible.

Among these peoples the rebus form of writing prevailed, based, as has been stated before, on the familiar game which our children play, of making up the name of one object from the pictures of several others.

That this was so has been shown by the researches of the Archeological Department of the University of Pennsylvania, which, by excavations in the ancient cities of the Mesopotamian plain, have shown that the Akkadians and the Sumerians used pictures, the names of which spelled out their words. Their writing materials were bricks, made of the mud of the valley, and their instrument was a cut reed, which, being wedge-shaped, made the drawn forms angular and more conventionalized at the start than the early forms of other races who did not use this stiff arrangement of reed and wet mud.

When the bricks were fully written on they were baked, either in ovens or in the sun and were then ready to be used as records or stored away, to be read, as books.

In time the writing-instrument, which had to be freshly cut every little while, tried the patience of people who were coming, more and more, to depend on writing, and so they made the reed in wood or perhaps in copper. Now the pictures became more and more standardized and before long they had lost much of the pictorial quality, so strong in the very early Babylonian forms.

When the Semites and the Caucasians finally arrived in the valley they took possession, driving out many of the Sumerians and Akkadians, but these two blood cousins had, in the usual way of humanity, been scrapping with each other steadily ever since the settlement of the valley, so many of them accepted the rule of the more aggressive Semites, who had also a greater talent for political organization; and the Caucasians leaned more to the Semites than to the Mongolians.

The first great Semite king was Sargon I, about the fourth millennium, B.C., and it is in his reign that the picture writing of the valley at last got itself set into the highly conventionalized and very beautiful cuneiform writing which was used right up to the time of the destruction of Babylon by Darius the Great in 666. B.C.

The Persians and the Medes had already partaken of the culture of the valley and were cuneiform users.

They now simplified the writing of the valley, greatly eliminating many of its more archaic forms and cutting off "its cumbersome homophones, polyphones, ideographs and determinatives," as Rawlinson, the great authority on cuneiform writing, tells us. They now had twenty consonants, to which they added four vowel sounds and a number of syllable formations, with several others which were really ideographs and thus had a thing which was much nearer a real alphabet than anything that Egypt had even achieved.

They also wrote from left to right, which has continued to be the tendency of all Aryan nations, as against the Oriental tendency to write from right to left.

It is amazing to reflect that all this was lost to the world for thousands of years and that scarcely more than a hundred years ago there was not a person who could read the great array of cuneiform writings which were not only to be dug up by any traveler on the sites of Babylon and Nineveh, but which were to be seen everywhere in museums. The story of how this lost writing has been restored to us is one to thrill the imagination, and also to cause us to wonder at the fact that it is three "inscribed stones" to which we owe almost our entire knowledge of ancient writing.

On the great rock façade of Behistun, a mighty cliff rearing its gigantic head over sixteen hundred feet above the plain, there had for two thousand years been an awesome sight—immense figures sculptured in the solid and gloomy rock, surrounded by mysterious wedge-shaped characters. This rock had been feared, worshiped, speculated on, but no one had ever had even a remote idea of what it really was until in 1802 a German scientist, Dr. Georg Fridrich Grotefend, after long contemplation of the rock, believed that the name of Darius was to be found in some of the characters which were incessantly repeated.

Nothing more was done, though, until in 1851. Sir Henry Rawlinson, who had started to work on the basis of Dr. Grotefend's findings, and who had given many years to the matter of research, finally wrested from the haughty rock its historic secret. No single scholar, before or since, has equaled this feat, for there was nothing to go on, not a shred with which to start. Thousands of these inscriptions have been deciphered since that time, and to-day the *savant* can read cuneiform writing almost as easily as he does any language other than his own, to which he has to give a little special attention because of difference in idioms.

The inscription on the Rock of Behistun is a piece of the silliest self-praise that a poor mortal ever wrote and set up for the world to laugh at, but it has served a purpose, a purpose so superb that the primitive mind of the man who caused it to be put there, by the terrible labor of slaves, could not even have imagined that purpose. It is a laudation of King Darius and begins with the usual sickening phrase of antique royalty:

FROM THE ROCK OF BEHISTUN

"I am Darius the great King, the King of Kings, the King of Persia, the King of the provinces. . . . From antiquity we are descended; from antiquity has our race been Kings." And so on and on. The import of the Rock is less than nothing, in itself, but it was the key that opened a whole section of the ancient world to us.

The old sculptors and artisans who did the job, however, knew their business. *Their* work is beautiful. The unfortunate captives, the arrogant king, the nine princes with chains around their necks, and the wonderful, precise characters of the cuneiform writing, may well excite our deepest admiration for these artisans of so long ago.

Those who remember their Bible well are familiar with the names of many nations which are to the rest of the world totally unknown. The Hittites and the Amorites—who that has read the graphic accounts of their wars, reconciliations, forays, sieges and bouts with the Hebrews, can ever forget them?

These nations, which so ringed around and harassed the land of Palestine, in ancient times, were users of cuneiform writing not only undecipherable, but utterly lost, because the very towns and tablets and pottery which, with other ancient races, gave us evidence of their existence, had been so destroyed and buried by the fanatical Moslems that little of that writing had ever been found, until the time that the scholar, Burkardt, in 1812, discovered a very unusual stone imbedded in the wall of one of the native houses at Hamah, in Syria—the ancient "Hammath" of the Bible—and soon found five more in other walls. These were identified as records of the great kingdom of the Hittites; and there are now many more discoveries, far too numerous to mention here, which bring out the richness and power of this old kingdom and—what is more pertinent to our present interest—establish a new link with the alphabet.

This cuneiform writing of the Hittites was the connecting-link between the Hebrew and the Phœnician alphabets.

At last, after going through the records of hundreds of thousands of years, we are approaching a place in history where our interest must quicken, for we are coming to the beginnings of the very characters wherewith these statements are written.

These Hittites, with their cultural but less powerful sister nation, the Amorites, were spread all to the north and east of what afterward would be known as the land of the Phœnicians. That they were an exceedingly ancient people, and that they were enormously powerful, is evidenced repeatedly throughout the records of the ancient world. To-day, on the walls of the great temple of Karnak, at Luxor, in Egypt, we may read, as sharply incised as the day that it was put there, thirty-seven centuries ago, the treaty of peace between Rameses II and Kheta-Sira, the Hittite king. The inscription is a faithful copy of the original treaty, which, carved on a silver tablet, was taken to Egypt by the emissaries of the Hittite king. The inscription in Karnak specifically states this.

By the time that the Phœnicians, keen adapters of all the arts of other nations, clever craftsmen, good imitators, fine traders and good scholars, came on the scene, the Hittites had gone far into making an alphabet of their own. And they were not the only ones. Far and wide, over the earth, the nations were simplifying their writing and searching for the true idea of an alphabet, a thing which, up to that time, had not existed.

What is an alphabet?

It is the giving of concrete and simple and standard symbols to every sound which is in a language.

The number of these symbols has varied, as the sounds of different languages have varied. The Russian alphabet, for instance, contains thirty-six, nineteen of them being direct heirs of Phœnicia, and of Greece and Rome, as our own are, and others coming from the roundabout Croatian source, which was the heritage of the cuneiform in ancient times, and several invented in modern times. It is said that the old alphabet of forty-eight symbols really covered the case better. Any one who has listened to Russian, spoken by an excitable crowd with different dialects of the language, can well believe that even forty-eight would be scanty, as a vehicle for the strange vocables.

The Phœnicians were essentially men of the sea and traveled far. Theirs was the first merchant marine of history and it was a good one. They mined minerals in Cornwall, on the Cornish coast, had settlements and sold their wares in Egypt, knew the "far Isles" which were afterward to be Greece and Rome. They had but two important cities, Tyre and Sidon, but out of those cities went a good third of all the fine manufactured articles in the then world of culture. They were famous for their crafts. The Bible has repeated assurance for us of the position which the Phœnicians held in this respect. Solomon contracted, we are told, with Hiram, the King of Tyre, for expert works and advice in the putting up of the temple in Jerusalem, and in Chronicles II, ii, 14 we have a very specific statement:

". . . his father was a man of Tyre, skilful to work in gold, and in silver, in brass, in iron, in stone, and in timber, in purple, in blue, and in fine linen, and in crimson; also to grave any manner of graving, and to find out every device which shall be put to him . . ."

As a recommendation, no workman ever had anything better than that!

By the time that we really get to know of the Phœnicians they were all of this, and were also traders, miners and merchants of superb quality. We should not,

LAST LINE OF MOABITE STONE

however, think of them as merely practical people. They were essentially linguists and scholars, translators and students of history; knowing geography as no other race did and having the political cleverness to stay out of a great many racial broils of the time.

Like the Rock of Behistun and the Rosetta Stone,

the "Moabite Stone" which was found near the Dead Sea, in 1868, by an unscientific missionary, was the key which opened great historical doors.

The Arabs, true to form, tried to break it up as soon as they thought that it was of value to any save themselves, but "squeezes" had been taken of the stone when first found and this allowed the broken parts of it to be reconstructed, when it was at last rescued.

It was near Dibon, the ancient Moabite capital, that it was found, and for this reason it is called the Moabite Stone. It is at least two thousand and seven hundred years old and records the triumph of the Phœnician king Mesha over Jehoram of Judea, who reigned from 896 to 884 B.C. In the illustration is reproduced the last line of this long inscription, which is produced from the reconstruction of the old stone, by Mark Lidzbarski.

Here, then, we begin to recognize forms that are not wholly alien to our eyes. The old picture forms are all gone. Here is *the alphabet.*

The first letter on the reader's right is a *t,* the next is *sh,* then *q,* then *I,* then *f,* then *a* and the next *n.*

In looking carefully at these letters we have to remember that they were written from right to left and that this reverses some of their forms. In this stone, carved almost three thousand years ago, the words are separated by small dots. Sentence arrangement, margins and paragraphing had not yet been thought of —were not to be thought of, for thousands of years to come.

Here are the forms which have come up through all the ages since primitive man first started out with that standardized head of the ox, and with the other standardized picture forms which were slowly to lose their detail and become abstract figures; here is the concentrated essence of the efforts of tens of thousands of men, painfully trying to make the little black symbols tell the story of their thoughts and feelings. Here, at last, is entire absence of the picture and the presence of the pure symbol.

This was in the ninth century B.C., and with that period real education and real culture began.

However, to have such a perfect alphabet it was inevitable that it should have had a long previous history, such, for instance, as the English language has had, slowly coming together out of its various elements and not even a concrete thing until Chaucer's time.

But the Phœnicians did not have a monopoly of the alphabet. Their neighbors all around them had portions of the same idea. The Hebrews borrowed of them so liberally that the Hebrew alphabet, like our own, bears traces of the borrowings.

During that period of Hebrew history known as the Captivity, a form of the Phœnician alphabet was used by the Hebrews which was called the Aramean. This crept into use in Babylon and was used extensively in Aram and Syria and the Jews in Palestine used it until the second century B.C., when something of the square form of Hebrew began, the form which has ever since been used, but in which the old Phœnician forms can be detected, even as they can be detected in the letters of which this book is made.

The Aramean alphabet is the foundation on which the curious "shorthand," which is Arabic, is founded.

The letter forms of Arabic are the most inconclusive and unformed of any which came out of the great sources of Phœnician culture, and the forms have been so denuded that the analogy is hard to trace—nevertheless, we know that it exists.

The Phœnician letter forms, it is worth noting, are the foundations for Arabic and all its tributaries, and for Hebrew and all its near and far relations, and for Greek and Latin, and all their near and far relations. A noble family tree, indeed; and what a tiny parent stem!

The first four letters of the alphabet are marked by names which are practically the same, in many diverse languages. The Syriac are *olaf, beth, gomal, dolath.* The Arabic are *alif, be, jim, dal.* The Slavonic are *az, buki, glagol, doboro.* The Indian are *alf, bet, gemel, dent.* And the Greek, of course, are *alpha, beta, gamma, delta.*

The Phœnicians were a race of full development when the Greeks were question-marks in the history of the world—wandering tribes whose culture was not sufficient really to leave a trace.

But if we look to the island of Crete we shall find that there was a civilization and a culture which was very wonderful, and a system of writing which, while it was of the rebus variety, had very definite meanings, although its forms were strictly those of the picture. The illustration, which is of an engraved seal, is of an antiquity which makes it impossible for us to read the meaning, and yet meaning there was. When we *do* get to the period when we can make an effort at approximating the meaning of the Cretan pictographs we find all the paraphernalia of civilized life in full swing: soldiers, marriage, temples, taxes, kings and courts, laws of inheritance, representatives of the people at court, jewelry, good cooking, specialized orchards, butchers, wine and beer and bread—it is not recently matured culture which we are brought to see, but something taking tens of thousands of years to

VERY ANCIENT CRETAN SEAL

develop—and all this was long before "the glory that was Greece."

Writing, in Crete, was certainly practised long before it was even thought of in Greece. Minos, king of Crete, was the first law-giver of Greece. Arthur J. Evans, to whom the world owes so much of its knowledge of ancient civilizations, discovered in the ruins of the palace of Knossos, Crete, a large number of inscriptions which have to do with this king and which show him a great philosopher and law-giver.

The peak of civilization in Crete lasted for over twelve hundred years and it is no doubt from Crete that Greece got her culture. She did not get her alphabet from there, for Crete did not have one. She got it from her neighbor, the Phœnician nation. Nevertheless, along with the pictographs of Crete there were the beginnings of alphabetical forms. The illustration shows linear script found by Evans in the island and does, as the finder says, "present a European aspect." These were conventionalized forms, the remnants, as it were, of such picture forms as the head of the ox which ultimately became *alpu* of the Babylonians.

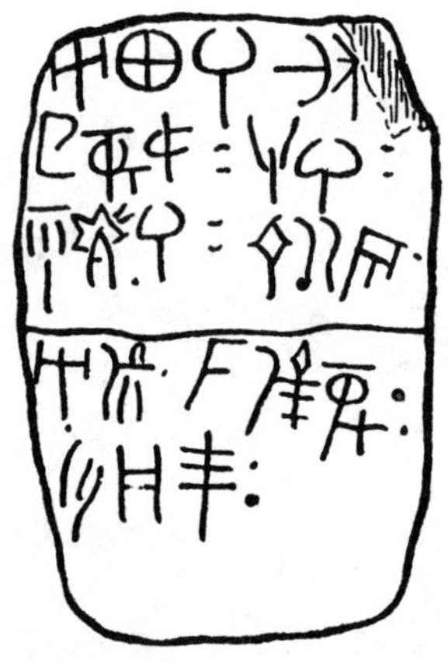

CRETAN, ABOUT 1800 B.C.

Professor Flinders Petrie, the great Egyptologist and one of the first scientists to reveal the sources of the alphabet to us, has this to say of the origin of all the various semi-alphabetic systems found in Crete, in Cyprus and in all the countries abutting on the Mediterranean:

"A Great Signary (not hieroglyphic, but geometric, in appearance if not in origin) was in use all over the Mediterranean 5000 B.C. It is even found in Egypt at that period and was split in two, Western and Eastern, by the cross flux of hieroglyphic systems in Egypt and among the Hittites . . . it developed variously but retained much in common in different countries. It was first systematized by the numerical values assigned to it by Phœnician traders who carried it into Greece, whereby the Greece Signary was delimited to an alphabet. . . . That the signs were used for written communications of spelled-out words in the early stages, or as a real alphabet, is far from probable. It was a body of signs with more or less generally understood meanings; and the change of attributing a single letter value to each, and only using signs for sounds, to build into words, is apparently a relatively late outcome of the systematizing due to Phœnicians."

Professor William N. Bates, of the University of Pennsylvania, in a lecture on "The Origin of the Greek Alphabet" says: "So much, I think, we may regard as sure: that the Greek alphabet originated in Crete. Furthermore, in the light of our present knowledge, it seems likely, though it is not yet proved, that the Phœnicians simplified the characters which they got from Crete and made the alphabet better known."

Since the time that Petrie made his researches, we have learned a great deal more about the Hittites and all the nations which were the forebears and contemporaries of the Phœnicians and the consensus of opinion now is that the full tide of writing—rising from the oldest Babylonian and the oldest Egyptian, through all the many streams that we have so lightly sketched, at last found the right receptacle in the Phœnician genius.

So—now we may return to the quotation with which this section of this book began and say:

The Phœnicians did not invent the alphabet, which had been coming into being since man first standardized the head of an ox, his first possession; but they did a great deal to make it thoroughly practical and to make it known.

And—civilization did not begin on the banks of the Nile or on the banks of the Euphrates or on the banks of the Ganges or on the banks of the Yang-tze, but on them all. And not "five thousand years before Christ," but perhaps a hundred thousand years before—which is a conservative estimate.

With the Greeks and their alphabet, we are in modern times. Not only in regard to the alphabet itself, but in regard to the politics, the marriage conditions, the drama, literature, the arts and architecture.

The Greeks, themselves, called their alphabet "Phœnician letters," thus acknowledging their debt to their little neighbor. We get the idea, so prevalent in literature even to-day, that "Cadmus invented the alphabet," from one of the casual and general statements of our genial friend, Herodotus. "Cadmus, the Trojan, and the followers whom he brought into the country from Phœnicia," says Herodotus, were the ones who "invented" the alphabet. In this, as usual, Herodotus was more interested in saying something startling than he was in being accurate. He would have made a wonderful writer for the modern press, would Herodotus!

Up to about 500 B.C. all the Hellenic states had alphabets of their own, but in the year 403 the Ionic alphabet was adopted at Athens and later was taken up by all of Greece. This is known as classic Greek

PHŒNICIAN AND GREEK ALPHABETS

and some of the finest inscriptions of classic times are written in it.

Rome, creeping into the light of the historical day, is not Rome proper, but the crude and yet not unlettered Pelasgians and the less crude and more lettered Etruscans, and finally, the Latins. From the tenth

EARLY ETRUSCAN

century B.C. the art of writing was seeping into the part of the world which we now know as Italy. Rome, as William A. Mason remarks, "owes everything to the earlier culture prevailing in the peninsula before the arrival of the Latins."

The Pelasgians and the Etruscans, hardy, honest and morally clean, gave, with their blood, stamina to the souls and bodies of the Latins and culture to their minds.

The Pelasgians and the Etruscans were foes; the Etruscans either absorbed the Pelasgians by slavery or marriage or drove them out, and the Latins for six hundred years fought the Etruscans and finally absorbed them or drove them out, but the vanquished left behind a priceless heritage—the learning which they had acquired in their mercantile intercourse with the seafaring Phœnicians.

The very earliest writing that is found, of the proto-

Roman style, has the letter formations which we know.

The illustration is taken from the oldest example of Roman-Greek writing. It was found scratched on a vase in a tomb near Cervetti, Italy.

OLDEST ROMAN LETTERS KNOWN

This habit of inscribing the complete alphabet, as a decoration, on vases which are placed in tombs, shows that learning, as such, and the alphabet as the means of learning, had tremendous veneration. And yet, learning and the alphabet could not have been such rare possessions, since many of these inscriptions are obviously written and scratched by people who are not experienced writers, not the professional scribes who usually did such inscribing. So we may see that writing, even writing which is that of our own times—practically—was being done centuries before Christ.

Thus, the very early Etruscan inscription in the illustration reads *from left to right*—which is distinctive of Western writing. We find the Phœnician *M, N* and *E* here, as well as a number of forms which later were to be the real Greek. As an instance of good hand printing, it is most interesting and as an illustration of the age of the letters wherewith we now write, it is thrilling.

When the Latins at last got settled in Rome and had some breathing-space, they started to clarify the alphabet some more. They did it. No more beautiful letters were ever evolved than Roman capitals and these are the capitals which are used in this and every other book of the Western world to-day. Greece, fighting her gallant way down through disaster and final death, left behind her her deathless legacy to the world: her culture, her beauty—and the alphabet which she had caught up from the failing hand of the Phœnicians and passed on, over her trampled body, to Rome.

When Rome was falling beneath the blows of the barbarians from the North, and when the remnants of

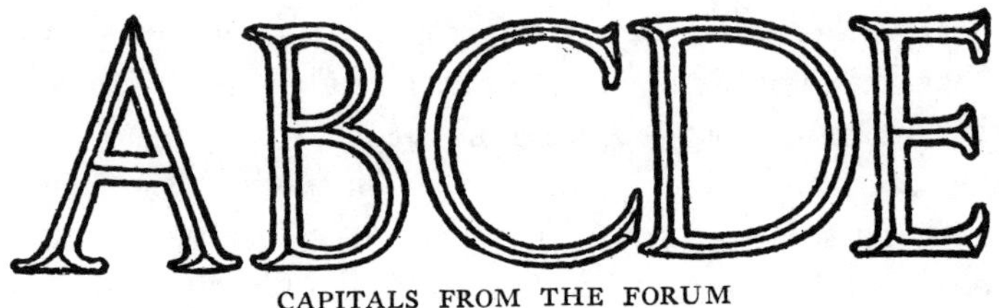

CAPITALS FROM THE FORUM

the ancient world were breaking into still smaller pieces, from which we would eventually have the Europe of to-day, the world of culture was writing practically everything in either what we call Roman capitals, or in smaller letters which were just the same in form, except that they were written more hastily and that sometimes a slight stroke connected them.

The small letters which we call "Roman" to-day, to distinguish them from "italics," and which are really "minuscules" and which the printer coldly calls "lower case," had not been evolved and neither had the italics.

As time went on they got to making a letter which was called "uncial" because it was an inch high. It was a sort of queer small letter or "lower case" letter.

Until the time when Rome went down, under the

wolves of the Hinterland—the Goths and Visigoths and what not of the races at the Back of Beyond—writing was a fine thing. It was mainly in the Roman letters known to us as capitals (of which the letters from the Forum are fine examples).

But with the coming of the Dark Ages writing fell into the slough of ignorance. Culture was not. Gentle breeding and learning were the rarest things in the world. Handwriting, that delicate barometer of human intelligence, fell and fell. People forgot how to write, and even the priests, who alone tried to carry on the great traditions, lost them. In the darkest of the Dark Ages it is quite safe and even conservative to say that not one person in five thousand could either read or write.

What was more, the very highest in the land could not. King Arthur, of legendary fame, a big enough chief and a strong enough character to bite the outline of his personality into the fabric of history, was "no scholar" and spent weary hours trying to be one. Many of the fine ladies and gentlemen of feudal times could no more have written a letter than they could have taken to themselves wings and flown over the mountains. The sword and the strong arm were again rampant on the earth and the mind of man dozed off, taking the sort of nap that it had known prehistorically—when all that it registered were only those things needed to make a good hunter.

However, the priests passionately sought to hold on to the helm of learning, and they almost succeeded. The church has a great deal to answer for, one way and another, but almost anything that she has done may be forgiven for what she did during the Dark Ages when that "education and culture" which began so many thousands of years before Christ, on the banks of all sorts of rivers, seemed about to depart this life permanently.

FROM A MEDIEVAL MISSAL

The monks, in monasteries, had little rooms which they called their "scriptoriums" and there, with pen and ink and parchment, they valiantly strove to stem the tide of ignorance which had set toward them. They lovingly embellished the forms of letters, instituted the paragraph, made efforts to punctuate, and started the custom of the margin.

Along with this finest of writing, examples of which are to be found in every good museum, there existed the crudest of writing among the people, who had forgotten everything that was known by even the ordinary "mercenaries" of Phœnicia, who left bits of fine writing all over the world, wherever the ships stopped. All through the Dark Ages and up into the Middle Ages this ignorance and this strange contradiction in life continued. Writing was either a lost art or was practised meticulously.

The first school for writing in the new world, which was founded on the ruins of the classics, was that established by Alcuin of York, who was invited to come to France, to the Court of Charlemagne, to become an instructor in the school of the palace.

Alcuin established a school of calligraphy at the Abbey of St. Martins at Tours, in 796, and it was from this school that most of the monks of the following hundred years got their training. The Benedictine monks were especially interested in writing and it is to them that we owe almost all of the writing which we now have, as well as records of science and religion and art.

From the Irish monasteries, at this time, there came a very beautiful "hand" which was taken up by the monks in their scriptoriums.

About the tenth century we find that paragraphs are found, that a set space between the words is used, that punctuation-marks are coming into use, that the page begins to look like something which is familiar to us.

After the tenth century, when the writing was still more or less formal, it began to be used by almost everybody. The scholarship of the world was again seeping downward and affecting the very ordinary man and the occasional woman.

But, so long as the mind of man and the habits of

man and the actions of man were shackled by all the restrictions of the feudal ages, the *hand* of man was shackled too. He could make only the set formations of the set type. He practically "printed" all that he wrote, no matter how rapidly he did it, or with what cursive forms he tried to amalgamate the set forms. Something was lacking. The human mind and the

LOMBARDY, A.D. 1253

ITALIAN, EARLY THIRTEENTH CENTURY

human will were cast in a mold which could not break, until the cosmic forces were ready.

About the eleventh and the twelfth centuries there began to creep into the writing of the scribes and the "bookmen" or scholars something which was not a running hand but which was close to it. Capitals were taking on their modern form and the small letters, although fashioned about the same as the capitals and thus remaining still the true Roman, were written more slantingly and a slight connecting-stroke was used, though by no means consistently.

It was the Irish monks who were most influential in making changes in handwriting before the Renaissance. They were cut off from the schools of the mainland and of Europe, and with a culture which was innate and individual, they soon introduced many innovations. The Irish "book-hands" were famous, even in the ages when many a scribe rose to fame and riches because of his special skill in writing.

The noted "Book of Kells," a relic of a monastery, founded in the sixth century by Saint Columba, which was for a long time a famous seat of learning, is actually extant to-day, and is in the library of Trinity College in Dublin. How it escaped the continual sacking of the Emerald Isle is one of those mysteries of history which are unfathomable.

With two elements straining at each other, then, writing went forward. One element strained toward beautiful uniformity and exactness and in this the monks so succeeded that they produced hundreds of books so wonderfully done that it does not seem that the variable human hand could have produced them. The other element strained toward something easier to write than these stiff and accurate formations, which required a hand trained throughout a lifetime for their production. Lifting the writing-instrument after each letter involved too great a waste of time and checked the expression of thought. People all over the world were writing, now. Making accounts, writing letters to one another, keeping diaries, writing household recipes, poetry, messages, notes—the writing-instrument slipped along without being really lifted, and the letter forms were more and more simplified, that greater speed might be made. The stiff action of the hand in making letters which stood upright on the paper was loosened to the easy angle at which the hand could function without difficulty and thereby produce the writing which leaned to the right.

By the tenth century writing, all over the continent of Europe, was getting to be quite an average thing and when William the Conqueror swept down on Britain he brought with him the great traditions of the Normandy and Lombardy scholars, to add to the indigenous culture which had been progressing more or less steadily since the day of the Roman occupation.

ITALIAN RIBBON LETTER

ITALIAN, SIXTEENTH CENTURY

About the tenth century, then, we begin to see nationality creeping into writing. Italian letter forms are rather florid. Spanish letter forms have a grave graciousness and yet a lightness of design, like their early ornament. German letters have the extraordinary heaviness which they have maintained right up to the present time (in the German script). The writing of the Gauls was simmering down into the precise elegance and distinction which was, later, to be so distinctively French. The Arab was perfecting his decorative shorthand. Over in Britain—the great first western "melting-pot" of the world—people were starting to do, what they have continued to do ever

EARLY HISPANO-MORESQUE

RENAISSANCE, ABOUT SIXTEENTH CENTURY

since: to write with a freedom and ease and individuality which was not to be surpassed by any nation until another child of the west, with the blood of the world in her veins, should arise in a still more western place.

From the earliest times, as has been said, there were always two elements straining away from each other, in this matter of writing. One element strove to make the writing formal and regular and the other strove to make it easy and individual. The time had now come in the history of writing when these two elements were no longer to be antagonistic to each other.

It was Aldus Manutius, of Venice, in 1495, who invented "the Italian running hand," which was the parent of all the writing since used in the greater part of Europe, including the British Isles and her dependencies, and in the North and South Americas. This handwriting uses the Roman capitals, which are directly ancestored from the Phœnician and from them to the Greeks; and the small letters, which also have the same source, but have passed through the deep alembic of the ages since Rome fell.

Aldus Manutius, like all writing masters, expressed the feeling of his time. He invented the writing which would express the new freedom that was in the world, the ability to function well without the old set forms. It was a fluid, flowing writing which he invented. A pity that statues are not put up to him, who did so much more for the world than he knew.

At the end of the fifteenth century printing had already made such strides that the old art of making books by hand was dead forever, but the art of writing, by the individual, for individual purposes, had enormously increased. In this writing, we see, as we see in writing of to-day, the old Roman capitals and the Greek letter forms, the two transfused into twenty-six large forms and the same number of small forms which will continually speak to us of the many thousands of years on which this art of writing is built.

Says William A. Mason: "In the sixteenth century letter-writing began to be quite an ordinary accomplishment among intelligent people, but the *'hand' in which correspondence was written varied as much as the individuals who penned it."* (The italics are not Mason's.)

The fact was that writing, for the first time in the world, was becoming individual. It had expressed race and time, social and mental conditions of the periods, art, culture and human intelligence, but never before in the history of the world had it *shown much of the individual.*

It is recorded that Michelangelo and Tasso wrote very individual "hands"; that Lady Jane Grey, who was undoubtedly a fair scholar, used a writing of great beauty; that Queen Elizabeth habitually "printed" her writing (indicative of the Constructive type, the "builder and ruler") ; that Mary Queen of Scots habitually used rounded formations (her yielding nature, the way in which she allowed men to influence her, and her love of pleasure, are shown in this rounded writing) ; and as for the "hand" of the immortal Will, it is so individual that he is not, and cannot be, the mystery to the graphologist that he is to even those who specialize on him and his history.

Printing, while really a modern thing, has also had quite a history. As early as the times of William the Conqueror charters and legal papers were stamped with engraved seals, and travelers in Oriental countries had not failed to bring back accounts of printing from wooden blocks, long practised in that region of the earth while yet the western world was little more than a jungle. People were now reading in such increasing numbers that it was humanly impossible to supply them by means of the handwork which, up to that time, had been all that was known of the making of books.

So now we have the invention of xylographic printing in which each page was printed from a block of engraved wood. The block, inked, was pressed on the paper and the impression taken off by means of rubbing the back of the paper. The difficulty of this work was such that only a few sheets were ever bound up together as a volume. The form in which they were made and bound gave them the name of "block-books." The church was responsible for these, for they were mostly religious books, often with crude pictures added, and were intended for the lower classes.

Gradually these pictures grew better. The art of wood-engraving and of printing rose, as one, into beauty and utility.

So far there was not the idea of movable type. The wooden block had to be cut—a most laborious process.

There are always several who have had the glory of great discoveries or inventions claimed for them and the invention of printing with movable type is no exception to this rule. However, it is popularly believed that Johann Gutenberg was the first person actually to put this idea into practise. He had a partnership with Johann Fust in Mainz (Mayence), Germany, from 1450 to 1455, though what books they produced, if any, cannot be proved. Almost the only evidence we have that this was the real beginning of the art of printing lies in the records of a suit at law which Fust brought against the impecunious inventor and in the record that Charles VII sent a man to the inventor to see if his secret of "printing with metal characters" could be begged, borrowed or stolen.

After Gutenberg was declared a bankrupt, Fust went into partnership with Schoffer and together they brought out a "Psalterium," being the first printed book with a date, that of August 14, 1457.

In Holland, Lourens Janszoon Coster, of Haarlem, began printing with movable characters somewhat earlier.

The famous "Gutenberg Bible" or "Mazarin Bible" was found in the library of the Cardinal, and is considered to be the first Bible ever printed. It consists of a fine work of 1282 pages, in "black letter" with spaces left for the capitals and decorations, which were drawn in by hand. It would be a beautiful piece of work, to-day, from the most wonderful of our presses, and when we consider that it was produced with the crudest of machinery and that the operatives who made it were not even used to their job, we may well look on it as the first great high point of modern printing.

With this achievement and at this point, the two elements which had been straining against each other for so long were at last permanently separated and at peace.

Printing took up again the old Roman letters, revived them and brought them to living use.

Handwriting, released from its need to use the stern outlines of old Rome, went right on to find true expression.

Far, far from Oog! Far, far from the picture-writing of the great civilizations of antiquity. Far from the casual shorthand of bedeviled scribes, seeking for some way to make notes of what their masters had dictated. Far from the "charter" hand which the lawyers of Europe had used for the records, the deeds and the instruments of history and law. Far even from the tenets of the formal writing master. Handwriting took to itself a vital life of its own, worthy of its marvelous history, leaving its mechanical twin, printing, to remain, like all mechanical things, of great use but not of innate life.

With the Elizabethan age handwriting was released from every shadow of the old formality. It became possible for an individual to write his own distinctive "hand."

Here, in 1632, the student of handwriting and of graphology turns from the study of the development of the alphabet, which is also the history of handwriting, to the consideration of the latter science. All previous history, up to this important date, has been a preparation for the understanding of the revelation of character, racial national and individual, in handwriting.

GENERAL REMARKS ON FAMILIAR SIGNS

The so-called "Roman numerals" are neither Roman nor numerals. They are, perhaps, the most primitive signs now extant and are the record of the time when we counted on our fingers and probably had no words for the numbers.

I is one finger; II, two fingers; III, three fingers; IV, the spread fingers with the thumb crossed down; V is the spread hand, held up; VI is the spread hand and a finger from the other hand; VII is the spread hand and two fingers from the other hand; IX is both hands, spread, with one thumb crossed down; and X is the sign for the two spread hands, crossed over each other.

It is likely that for many thousands of years this sign language was the only way in which the human could count. It is still the way that much of our counting is done, although we have forgotten how we started it.

ARABIC NUMERALS 1, 2 3

The Arabic figures with which we do our real mathematical calculations do not seem to have any reference to this sort of primitive counting; but to see that here, too, there was a visual system we have only to look at one, two and three, as the Arabs really write them, to see that *their* counting began with sticks. One is a stick, two is two sticks, three is three sticks, four is four sticks and so on. The Arabic, which runs from right to left, makes it easier to draw these figures in this way than when we try to write them from left to right.

Another set of very old formations are those which are found in the signs of the Zodiac.

Aries, the ram, undoubtedly came into use just after Alpu, the ox, as a standardized sign, or Taurus, the bull.

Leo, the lion; Cancer, the crab; Scorpio, the scorpion; Pisces, the fishes; the Twins—all have the most remote ancestry.

The lion was the first mammal to receive deification. The scorpion and all aquatic insects having this peculiar form have always been considered signs of evil. The water carrier, Aquarius, is, of course, just the sign for water. Capricornus, the goat, did not come into use until civilization had long domesticated him. Libra, the scales, is a very late sign, too, coming down almost to the time of known history. Mercury, Venus, Mars, and Jupiter were probably not used until Chaldea was in the full glory of its great study of the heavens.

The sign for the crab is its two claws; the sign for the lion is his tail; that for the Twins is obvious; Aries has his horns; and the Archer his arrow. Capricornus is a most extraordinary sign, for, although there is not a real picture, there is something indescribably goatish and lustily coarse in the outlines of this sign. Mercury is represented by his caduceus; and Venus, very appropriately, by her looking-glass. Mars has his shield and spear; and the sign for Jupiter is a highly conventionalized head of the eagle, Jove's own bird.

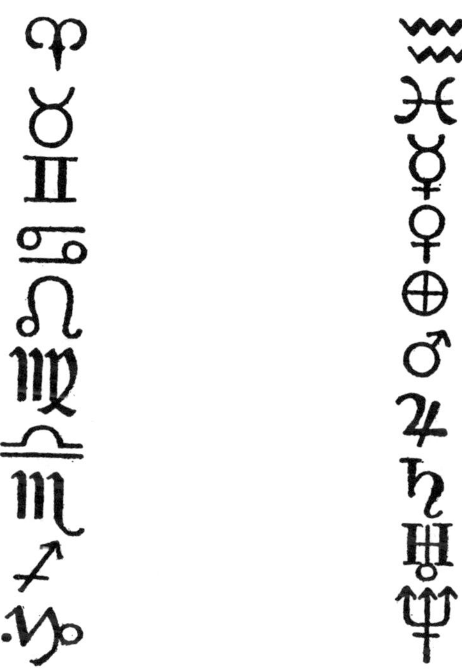

SIGNS OF THE ZODIAC

It will be noticed that this sign bears a close resemblance to that which physicians use on prescriptions. Here we have an instance of the fact that every writing form in the world has a long page of history behind it, if only we know enough to read it. For hundreds of years, this sign, persistently used by physicians all over the Aryan-Western world, has had little meaning, but it did have a significance when a Roman physician used it: thus he piously invoked the aid of Jupiter by using the insignia of the god.

Among the signs of the Zodiac, Saturn and Neptune are comparatively newcomers. There is the cycle for Saturn, who was called the reaper, and the trident for Neptune, who was never much of a real god even among those who invented him, but far more of a literary and poetical abstraction.

The sign for Uranius is wholly modern. Herschel, the discoverer of Uranius, is immortalized in the sign which stands for the planet—which is really a capital *H*.

This process of making new meanings out of old signs is still going right on.

There has always been a great deal of discussion as to the origin of the American dollar-mark, and much remark as to the curious fact that nowhere can we find even an inkling of the adoption of this sign. It just appeared from nowhere and everywhere, when the coin was first in use. The truth is, like all historical fact, both unique and simple.

The coin which was more or less the standard of the world for centuries before the coining of the dollar was the Spanish "piece of eight." This was often written *8*.

Now, when the dollar was a coin, in the very earliest days of its making, the world, so accustomed to write *8* for a coin which was of the same value, continued to write *8*. And then, to indicate that this was not the old Spanish coin, although of the same value, people started putting a line through the figure, and then two lines. Then they found it easier to make the *8* into an *S*—and the thing was done.

The character of "pound sterling" in English money is merely a capital *L* with a stroke through it, and this *L* is the initial of the Latin word, *Libra*—the scale.

Our abbreviation for the word "pound" is made up of the first and third letters of this same word.

The character *&* is composed of the Latin word *et,* the *e* and the *t* being run together.

The interrogation-mark was produced by using the first and the last letters of the Latin word, *questio* and then by writing them one on top of the other. The exclamation-point is the old Latin word *io*—"joy"—the two letters written one over the other. There is no doubt that we owe these abbreviations, which have now become separate forms, to the old monks, who made them in the process of inventing punctuation-marks by which they strove for greater clarity: a clarity the aim of which was to make it possible for the slow-reading, slow-witted people of that age really to get at the meaning of the written word. Thus, again, as so often in the consideration of this subject of writing, we see how beauty and grace and sophistication have grown out of that which was, in the first place, sheer utility.

In the alphabet itself, we have seen that we have the remains of many old pictures. The capital *A* being the head of an ox; *B,* two tents side by side; *S,* the sign for water and also for snake; and the capital *I* in all its forms needing very little to return it again to the primitive "toothpick man" from which it has been derived.

It is likely that in *D* we have the sign of the first architectural effort, which mimicked the round tent and became the stone arch. Lay the letter down and this is clear. (It must be remembered that the wholly upright form of our alphabet is a modern thing.)

Adding the faint outline of a thumb to *G* will give us a symbolized outstretched hand, which would mark the coming of commerce—which, in the primitive days, was the "swapping" with which our childhood still simulates the ancient business. *E,* its open end laid down, would give us a perfect picture of a portico with end and central columns. *H* is really a gate and may show us the time when the enclosed garden became a precious thing; it could not have been until late in history, for the very idea of walling up ground is still alien to the farflung outposts.

L already has been shown to consist of the various angles at which the lion reclines. *O,* the *Omega* of the Greeks, is undoubtedly derived from, first of all, the double arch of the heavens, which represented the horison reflected in water and which was one of the earliest symbols of eternity. After that, the cord, tied to form a circle, became the symbol, as did also the snake with its tail in its mouth.

To see what *T* may represent, we may, with two strokes of the pencil, add round formations at each horizontal end and so have a crude ox-yoke and thus the sign of the inception of agriculture and plowed ground.

GENERAL REMARKS ON FAMILIAR SIGNS

Some of these indications as to the capital letters are still scarcely more than conjecture; but scientific research is steadily bringing to light greater and greater confirmation of them.

RACIAL AND OTHER INDICATIONS IN HANDWRITING

In considering the racial and national characteristics, as shown in handwriting, it will be interesting to go back and observe how writing has always carried the spirit of its age, and how all the arts have been in tune with it.

EGYPTIAN COLUMN

The Egyptian column, heavy and yet daring, with the *feeling* of the primitive world's overgrown vegetation clustered about its head (the ancient forest, in stone) has the same spirit as these heavy and yet elastic formations of the Egyptian "alphabet" and pictographs, where the primitive mind of man peers out from the sophisticated meanings of a later time.

Greek letters *belong* to Greek architecture. In decorative value the Greek alphabet and the Greek

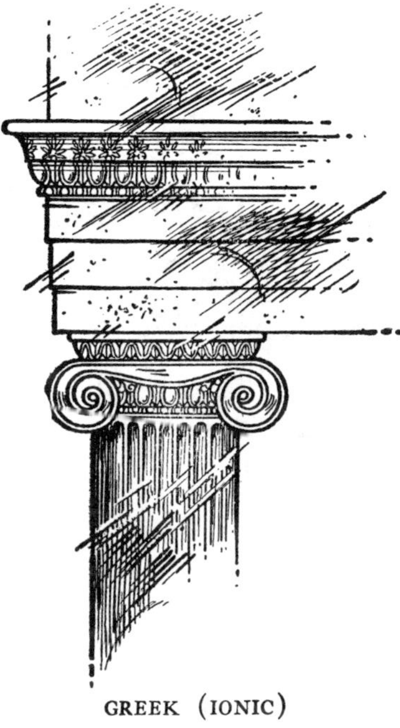

GREEK (IONIC)

column and its appurtenances are one. The Gothic arch and the ornament that it has, is of a piece with the incised and elaborated letter which we can find even in printing, up to the seventeenth century and which we still use for ornament at the beginning of chapters, in certain formal and important books.

The Roman architecture was not as good an exponent of the Roman letter forms, nor as much in sympathy with them, as we might expect, but those familiar with Roman history will not wonder at this.

Rome never imbibed feeling for art as she did actual knowledge and practical science. Her architecture is utilitarian when it is good, and a mere imitation when

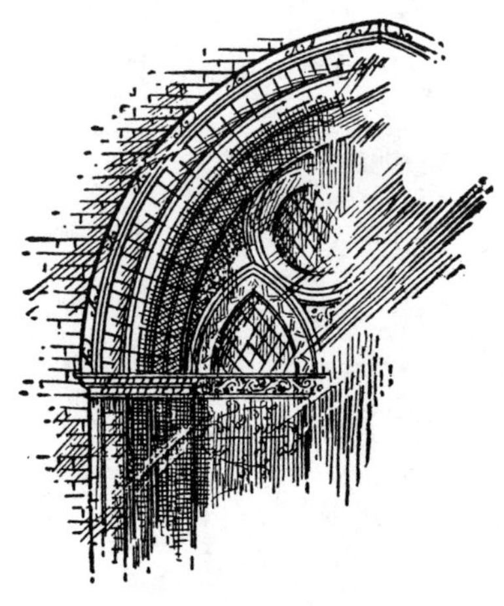

GOTHIC ARCH

it is not. Her famous arch, severe and accurate, cannot be equaled, but her column is a bastard in the noble family to which the Egyptian and the various Greek columns belong.

Nevertheless, if her column is denuded of ornament which was palpably applied, not being an integral part of the design, we shall see the simplicity and the strength in the outlines which agree with her noble alphabet.

The sinuous and abbreviated formations of the Arabic, Burmese, Annamese and other similar writings need only be placed beside the lace-like ornamentation

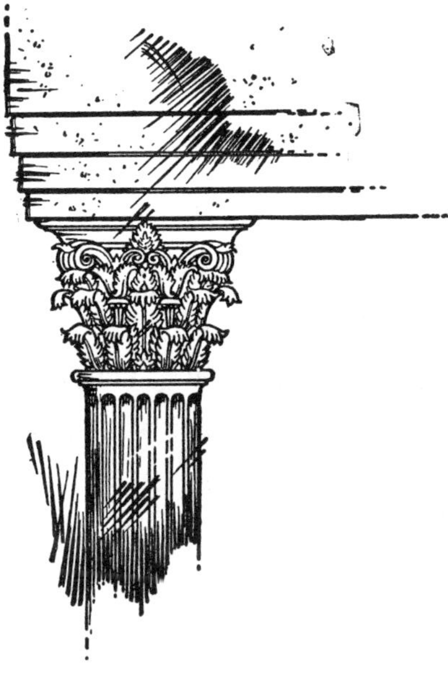

ROMAN CAPITAL

of those races to have the kinship of the writing and the ornament proclaimed.

Japanese writing, which is in theory just the same as the Chinese, can be detected as separate from it by even persons who know not one form of Japanese or Chinese writing. There is in every brush-stroke the elfish and tricksy spirit which is also elusively spiritual and dreamy. Chinese writing, technically the same, is solidly of this earth and humorously Falstaffian in its heaviness and spontaneity. It is suggested, as an exercise in training the eye, that the graphological student go to the Oriental room of any good library and look attentively at specimens of writing and reproductions of architecture of various nations which will be found there. The very forms of the ornamented door and window-frames, the bits of embroidery, the patterns of cloth, such as the cotton fabrics of ancient Egypt, India and Persia of to-day, and the small objects in daily

GERMAN, SIXTEENTH CENTURY

use in all those countries, will show the close relationship in feeling which writing has to the arts of a race or a nation.

It is worth noting that one of the most pronounced of graphological rules will open a whole new world of speculation to us. That rule is:

As we get away from the primitive in peoples, in nations and in races, the relationships between writing and art and architecture diminish.

Thus, France and the British Isles and the United States have little that provides analogies between arts, architecture and handwriting. Spain and Germany have more analogies. So do Italy and Russia. The Balkans, modern Greece, modern Turkey—all show a good many of these correspondences and analogies. Among French and English and American writing we would have difficulty in making individual differentiations as to nationality. Many English, especially those whose minds are trained to specific ends, use the small, delicate and clipped letter formations, the writing of small size and the capitals graceful, of the "typical" French hand of the same mental strata. So, for that matter, do many Americans, while the more aggressive and keenly ambitious French write a "typical" American salesman's hand, and many Americans use the "characteristic" incurve of the English.

Graphology, revealing the innate likeness and unlikeness of temperaments, shows, therefore, that the curious attraction which these three nations have for each other is founded on real relationship, that of the possible interplay of motive and spirit. To those who point out that the loss of national spirit and race feeling leaves us without the richness of color that the more primitive races give us, I wish to suggest that there is no period of the human being which is quite so unattractive as that which is neither childhood nor youth but the indeterminate stage between. The three races mentioned are at the indeterminate stage. Therefore, the loss of what may be characterized as racial local color ought, in the course of some few thousands of years, to find ample compensation. If these few thousands seem long, in anticipation, one needs only to cast a mental eye backward, for comparisons!

Primitive people—or what it is convenient to call

primitive people—do what children do: they instinctively and emotionally react, throughout their beings, to vibrations. This explains the unification of all their arts and of their writing. The ancient Aztecs, for instance, were by no means simple. Their ideation and emotional reaction was fully as complicated as the ancient Egyptians, and also as "primitive." The accom-

ANCIENT MEXICAN

panying illustration for the numeral "twenty" is the Aztec sign, also, for the twentieth month of their year, which was the month of harvest, a fact indicated by a

"A HEART ON A HILL"

quite realistic representation of teeth. With another sign or two, this form would also mean "riches," "a fat body," "happiness," "peace," "a healthy old age," and so on. Nothing very primitive about such ideas.

The very beautiful form shown in the second illustration, which looks like the most sophisticated of our decorative drawings, is really the name of an Aztec town. That name is, literally, "a heart on a hill." It was, without doubt, a name which told of a place of ancient human sacrifice, for offering the human heart on high places was part of the Aztec rites. The imagination of the best trained of our decorative artists could produce nothing better.

The handwriting of these people in whom the sense of form, color and art is so strong is never the individualized handwriting. It is too unified, too at one with art, to be that.

The student of graphology will at once see that this rule, at which we have arrived by a series of progressive reflections, tells us the reason for the odd unindividuality of the average artist. And the fact that a reflection bearing so strongly on one of the most modern of graphological problems is the derivative of those which have to do with fifty thousand years ago, will show the graphological student why it has been of such importance that that vast, shadowy and yet intricate background to present life should have been so fully considered.

WORDS USED IN CONNECTION WITH WRITING

Paper: From *papyrus,* the reed which grew in such profusion on the banks of the Nile, from which the earliest paper was made. It resembles wood-pulp and was handled by the ancient Egyptians in much the same way as such pulp is handled to-day, although of course they did not have our wonderful machines.

Bible: This did not originally mean a sacred book, at all. It is from *biblos,* meaning a book of any kind. It came into its present use because, when the Christian missionaries went out into the hinder part of Europe, they had the only "book" which their savage hearers had ever seen.

Library: From the Latin *liber,* which was a tree, the pulp of which was used for writing-material.

Book: From the Anglo-Saxon *boc,* meaning "beech," the bark of which was used for writing-material.

Tablet: From the Latin *tabula,* which meant "a board." On a piece of smooth board they spread hot wax and when it had cooled and made a surface the person who wanted to write a letter indited his words. After such a board had been used once, it could be held close to heat, smoothed over and used again and again.

Stylus: A three-cornered pen, which was a copy of the original three-cornered reed with which writing was first done. We now say "his style is good," meaning that he writes clever words—and that is from this old implement.

Pen: From *penna,* meaning a feather. The earliest pens, even those of our great-grandfathers' times, were the wing-feathers of a large bird, cut to a point.

Quill: From Old English *quylle,* meaning the wing-feather of a bird, but originally meaning a reed.

Pencil: From a Latin word meaning "a tail." This does

not seem to make sense until we remember that the original pencil was a brush! This brush was made from the hair of tails of horses, pigs and mules, dipped in colors or in ink, and used as a hastier way of writing than that afforded by the stylus. When the real pencil with the lead came into being, the name survived.

VOLUME: From the Latin *volumen,* which meant a roll of paper fastened to a cylinder of wood. This is the form in which all books appeared in classic times.

PARCHMENT: From Pergamus, a city in Asia Minor, where skins were extensively prepared for the purpose of writing.

ENCHORIC: Native to a country. Especially said of a language which is native to a country.

EPIGRAPHY: The art of writing inscriptions on stone or other substance and the art of deciphering such inscriptions. Often used in the writing of experts who have made a study of ancient writings.

HOMOPHONES: Words which sound alike but have different meanings: as, "all" and "awl."

GRAFFITI: "Mere scratchings." Said of the earliest forms of drawings found in rock caves.

KYRIOLOGIC WRITING: Writing in which forms represent sounds or ideas. Our own writing is this, since our alphabet represents sounds.

IKONOMATIC WRITING: Writing in which the figure of one thing is made to stand for the meaning of something else: as when the sun stands for "day"; the stars for "night"; etc.

MELONYMY: Where the part of a figure represents the whole: as the hand means the whole body; a ship a fleet; etc.

ACOLOGY: The use of a picture to represent the word or name: as when Richard the Lion-Hearted was represented in Saracen literature by a heart and a lion.

SYNEDOCHE: Using a part of an object to show the whole: as, in many early languages, legs bent showed jumping, etc.

BIBLIOGRAPHY

ANCIENT HANDWRITINGS. *William Saunders.*

BEGINNINGS OF WRITING. *William J. Hoffman.*

DAWN OF CIVILIZATION. *Gaston Camille Maspero.*

THE EUROPEAN DIFFUSION OF PICTOGRAPHY IN ITS BEARINGS ON THE ORIGIN OF SCRIPT. *A. J. Evans.*

THE FORMATION OF THE ALPHABET. *William M. Flinders Petrie.* Geographical Journal, 1912.

MATERIALS USED TO WRITE UPON BEFORE THE INVENTION OF PRINTING. *Albert Maire.* Smithsonian Institute Report, 1904.

THE MEDITERRANEAN SIGNARY. *W. M. F. Petrie.*

THE STORY OF THE ALPHABET. *Edward Clodd.*

THE STORY OF PRIMITIVE MAN. *Edward Clodd.*

ANTHROPOLOGY. *Edward B. Taylor.*

EARLY HISTORY OF MANKIND. *Edward B. Taylor.*

EVOLUTION IN ART. *A. C. Haddon.*

SCIENCE OF LANGUAGE. *A. H. Sayce.*

EARLY BABYLONIAN HISTORY. *Hugo Radau.*

EXPLORATIONS IN BIBLE LANDS. *Herman V. Hilprecht.*

A HISTORY OF SUMER AND AKKAD. *Leonard W. King.*

LIGHT ON THE OLD TESTAMENT FROM BABEL. *Albert T. Clay.*

THE DEVELOPMENT OF CHINESE WRITING. *L. C. Hopkins.*

ANTHROPOLOGY AND THE CLASSICS. *Arthur J. Evans.*

HISTORY OF THE ART OF WRITING. *William A. Mason.*

A HISTORY OF EGYPT. *James H. Breasted.*

LIFE IN ANCIENT EGYPT. *Gaston Camille Maspero.*

A THOUSAND MILES UP THE NILE. *Amelia B. Edwards.*

AN INTRODUCTION TO GREEK EPIGRAPHY. *E. S. Roberts.*

THE HITTITES. The Story of a Forgotten Empire. *A. H. Sayce.*

History of Art—in Phrygia, Lydia, Caria and Lycia; History of Art in Sardinia, Judea, Syria and Asia Minor. *Geo. Perrot and Charles Chipiez.*

Styles of Ornament. *Alexander Speltz.*

Alphabets, Old and New. *Lewis F. Day.*

History of Antiquity. *Maximilian W. Dunker.*

Herodotus. *George Rawlinson.*

Considerations of the Art of Picture Writing . . . of North American Indians. *Henry R. Schoolcraft.* 1844.

Archives of Aboriginal Knowledge. *Henry R. Schoolcraft.* 1860.

Book of Kells. *Sir Edward Sullivan.*

The Court Hand. *Hilary Jenkinson.*

The Development of the Book Hand. *Williams.*

Palæographical Album of Facsimiles of Writings of All Nations and Periods. *J. B. Silvestre.* 4 Vols. 1841.

The Story of Phœnicia. *George Rawlinson.*

A History of the Art of Printing. *H. Noel Humphreys.*

The Practice of Typography. *Theodore L. De Vinne.*

The Italic Alphabets. *Isaac Taylor.*

The Old Northern Runic Monuments of Scandinavia and England. *Dr. George Stephens, F.S.A.*